One-Minute WordPerfect

1. Type *WP* then press the ⏎ key to start WordPerfect.

2. Type your document.

   Indent with the Tab key.

   End paragraphs (not lines) and insert blank lines with the ⏎ key.

   Erase mistakes with the Backspace or Del key.

   Get help with the F3 key.

3. To print your documents, hold down the Shift key while you press the F7 key, let go of them both, then press the 1 key on the top row of the keyboard.

4. To save your document, press the F10 key, type a name up to eight characters long, then press ⏎.

5. Press the F7 key, then *N* twice to clear the screen and start over. Repeat steps 2 to 4 to produce another document.

6. Press the F7 key, *N,* then *Y* to exit WordPerfect.

The ABC's of WordPerfect 5

The ABC's of WordPerfect® 5

Alan R. Neibauer

San Francisco • Paris • Düsseldorf • London

Cover design by Thomas Ingalls + Associates
Cover photography by Michael Lamotte
Series design by Jeffrey James Giese
Chapter art and layout by Ingrid Owen
Screen printing produced with XenoFont from XenoSoft, Berkeley, CA

Library of Congress Card Number: 88-60894
ISBN 0-89588-504-2
Manufactured in the United States of America
20 19 18 17 16 15 14 13 12 11
10

To Barbara, for her support and understanding

Acknowledgments

The dedication of many professionals goes into creating a book such as this. Working against deadlines, and trying to give readers accurate and useful information on software that's still in development, can be a frustrating task. But somehow the excellent team at SYBEX brings it all together.

These professionals should be recognized for their efforts—professionals such as David Kolodney, supervising editor, and Eric Stone, copy editor, who tie up the loose pieces and make it all work. Technical editors Brian Atwood and David Clark ensure the accuracy of the text. Jocelyn Reynolds, word processor, Olivia Shinomoto, typesetter, Kristen Iverson, proofreader, and Paula Alston, indexer, make the transition into a finished form. Chapter designer and layout artist Ingrid Owen, book designer Jeff Giese, and graphics technician Michelle Hoffman guarantee a readable and attractive product.

Thanks also to Barbara Gordon and Dr. Rudolph S. Langer for such a well-running group, and to Dianne King, for thinking of me.

Special thanks to Rebecca B. Mortensen and her colleagues at WordPerfect Corporation. WordPerfect just seems to get better and better.

Last, but definitely not least, my sincere appreciation to my wife, Barbara. She always seems to fit me into her schedule at the Philadelphia College of Pharmacy and Science, to do those things she does best as a colleague and friend. It is not easy being the wife of a writer and teacher.

Contents
at a Glance

Introduction | xxiii
1 Creating Your First Document | 2
2 Improving and Correcting Your Document | 18
3 More Efficient Revision Techniques | 32
4 Enhancing the Appearance of Your Documents | 50
5 Formatting Characters for Emphasis and Variety | 68
6 Centering, Flush Right, and Other Text Alignment | 86
7 Right and Left Indents and Other Paragraph Formats | 102
8 Page Formatting for a Professional Look | 118
9 Adding Headers, Footers, and Page Numbers | 134
10 Editing Entire Blocks | 146
11 Streamlining Your Editing with Search and Replace | 156
12 Creating Multicolumn Layouts | 164
13 Creating Personalized Form Letters | 176
14 Adding Footnotes and Endnotes | 190
15 Advanced Printing and Setup | 202
16 Automating Keystrokes with Macros | 218
17 Word Tools: The Speller and Thesaurus | 228
18 Enhancing Your Documents with Graphics | 240
A How to Make Backups | 259
B Installing WordPerfect | 265
C How to Designate Printers | 269
Index | 278

Table of Contents

Introduction   xxiii

    How to Use This Book   xxiv
    The WordPerfect Keyboard   xxv
        Special Keys   xxvi
        Function Keys   xxviii
        Numeric Keypad   xxix
    Interacting with WordPerfect   xxx
        Prompts   xxx
        Selection Lines   xxx
        Menus   xxxi
    Get to Know Your Hardware   xxxii
        Monitors   xxxii
        Display Cards   xxxii
        Disk Drives   xxxiii
        Printer   xxxiii
    Conventions Used in This Book   xxxiv
        Combining Keystrokes   xxxiv
        Following the Instructions   xxxv

1 Creating Your First Document   2

    Lesson 1—How to Start WordPerfect   2
        Hard Disk   2
        Floppy Disks   3

Lesson 2—The WordPerfect Screen   4

    Scrolling Text on the Screen   5

Lesson 3—How to Type in WordPerfect   5

Lesson 4—How to Move the Cursor   7

Lesson 5—How to Insert Text   9

Lesson 6—How to Print Documents   11

Lesson 7—How to Save Your Document   13

    Saving New Documents and Quitting WordPerfect   13

Lesson 8—How to Get Help   14

2 Improving and Correcting Your Document

18

Lesson 9—How to Recall a Document from Disk   18

    Recall by Name   18

    Recall by Directory   18

Lesson 10—How to Move the Cursor More Efficiently   20

    Moving Down through a Document   20

    Moving Up through a Document   20

    Moving Left   22

    Moving Right   22

    Moving to Specific Locations   23

Lesson 11—How to Delete Text   23

    Deleting Characters   23

    Deleting Words   24

    Deleting Lines   25

    Mass Deletion   25

    Deleting Parts of Words   25

    A Summary of Deletion Commands   26

Lesson 12—How to Restore Deleted Text **26**

Lesson 13—How to Save a Document after Revisions **28**

Saving and Continuing with the Same Document **28**

Saving and Starting a New Document **29**

Quitting WordPerfect without Saving the Document **29**

3 More Efficient Revision Techniques **32**

Lesson 14—How to Use Typeover **32**

Lesson 15—How to Work with Codes **34**

Revealing Codes **34**

Working with Codes Revealed **37**

Lesson 16—How to Split and Combine Paragraphs **37**

Combining Two Paragraphs **38**

Splitting a Paragraph into Two **38**

Lesson 17—How to Repeat Keystrokes **39**

Adjusting the Screen after Editing **40**

Lesson 18—How to Work with Multiple Documents **41**

Displaying Two Documents **42**

Clearing Windows **44**

Displaying the Scale Line **44**

Lesson 19—How to Add the Date to Documents **45**

Changing Date Formats **47**

4 Enhancing the Appearance of Your Documents **50**

Lesson 20—Default Values and Format Changes **50**

Lesson 21—How to Change Left and Right Margins   **51**

    Deleting Margin Set Codes   **57**

Lesson 22—How to Adjust Line Spacing   **57**

Lesson 23—How to Control Page Breaks   **58**

    Deleting Page Breaks   **60**

Lesson 24—How to Add Document Comments and Summary   **61**

    Document Summary   **61**

    Comments   **63**

    Editing and Printing Comments   **64**

5 Formatting Characters for Emphasis and Variety   **68**

Lesson 25—How to Boldface and Underline Text   **69**

    Boldfacing and Underlining as You Type   **69**

    Boldfacing or Underlining Existing Characters   **70**

    Deleting Boldface and Underline   **72**

    Underline Styles   **72**

Lesson 26—How to Control the Uppercase/Lowercase Option   **74**

Lesson 27—How to Change the Appearance of Characters   **74**

    Changing the Appearance of Characters As You Type   **75**

    Changing the Appearance of Existing Characters   **77**

    Summary   **78**

Lesson 28—How to Change the Size and Position of Characters   **79**

    Changing Font Families   **82**

    Changing the Position or Size of Existing Characters   **83**

    Font Sizes and the Position Indicator   **83**

6 Centering, Flush Right, and Other Text Alignment 86

Lesson 29—How to Center Text   86
  Centering New Text   86
  Centering Existing Text   87
  Uncentering Text   88
Lesson 30—How to Align Text Flush Right   88
  Aligning New Text on the Right   89
  Aligning Existing Text on the Right   89
  Returning Flush Right Text to Normal   90
Lesson 31—How to Set Tabs   90
  Column Alignment   90
  Setting Tab Stops   91
  Aligning Columns As You Type   95
  Changing Tabs   98

7 Right and Left Indents and Other Paragraph Formats 102

Lesson 32—How to Indent Paragraphs   102
  Indenting from the Left Margin   102
  Indenting from Both the Left and Right Margins   105
Lesson 33—How to Create Hanging Indentations   107
  Numbered Paragraphs   107
  Changing the Format of Existing Text   109
Lesson 34—How to Set Justification   109

Lesson 35—How to Hyphenate Text   110
   Entering Hyphens Yourself   110
   Manual Hyphenation with Assistance   111
   Automatic Hyphenation   112
Lesson 36—How to View Documents   113

8 Page Formatting for a Professional Look   118

Lesson 37—How to Set Top and Bottom Margins   118
Lesson 38—How to Set Page Size and Shape with Forms   119
   Entering Smaller Sizes without Defining Forms   123
   Forms and Page Feed   124
Lesson 39—How to Eliminate Orphan and Widow Lines   125
Lesson 40—How to Create Title Pages   126
Lesson 41—How to Print Envelopes   128
   Defining the Envelope Form   129
   Selecting the Envelope Form   129
   Setting Envelope Margins   130

9 Adding Headers, Footers, and Page Numbers   134

Lesson 42—How to Create Headers and Footers   134
   Header/Footer Suggestions   138
   Editing Headers and Footers   139
Lesson 43—How to Insert Page Numbers   139
Lesson 44—How to Suppress Headers, Footers, and Page Numbers   141
Lesson 45—How to Set New Page Numbers   143

10 **Editing Entire Blocks**   **146**

Lesson 46—How to Delete, Move, and Copy Blocks   **146**
Converting Text into a Comment   **150**
Lesson 47—How to Move Text between Documents   **150**
Multiple Documents   **151**
After Exiting a Document   **151**
Lesson 48—How to Print Blocks   **152**
Lesson 49—How to Save and Append Blocks   **153**
Saving Blocks   **153**
Appending Blocks   **154**

11 **Streamlining Your Editing with Search and Replace**   **156**

Lesson 50—How to Search for Text   **156**
Searching for Codes   **158**
Lesson 51—How to Replace Text   **159**

12 **Creating Multicolumn Layouts**   **164**

Lesson 52—How to Create Newspaper Columns   **164**
Defining Column Layouts   **165**
Typing Columns   **166**
Lesson 53—How to Create Parallel Columns   **168**
Defining Parallel Columns   **170**
Typing Parallel Columns   **171**

13 Creating Personalized Form Letters 176

Lesson 54—How to Write the Form Letter **176**
    The Primary Document **176**
Lesson 55—How to Assemble the Variable Information File **180**
    Handling Missing Information **183**
Lesson 56—How to Merge Files **184**
    Merging Form Documents to the Screen **185**
    Merging Form Documents to the Printer **186**

14 Adding Footnotes and Endnotes 190

Lesson 57—How to Enter Footnotes **190**
    Adding, Editing, and Deleting Footnotes **194**
Lesson 58—How to Change Footnote Options **194**
Lesson 59—How to Enter Endnotes **196**

15 Advanced Printing and Setup 202

Lesson 60—How to Customize WordPerfect **202**
    Backup **202**
    Fast Save **208**
Lesson 61—How to Set Print Options **208**
    Document on Disk **209**

Type Through   **210**

Binding   **212**

Number of Copies   **212**

Graphics Quality   **212**

Text Quality   **213**

Lesson 62—How to Control Printing   **213**

16 Automating Keystrokes with Macros — 218

Lesson 63—How to Create and Use Macros   **218**

Defining Macros   **219**

Using Macros   **221**

Lesson 64—A Macro Library   **224**

Go Command for Hand-Fed Paper—Alt-G   **224**

Macro for Resetting to the Default Format—Alt-F   **224**

Macro to Center Text on the Page—Alt-P   **224**

Double Space Macro—Alt-D   **225**

Page Number Macro—Alt-N   **225**

Legal Paper Macro—Alt-L   **225**

Save Named Text Macro—Alt-X   **225**

Font Change Macros   **225**

17 Word Tools: The Speller and Thesaurus — 228

Lesson 65—How to Check Your Spelling   **228**

Floppy Disk Systems   **228**

Checking Spelling   229
Other Spelling Options   232
Lesson 66—How to Use the Thesaurus   233

18 Enhancing Your Documents with Graphics 240

Lesson 67—How to Add Vertical and Horizontal Lines   240
Horizontal Lines   241
Vertical Lines   243
Lesson 68—How to Enclose Text in a Box   245
Lesson 69—How to Add Graphics to Your Documents   252

Appendices

A How to Make Backups 259

Systems with Two Floppy Disks   259
Hard Disk Systems with One Floppy   262

B Installing WordPerfect 265

Configuration File   265
Floppy Disk Systems   266
Hard Disk Systems   266

C How to Designate Printers

269

Setting Up WordPerfect for Your Printer **269**
Changing Printer Definitions **276**
Quitting WordPerfect **277**

Index

278

Introduction

If you've never used WordPerfect before and want to learn how, or have tried out an older version of WordPerfect, then this book is for you. You will learn how to create and print documents in short, easy-to-understand lessons. Each lesson takes only a few minutes, so you can complete several lessons in one session, learning a complete useful task easily and quickly.

As your skills increase, the lessons will start to cover more sophisticated functions of this remarkable word processing tool—including the powerful graphics and desktop publishing functions. But even these "advanced" lessons are clear and concise, designed to get you working in just minutes without the need to refer constantly to manuals.

WordPerfect comes in several versions and for a variety of computers. This book covers version 5.0 for the IBM family of personal computers and those compatible with them. The program is basically the same whether you're using DOS or OS/2 as your disk operating system. So if you have an IBM PC/XT, AT, PS/2, or similar computer, you can just follow the instructions in this book.

Of course, WordPerfect comes in versions for other computers using other operating systems. While the differences are too numerous to be covered adequately in an introductory book, once you've learned the elements of WordPerfect presented here, it will be easy to apply your knowledge to other versions if the need arises.

Why use this book when you already have the manual that came with WordPerfect? The manual is a well-written and complete reference to WordPerfect. But it is designed as a reference, not as a learning aid. Its primary function is to explain in detail—in over 500 pages—every technicality that even the most advanced user needs.

This book, on the other hand, is designed for the beginning Word-Perfect user. It can be used even if you are just learning how to use your computer system. It shows you how to copy and install Word-Perfect, and how to create, edit, and print documents of all types. If you are already using WordPerfect's basic functions, then the advanced lessons later in the book will teach you the more difficult tasks. And even if you're quite experienced with older versions of the program, you'll quickly learn the major differences needed to stay productive with the new version.

*H*ow to Use This Book

Each chapter is made up of several lessons. Most of the lessons include a series of easy-to-follow numbered steps. To learn how to use WordPerfect, just sit down at your computer and do what each step instructs. You'll be amazed at how easy it is.

If you just purchased WordPerfect, the first three appendices will be invaluable. There you'll learn how to make a copy of your disks, install WordPerfect on your computer, and tell WordPerfect what printer you're using. Go directly to these appendices if you have not yet used the program or are not sure that you've set it up correctly.

The lessons in the first chapter show you how to start WordPerfect and how to type, print, and save a simple document with the fewest keystrokes possible. Not every detail of editing, saving, or printing is given in these beginning lessons, just the basic keystrokes. This is to demonstrate how easy WordPerfect really is, and to test your hardware and printer before going any further. It also lets you type and print those simple documents that you need right away.

The chapters that follow include lessons covering every aspect of WordPerfect. In Chapters 2 and 3 you'll learn about editing your text, while Chapters 4 through 8 show you how to format it for printing. In Chapter 9 you'll learn how to add "headers and footers" to your documents, and how to number pages. Chapter 10 shows you how to work with blocks of text, and in Chapter 11 you'll learn how to search for and replace words or groups of words automatically.

The remaining chapters cover WordPerfect features that, while appearing to be more specialized, are actually useful in a great variety of applications. In Chapter 12 you'll learn how to create columns of text, and Chapters 13 and 14 show you how to produce form letters and add footnotes to your documents. In Chapter 15 you'll learn how to use some advanced printing features, and in Chapter 16 I'll show you how to create labor-saving "macros." You'll learn how to use WordPerfect's powerful Speller and Thesaurus features in Chapter 17, and how to add lines, boxes, and drawings to documents in Chapter 18, taking full advantage of WordPerfect's desktop publishing features.

While there is a normal progression in learning a program such as this, you can jump ahead to more advanced lessons if you need that information to complete your work. For example, while following an earlier lesson you might need to move an entire section of text from one location to another. This is called a *Block* function. Just look in the table of contents or index and go directly to that lesson. Follow the steps and, when done, return to the earlier chapter and continue.

However, this is only recommended when absolutely needed. Because the lessons are short and designed to teach you quickly, you'll reach the advanced chapters before you realize it.

The WordPerfect Keyboard

For typing, the computer keyboard is no different from a regular typewriter. It doesn't matter if you have the original IBM/PC keyboard shown in Figure I.1, the keyboard first sold with IBM PC/AT's (Figure I.2), or the newer "enhanced" keyboard now shipped with most IBM's including the PS/2's (Figure I.3). The middle section of the keyboard (or the area on the left on the enhanced keyboard) includes the keys for letters, numbers, and punctuation marks needed to enter your text.

But the keyboard also includes special keys not found on a typewriter. These keys allow you to harness the power of the computer for word processing. During the lessons that follow, you will be taught to use these special keys, both alone and in combination.

Figure I.1: Original IBM keyboard

Figure I.2: Older IBM PC/AT keyboard

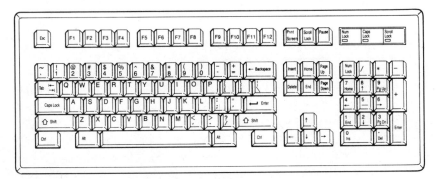

Figure I.3: Enhanced IBM keyboard with PS/2 windows

Special Keys

Look at your keyboard for the following keys:

 This is the TAB key. When an instruction says to press TAB, press this key.

This is the SHIFT key. When an instruction says to press SHIFT, press this key. You can press either of the two shift keys on the keyboard.

 This is the ENTER key—one of the most important keys you will be using. You will use the Enter key to end paragraphs or to insert blank lines into the text. The Enter key is also called *Return*. To avoid any confusion, we'll use the symbol ⏎ throughout this book. So when an instruction says to press ⏎, press this key.

 This is the BACKSPACE key. You use it to delete unwanted characters.

 When an instruction says to press ESC, press this key, the ESCAPE key. This key is used to repeat characters and commands automatically.

 When an instruction says to press INS, press this key. This is the INSERT key, which switches between the Insert and Typeover modes. In the Insert mode, existing characters will move over to make room for new ones that you type. In the Typeover mode, new characters will replace existing ones.

 When an instruction says to press DEL, press this key. This is the DELETE key, usually used to erase characters from the screen.

 When an instruction says to press ALT, press this key, the ALTERNATE key. It is used with the function keys described below.

 When an instruction says to press CTRL, press this key, the CONTROL key. It is also used with the function keys.

Function Keys

Depending on your computer you have either ten or twelve special keys, labelled F1 to F10 or F12. They are either on the left side of the keyboard or above the top row, as on the IBM enhanced keyboard. They operate exactly the same in either location.

These keys have been "programmed" by WordPerfect for special functions, and they provide quick and easy methods to perform some complex tasks. Certain functions are performed by pressing a function key by itself. Other functions are accomplished by pressing them in combination with the Alt, Shift, or Ctrl key. At first, you might be overwhelmed by the large number of function keys available. But you'll quickly learn the most important ones and before long you'll master them all.

You received two templates describing these function keys with your WordPerfect manual. The square template with the cutout in the middle is designed for keyboards with the function keys on the left. Place it over the keys and refer to it as you type. The long template is for the enhanced keyboard—place it above the keys so you can refer to it when you want to use the function keys.

Notice that the templates give four different uses for each of the function keys. Some uses are printed in black, others in red, green, or blue. The task in black is accomplished by pressing the function key by itself. The other colors represent combining the key with either the Ctrl, Shift, or Alt key, as explained in the section "Conventions Used in This Book." The color code is:

COLOR	KEY + FUNCTION KEY
Red	Ctrl
Green	Shift
Blue	Alt

While this may seem difficult to remember, there's a little trick that may help. (This will not apply to users of certain keyboards, including the IBM enhanced.) Notice that on the template the functions are printed in the following order:

Red

Green

Blue

Black

Now notice that the corresponding keys are in the same order:

Ctrl

Shift

Alt

So for example, for the function printed on top (red), use the top key (Ctrl) with the function key. For the function printed second, use the second of the keys (Shift). Even people who are color-blind, like myself, can use the template.

If you have misplaced your template, see the inside cover of this book for a recap of the function keys.

*N*umeric Keypad

On the right side of the keyboard is a group of keys, serving as both the numeric keyboard and the cursor movement keys. These keys have both numbers and arrows printed on them. Normally, they act as the cursor movement keys explained in Chapters 1 and 2. But if you do a lot of numeric typing you might find it convenient to use these keys rather than the numbers on the top row of the middle section. To use the keypad for numbers you have to press the Num Lock key above the keypad. With Num Lock on, they are numbers and the characters *Pos* blink at the bottom right of the screen (as will be explained fully in Lesson 2). With some keyboards, a small light in the Num Lock key itself will be on when the Num Lock key is on. Press the key to turn the light, and the key, off.

Some keyboards have separate cursor movement keys and numeric keypad. If you have this type of keyboard, then use the keypad for entering numbers and the arrow keys to the left of the keypad for cursor movement.

Interacting with WordPerfect

WordPerfect has so many powerful features that there are not enough function-key combinations to represent them all. Certainly some tasks are performed by pressing only one or two keys—such as pressing F6 to make characters boldface or the Shift and F6 keys together to center text. But in many cases, pressing one of the function keys will display a message, a line of choices at the bottom of the screen, or even an entire screen of options.

Prompts

A *prompt* is a brief message at the bottom of the screen asking you to make a selection. For instance, if you press F7, the Exit key, the selection line will read

Save document? (Y/N) Y

This is the Save prompt asking if you want to save the current text or not. The Yes at the end of the prompt is the *default* value. Default values usually represent the most common choice and appear automatically for your convenience. You can just press ◄— to accept the default choice shown. If you do not want that default value, make another choice (here, you could choose *N*—you don't have to type the whole word *No*) or press the F1 key to cancel the command. F1, by the way, can always be used to cancel the effect of the last function key pressed.

Whether it displays a prompt, a series of choices, or information about the status of your document, the line at the bottom of the screen is generally called the *status line*. We'll discuss it in more detail in Chapter 1.

Selection Lines

Other function keys reveal a number of choices. If you press Ctrl and F8 the following *selection line* will appear at the bottom of the screen:

1 Size; 2 Appearance; 3 Normal; 4 Base Font; 5 Print Color: 0

This particular selection line is used to alter the appearance of characters. Notice that each choice is numbered and that one character of the choice, not always the first, appears in boldface. Press either the number of the desired choice or the boldfaced letter (such as *1* or *s* for *Size*) to select that option. Or, press the ⟵ key by itself to select the default option shown at the end of the line. In this case, the default 0 will cancel the action. Your selection might perform some action immediately or lead to additional selection lines. Continue picking the desired options.

You can always press F1 to cancel the selection line and return to the document.

Menus

A *menu* is a list of choices too long to fit on just one selection line at the bottom of the screen. Pressing the Shift and F8 keys together, for example, will change the screen to the Format menu shown in Figure I.4. Even though the menu takes up the entire screen, the document will return when you have completed your selections.

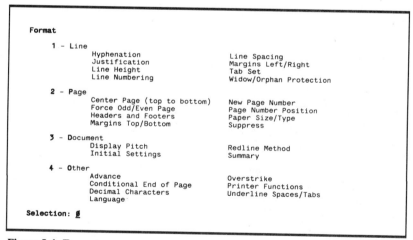

Figure I.4: Format menu

Notice that the menu has four options, numbered 1 to 4, and that one letter of each choice appears in boldface. At the bottom of the screen is a prompt:

Selection: 0

This is used to determine which of the four options you wish to select. As with selection lines, you press the number or boldfaced letter to select the menu option.

You can use the default value 0 to quickly "escape" from the menu. Press ◄—┘ to accept the default value (or press the F1 key) and return to the document.

What happens when you select an option other than 0 depends on the selection. In the case of the Format menu, selecting any choice will show a new menu of additional options. With other menus, however, making a choice will automatically change some setting or you may have to type in a new setting.

*G*et to Know Your Hardware

Now that you are familiar with the keyboard, make sure you understand the rest of your IBM PC or compatible computer.

*M*onitors

You may have either a monochrome, color, or composite monitor. A monochrome monitor displays "black and white" images. The color monitor can display at least sixteen different colors. The composite monitor is also considered black and white because it is not in color. However, shades of gray (or green or amber depending on your monitor) are substituted where colors would appear. For instance, yellow would be displayed as a lighter shade, red as a darker one.

*D*isplay Cards

The *display card* is the part of your computer that puts an image on the monitor. It matches your monitor in terms of having monochrome or color (including composite) capabilities. But the display card also determines the *resolution* of your image and the number of colors that can be displayed at one time. Resolution refers to the quality of the displayed image, how sharp and clear the characters and graphics will appear.

WordPerfect automatically figures out the type of display card and monitor you have when it starts.

Disk Drives

To use WordPerfect you must have two disk drives, in any combination of floppy (either 5¼ or 3½ inch) or hard.

If you have two floppy disk drives, they may either be side by side or stacked on top of each other. The drive on the left-hand side, or on top, is called drive *A*. The other drive is called *B*. When you insert a disk into the drive, you must first open the drive door. With horizontally mounted drives, insert the disk with the label facing up and the small *write-protect notch* toward the left. (With 3½-inch disks, the write protect notch is the small square window with the tab that can be moved back and forth.) For vertically mounted drives, the label faces the left and the write-protect notch faces the bottom. Never bend the disk or expose it to magnetic fields, extremes of hot or cold, or cigarette smoke. Store your disks in plastic or cardboard storage boxes.

Always hold 5¼-inch disks on the edge with the label. Never touch the areas exposed by the long oval slot, which goes into the drive first.

A hard disk is normally called *drive C*. So if you have a hard disk and only one floppy, you have drives A and C in your system. Your hard disk should already contain the disk operating system and you can start your computer without a floppy disk. The instructions in this book assume that if you have a hard disk, it is already set up with DOS or OS/2.

Printer

In Appendix C you will set up WordPerfect for your printer. WordPerfect is designed to work with hundreds of different printers so this will be an easy task. Just make sure you know the name and model number of your printer before continuing.

Conventions Used in This Book

Combining Keystrokes

As you have gathered, many WordPerfect commands require more than one keystroke to activate. These key combinations can be of two types. You might have to press two or more keys at the same time, or you might have to press several keys in sequence.

On the template and in the WordPerfect manual, all function commands such as these are given names. But if you lose your template, or just decide not to place it on your keyboard, you might have trouble remembering what keystrokes the names represent. So throughout this book, all functions are referred to by the actual keystrokes used. Instead of saying *press the Print key,* our instructions will say *press Shift-F7.*

Keys that should be pressed together are separated with a hyphen. For example, if an instruction says to press Shift-F7, this means that you should press and HOLD DOWN the Shift key; then press the F7 key. The sequence is this:

1. Press and hold down the first key listed.

2. Press and release the second key.

3. Release the first key.

Other key combinations must be pressed in sequence, one after the other. These are always separated by blank spaces. For instance, if an instruction says to press F7 N N, this means you should:

1. Press and release the F7 (Exit) key.

2. Press *N.*

3. Press *N* a second time.

This might seem to be a great number of keystrokes for one command. However, as you learn commands such as these, you'll find they become almost automatic. In most cases, you don't have to pause between keystrokes, so pressing three keys will not slow your progress.

The instruction Shift-F7 2 combines both types of instructions. First do Shift-F7 by pressing and holding the Shift key while you press F7. Let go of them both, then press the 2 key.

*F*ollowing the Instructions

Most lessons in this book take you step-by-step through a specific task. Just follow each instruction to master the technique discussed. You will see several types of instructions. So to differentiate between instructions, things you type, and things that WordPerfect displays on the screen, here are a few rules:

- When you are asked to type something in from the keyboard, what you are to type will appear in italic type, like this:

  Type *myfirst* or *b:myfirst*

- Sometimes you will be asked to type several lines of text, or even entire paragraphs. These lines will be indented and set off from the instruction, and they will be in colored type, like this:

  1. Type the following:

     WordPerfect allows the creation, editing, and printing of all types of documents. They can be saved at any time.

- When WordPerfect shows something on the screen in response to something you have done, that information will also be shown in colored type, like this:

  The prompt line changes to

  Save document? (Y/N) Yes

- When you are actually to do something on your computer, I will give you a series of numbered steps to follow:

  1.
  2.
  3.

Read and perform each step in the order given. But be sure to read all of the text that is in the step since, in a few cases, some optional instructions may be given, such as:

> If you want to accept the default value, press ⏎ then skip to step 18.

In this case, you could press the ⏎ key and go directly to step 18, skipping any steps in between. If you don't want to accept the default value, however, don't press ⏎ but continue reading and following instructions.

You're now ready to start WordPerfect. If you have not yet used the program, begin with Appendices A, B, and C.

1
Creating Your First Document

*F*eaturing

Starting WordPerfect
The WordPerfect
screen
Typing characters
The arrow keys
Inserting characters
Printing documents
Saving documents
Getting help

You're probably anxious to use WordPerfect. Good. But before using this powerful program for the first time you must do these three things that are explained in the appendices:

1. Make a copy of WordPerfect solely for your own backup.

2. Make a working set of floppy disks or install the program on a hard disk.

3. Let WordPerfect know what printer or printers you'll be using for your documents.

If you've already followed the installation instructions in the Word-Perfect manual, you are ready to start Lesson 1 right now. Otherwise, carefully follow the instructions in Appendices A, B, and C, then come back to this chapter.

Now that WordPerfect is ready, let's begin!

*L**esson 1 – How to Start WordPerfect*

When you start a program, you are actually transferring it from the disk into the computer's memory. Then the control of your program is passed from the disk operating system (DOS or OS/2) to the program itself.

With WordPerfect, only parts of the program are loaded into your computer. These are the functions that you'll use most often. Other segments of the program remain on the disk and are loaded only when you need them. So when you select certain more advanced commands, you'll hear your disk spin while these instructions are loaded. WordPerfect uses this technique so you'll have as much memory as possible available for your own documents.

How you start WordPerfect depends on whether you are using a computer with a hard disk or two floppy disk drives.

*H**ard Disk*

To start WordPerfect on the hard disk:

1. Turn on your computer. Respond to the date and time prompts if they appear. The *C>* prompt will appear.

2. Type *CD\WP50* and press ◄┘. (If you called your subdirectory something other than WP50, type that name instead.)

3. Type *WP* and press ◄┘.

*F*loppy Disks

If you are using floppy disks, you should have all of the WordPerfect disks handy when you are typing. Always start with the WordPerfect 1 program disk in drive A and a document disk in drive B. Use the disks you made in Appendix A, not the original WordPerfect disks. These should be stored in a safe location in case your copies become damaged.

To start WordPerfect with a floppy disk system:

1. Place the WordPerfect 1 program disk in drive A and turn on your computer. Respond to the date and time questions. The *A>* prompt will appear.

2. Place the blank formatted disk in drive B.

3. Type *WP* and press ◄┘. If you're using 5¼-inch disks, see the message

   Insert diskette labeled "WP 2" and press any key

   Then you should remove the WordPerfect 1 disk from drive A, insert the WordPerfect 2 disk, close the disk drive latch, and then press any key.

   An alternative method of starting WordPerfect will automatically save your documents on the document disk in drive B. After starting your computer and inserting your disks as described in steps 1 and 2, press *B:* then ◄┘ to "log onto" drive B. The prompt changes to *B>*. Now start WordPerfect by typing *A:WP* and pressing ◄┘.

If you are not ready to go on to the next lesson, press F7 N Y (the F7 function key—the Exit key—then *N* to the *Save Document?* prompt, then *Y* to the *Exit WP?* prompt). This exits the program quickly without saving the text on the screen.

*L*esson 2 – The WordPerfect Screen

If you are not already in WordPerfect, start the program as you did in Lesson 1.

When you start WordPerfect, the screen is entirely blank except for the blinking cursor and a small *status* line on the bottom of the screen:

Doc 1 Pg 1 Ln 1" Pos 1"

This line lets you know where the cursor is located in the document. Since you can work on two different documents at a time, the status line also tells you which document you are currently editing.

The four elements that are always on the status line are:

Doc   The document number, which can be either 1 or 2, depending on which document you are editing.

Pg   The number of the page you are currently viewing on the screen.

Ln   The distance of the cursor from the top of the page. With the default settings, a new page will start at 9.83".

Pos   A number indicating where the cursor is on the line in relation to the left margin. For example, using the default values, the text has a 1-inch, or 10-character, left margin. So when you are starting a line, the cursor will be in position 1" and the status line will show *Pos 1"*. (If you're using a laser printer and certain typestyles, your position indicator at the left margin might show something other than 1". You'll see why in Chapter 5.) If Pos is blinking, then Num Lock is turned on and certain keys will display numbers instead of moving the cursor. If POS is all uppercase, then the Caps Lock is on and you'll get all uppercase letters.

The lower left corner of the screen will usually be blank or contain the name of the current document. This indicates that you are in the *Insert* mode. If you enter characters within existing text, words to the right will move over and down to make room. If you press the Ins key (the *0* key on the keypad), the word *Typeover* will appear in the lower left corner. New characters typed will now replace existing ones.

Typeover   **Doc 1 Pg 1 Ln 1" Pos 1"**

Insert and Typeover are two basic typing modes that will be explained in Chapter 2.

Ins, by the way, is called a *toggle* key. You press it once to turn on a function; press it again to turn off the same function. So to get back into the Insert mode, press Ins again so the word *Typeover* disappears from the status line.

During word processing, various other messages and prompts will appear on the status line.

Scrolling Text on the Screen

The most obvious difference between the screen and the printed page is the number of lines they hold. The WordPerfect screen can display only 24 lines of text at one time. But don't worry—your documents can be as long as you want thanks to the features called scrolling and auto-pagination.

As you type, the cursor will move down the page and the Ln indicator in the status line will change. As you pass the last line on the screen the lines at the top will *scroll* up out of view into the computer's memory. You'll be able to scroll the text back down into view, as explained in Lessons 7 and 12.

As your text grows even longer, you don't have to worry about ending one page and starting another—just continue typing. After you type the 54th line on a page, a line of dashes will appear across the screen and the Pg indicator in the status line will increase by one. This is *auto-pagination*. If you later add or delete lines from a page, the page breaks will change so the default value of 54 typing lines will appear on each page. You can manually end a page at any time by pressing Ctrl-←.

Lesson 3 – How to Type in WordPerfect

If you've ever used a typewriter, you can start using WordPerfect. All of the letter, number, and punctuation keys on the four middle rows of the keyboard work just the same. You just type, letting the text scroll up and start new pages automatically. But don't worry if you've never typed a word in your life. I type using only three fingers, but I was still able to use WordPerfect to write this entire book.

Now let's look at one of the best features of word processing—word-wrap. Follow these steps:

1. Type the following text. *Do not* press the ⏎ key when the cursor reaches the right edge of the screen, just continue typing. If you make a mistake, press the Backspace key. This will move the cursor back through your text, erasing characters.

    WordPerfect allows the creation, editing, and printing of all types of documents.

    When you typed the word *types*, it automatically moved to the next line (see Figure 1.1); this is called *word-wrap*. (If you're using a laser printer or some other proportional spacing printer, your sentence may word-wrap at some other location.) WordPerfect senses when the word you are typing will not fit within the right margin. So it moves the word to the next line and lets you continue typing without having to listen for the margin bell and press ⏎ at the end of every line.

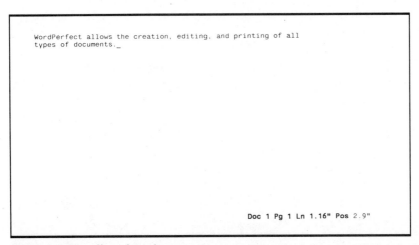

```
WordPerfect allows the creation, editing, and printing of all
types of documents._




















                                    Doc 1 Pg 1 Ln 1.16" Pos 2.9"
```

Figure 1.1: The effect of word-wrap

2. Complete the paragraph, noticing how word-wrap works at each line.

    WordPerfect allows the creation, editing, and printing of all types of documents. They can be saved on a disk and recalled at any time.

3. Press the ⏎ key. The cursor will move to the next line, under the last sentence typed.

4. Press the ⏎ key again to insert a blank line between paragraphs.

5. Type the following:

    Because WordPerfect is designed to use the full powers of your computer, you can format and manipulate text in ways unimaginable with a typewriter.

6. Press the ⏎ key and your screen will look like Figure 1.2.

```
WordPerfect allows the creation, editing, and printing of all
types of documents. They can be saved on a disk and recalled at
any time.

Because WordPerfect is designed to use the full powers of your
computer, you can format and manipulate text in ways unimaginable
with a typewriter.
_



                                              Doc 1 Pg 1 Ln 2.16" Pos 1"
```

Figure 1.2: *The completed example*

You can use the ⏎ key to end the paragraph, as in steps 3 and 6, or to insert a blank line in the document, as in Step 4.

*L*esson 4 – How to Move the Cursor

The cursor is that small blinking line or box on the screen that shows where the next character typed will appear. If the cursor is at the end of your document, characters you type will be added to the end of your text. But you can move the cursor anywhere in your document. If you want to add words to the middle of a paragraph, move the cursor to that spot and type.

Most of the cursor movement keys are located on the right side of the keyboard, either combined with the numeric keypad or to its left. If they are combined and a number appears on the screen when you try to move the cursor, press the key marked Num Lock.

The four most basic cursor movement keys are the directional arrows.

↑   This is the up arrow key. When you press this key the cursor moves up one line. If the cursor is on the first screen line, lines not shown will scroll down into view, showing text above the previous cursor position. Pressing the key has no effect if you are on the first line of the document.

↓   This is the down arrow key. When you press this key the cursor moves down one line, unless you are on the last line of the document. (To move beyond the last line press ←⏎.) If the cursor is on the last screen line, any lines not shown will scroll up into view, showing text below the previous cursor position.

→   This is the right arrow key. It moves the cursor one character to the right. When you reach the right margin, the cursor will move to the first character of the next line.

←   This is the left arrow key. It moves the cursor one character to the left. When you reach the left margin, the cursor will move to the last character of the line above.

To move more than one line or character at a time, hold down the directional arrow key.

Lesson 5 – How to Insert Text

Let's use the arrow keys to change your document on the screen. First make sure that the word *Typeover* does not appear in the status line. If it does, press the Ins key.

1. Press the ↑ and ← keys to place the cursor at the start of the first sentence, the *W* in *WordPerfect*.

2. Press the Tab key. The first sentence becomes indented five spaces (Figure 1.3).

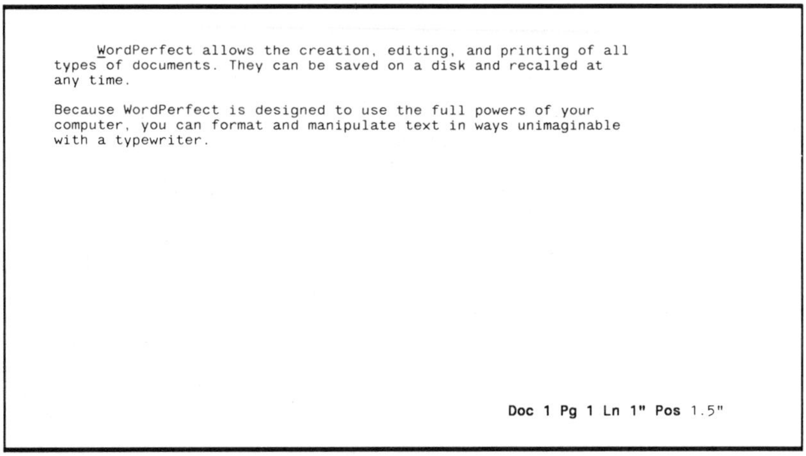

```
        WordPerfect allows the creation, editing, and printing of all
types of documents. They can be saved on a disk and recalled at
any time.

Because WordPerfect is designed to use the full powers of your
computer, you can format and manipulate text in ways unimaginable
with a typewriter.
```

```
                                          Doc 1 Pg 1 Ln 1" Pos 1.5"
```

Figure 1.3: A tab inserted to indent a sentence

3. Press any one of the arrow keys. The word *all* now moves to the next line and the entire paragraph adjusts to accommodate the tab (Figure 1.4). Moving the cursor adjusts text to the format settings.

4. Now insert a tab at the beginning of the next paragraph.

   a. Move the cursor to the beginning of that paragraph.

   b. Press the Tab key.

   c. Move the cursor in any direction to adjust the paragraph.

   The text is shown in Figure 1.5.

```
        WordPerfect allows the creation, editing, and printing of
all types of documents. They can be saved on a disk and recalled
at any time.

Because WordPerfect is designed to use the full powers of your
computer, you can format and manipulate text in ways unimaginable
with a typewriter.




                                              Doc 1 Pg 1 Ln 1.16" Pos 1.5"
```

Figure 1.4: The adjusted paragraph after moving the cursor

Let's insert some other text into your document just to see how it works.

5. Move the cursor to the letter *d* in *disk,* in the first paragraph.

6. Type

    floppy or hard

```
        WordPerfect allows the creation, editing, and printing of
all types of documents. They can be saved on a disk and recalled
at any time.

        Because WordPerfect is designed to use the full powers of
your computer, you can format and manipulate text in ways
unimaginable with a typewriter.




                                              Doc 1 Pg 1 Ln 1.83" Pos 1.5"
```

Figure 1.5: The text with both paragraphs indented

7. Press the Space bar after the word *hard* to insert a space between it and the word *disk*.

8. Now press any arrow key to adjust the paragraph (Figure 1.6).

```
        WordPerfect allows the creation, editing, and printing of
    all types of documents. They can be saved on a floppy or hard
    disk and recalled at any time.

        Because WordPerfect is designed to use the full powers of
    your computer, you can format and manipulate text in ways
    unimaginable with a typewriter.




                                        Doc 1 Pg 1 Ln 1.33" Pos 1.5"
```

Figure 1.6: Words inserted into the text

As you see, text or tabs can be inserted anywhere in the document. The paragraph will automatically adjust when the cursor is moved.

*L*esson 6 – How To Print Documents

WordPerfect has many powerful printing features. But for the impatient, let's print the text that is now on the screen. Make sure your printer is turned on and paper is ready.

1. Press the Shift-F7 (Print) function key to display the menu shown in Figure 1.7.

2. Press *1* for Full Document. (Since your document is only one page long, you could also have pressed *2* for Page.)

If you selected either *Sheet Feeder* or *Continuous* when installing your printer, the document will now be printed.

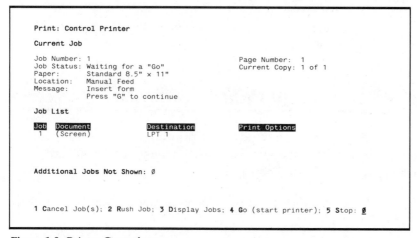

```
Print
        1 - Full Document
        2 - Page
        3 - Document on Disk
        4 - Control Printer
        5 - Type Through
        6 - View Document
        7 - Initialize Printer

Options
        S - Select Printer          Standard Printer
        B - Binding                 Ø"
        N - Number of Copies        1
        G - Graphics Quality        Medium
        T - Text Quality            High




        Selection: Ø
```

Figure 1.7: The Print menu

If you selected Manual, you'll hear a short beep telling you to load the paper into the printer. When the paper is ready, press *4* to display the Printer Control menu (Figure 1.8), then *G,* the Go option.

```
Print: Control Printer

Current Job

Job Number: 1                       Page Number:  1
Job Status: Waiting for a "Go"      Current Copy: 1 of 1
Paper:      Standard 8.5" x 11"
Location:   Manual Feed
Message:    Insert form
            Press "G" to continue

Job List

Job   Document              Destination        Print Options
 1    (Screen)              LPT 1




Additional Jobs Not Shown: Ø


1 Cancel Job(s); 2 Rush Job; 3 Display Jobs; 4 Go (start printer); 5 Stop: Ø
```

Figure 1.8: Printer Control menu

When printing with hand-fed, or manual, paper, you'll hear the beep after each page. Insert the next sheet of paper into the printer, then issue the Go command. If the Printer Control menu is already displayed, just press *G.* From the Print menu press *4 G.* If you've already returned to the document, press Shift-F7 4 G.

Press F1 until you clear the menus and return to the document.

*L*esson 7 – How to Save Your Document

When you are done typing your document, you must save it on the disk if you want to edit or print it later. How you save it depends on what you want to do next—whether you want to work on another document or stop using WordPerfect.

In this lesson, you'll learn how to save a document that you have just worked on for the first time. Later I'll show you how to save a document after you've recalled it from the disk to make revisions.

You need to save a document after printing it only if you think you'll need it later.

*S*aving New Documents and Quitting WordPerfect

Save the document you just created under the name *MYFIRST*.

1. Press the F7 (Exit) key. The prompt

   Save Document? (Y/N) Yes

   will appear.

2. Press ◄┘. If you change your mind about saving the document, just press *N*. Since you have not yet given this document a name, the prompt

   Document to be saved:

   appears.

3. Type *MYFIRST* if you have a hard disk system, or *B:MY-FIRST* if you have a floppy disk system and did not log onto drive B in Lesson 1, then press ◄┘.

   Document names can be from one to eight characters long and should start with a letter. Remember to begin the name with *B:* to store it on drive B unless you are using a hard disk or you logged onto drive B.

   Finally, the prompt

   Exit WP? (Y/N) No (Cancel to return to document)

   appears.

4. Press *Y* to return to the disk operating system.

If you change your mind at any step in this process, just press the F1 key until no prompts appear at the bottom of the screen.

*L*esson 8 – How to Get Help

Even with the template over the function keys, it is still difficult to remember which function key leads to which selection line or menu. WordPerfect is so powerful that there may be functions you use rarely, and between uses it is easy to forget how they work. So for just those times, WordPerfect has a Help function that you can reach by pressing the F3 function key.

If you are using floppy disks, make sure you have the Learning diskette handy. Hard disk users should have already installed the file WPHELP.FIL into the WP subdirectory containing WordPerfect. Here's how to get help:

1. Restart WordPerfect as you learned in Lesson 1.

2. Press F3, the Help function key.
   In a few moments, floppy disk users will see the following message on the status line:

   WPHELP.FIL not found. Insert Learning Diskette and press drive letter:

   Remove the document disk in drive B and replace it with the Learning Diskette. Close the drive door and press B.
   You can now get three types of help:

   - Press F3 again to display the template on the screen.

   - Press any function key, or combination, for a description of its uses.

   - Press any letter for an alphabetic index of functions and corresponding keystrokes.

3. Press the F3 function key a second time. A copy of the template will appear. You will see functions that are unfamiliar to

you, but don't worry. You will learn about all of them in the upcoming lessons.

If you have lost your template, and your printer is on and ready, press Shift-PrtSc to get a printed copy of the one displayed on the screen.

As long as you are still in the help function, let's explore the help explanations of function keys.

4. Press several function key combinations, and several letters, to see the type of help provided. When you are done, press the Space bar to return to the typing window.

5. If you are not ready to continue with the next lesson, press F7 and answer *N* (since you don't need to save what's on the screen) and then *Y* to exit WordPerfect.

2
Improving and Correcting Your Document

*F*eaturing

Recalling documents

Advanced cursor movement

Deleting text

Undeleting text

Typeover

Resaving edited documents

*L*esson 9 – How to Recall a Document from Disk

We all make mistakes. Errors in spelling and grammar or accidental keystrokes somehow find their way into documents. Surely at times you've spent a great deal of time changing—or correcting—what you had already typed. With a typewriter, this often means throwing away the page and starting over.

Well, one of the most important features of word processing is how easy it is to edit your documents, correcting errors without retyping the rest of the text.

Editing can be done on new documents as you type them, or on documents already saved on the disk. Of course, to edit a saved document you must first load it into the typing window.

Let's recall the document MYFIRST, which you created in the last chapter.

*R*ecall by Name

Since you know the name of the document you wish to recall, just follow these steps:

1. Start WordPerfect.

2. Press Shift-F10, the Retrieve key. The message

   Document to be Retrieved:

   appears on the status line.

3. Type *MYFIRST* or *B:MYFIRST* (if using two floppy disk drives) and press ←⏎.

The document will appear on the screen, with its name in the lower left corner.

*R*ecall by Directory

You've already recalled the document MYFIRST. But if you were not sure of the document's name, you could also recall it by first displaying the directory from within WordPerfect.

1. Press F5, the Directory Listing key. The letter of the current drive will appear on the status line.

2. Press ◄──┘ if that is the disk containing the document, or type the letter of another drive followed by a colon and press ◄──┘. A directory of the disk will appear on the screen (Figure 2.1). If there are more files on the disk than can be displayed, you'll see a small arrow at the bottom of the center line that separates the columns.

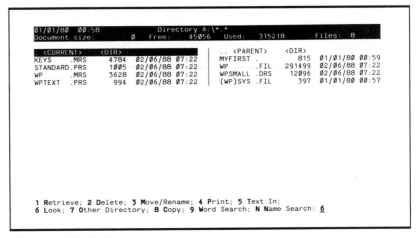

Figure 2.1: *File Listing*

3. Press the arrow keys. Notice that the "highlighting" moves from document name to document name, scrolling the listing up if there are more files than can be seen at one time. Highlight the name of the document you wish to retrieve.

   If you're not sure what you called the document, you can temporarily display its contents. Highlight one of the possible names, then press ◄──┘, 6, or *L* to select the Look option. The document will appear on the screen as shown in Figure 2.2.

   You can't edit the document while in this mode; you can just use the up and down cursor movement keys to look at its contents. Press Space bar again to stop it. Press F7, the Exit key, to return to the directory listing.

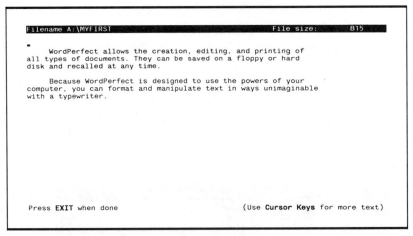

Figure 2.2: Displaying a document in Look mode

4. When you've highlighted the correct document, press *1,* but don't do this now or you'll get two copies of MYFIRST on the screen. Just press F7 to return to the editing window.

*L*esson 10 – How to Move the Cursor More Efficiently

While the arrow keys can be used to move the cursor anywhere in the document, there are faster ways of moving more than one line or character at a time.

*M*oving Down through a Document

Press the following keys or key combinations to move down through a document. As you move down past the last displayed line, the text will scroll up, displaying additional text if it exists.

Home Home ↓   Moves the cursor to the end of the document.

PgDn   Moves the cursor to the top of the next page in the document. For example,

	pressing this key while editing page 5 will place the cursor at the top of page 6.
Home ↓ or + (on numeric keypad)	Moves the cursor to the bottom of the screen or, if already there, displays the next 24 lines of text.
Esc *n* PgDn	Moves the cursor down *n* pages. Press Esc, enter the number of pages to move, then press PgDn.
Esc *n* ↓	Moves the cursor down *n* lines. Press Esc, enter the number of lines to move, then press the down arrow.
Ctrl-Home ↓	Moves the cursor to the bottom of the current page. The Ctrl-Home combination is called *GoTo*.

*M*oving Up through a Document

Press the following keys or key combinations to move up through a document. As you move up past the topmost displayed line, the text will scroll down, displaying additional text if it exists.

Home Home ↑	Moves the cursor to the top of the document.
PgUp	Moves the cursor to the top of the previous page. For example, if you are editing page 3, press this key to place the cursor at (and to display) the top of page 2.
Home ↑ or − (on numeric keypad)	Moves the cursor to the top of the screen or, if already there, displays the previous 24 lines of text.
Esc *n* PgUp	Moves the cursor up *n* pages.
Esc *n* ↑	Moves the cursor up *n* lines.
Ctrl-Home ↑	Moves the cursor to the top of the current page.

*M*oving Left

Press the following key combinations to move the cursor toward the left margin:

Home ←	Moves the cursor to the beginning of the line.
Esc *n* ←	Moves the cursor *n* characters to the left.
Ctrl-Home ←	Moves the cursor to the next column when typing multi-column documents.
Ctrl-Home Home ←	Moves to the first column on a multicolumn page.
Ctrl-←	Moves to the next word on the left.

*M*oving Right

Press the following keys or key combinations to move the cursor toward the right margin:

End	Moves the cursor to the end of the current line.
Home →	Moves the cursor to the right edge of the screen.
Esc *n* →	Moves the cursor *n* characters to the right.
Ctrl-Home →	Moves the cursor to the previous column when typing multi-column documents.
Ctrl-Home Home →	Moves to the last column on a multicolumn page.
Ctrl-→	Moves to the next word on the right.

Moving to Specific Locations

Finally, the GoTo combination (Ctrl-Home) can be used to place the cursor at a specific page or character.

Ctrl-Home *n*   Moves the cursor to the top of page *n*.

Ctrl-Home *x*   Moves the cursor to the first occurrence of the character *x* (it must occur within the nearest 2000 characters). For example, press Ctrl-Home M to place the cursor on the first letter *M* within 2000 characters of the cursor. The character can be any single keystroke—a letter, number, or punctuation mark.

Lesson 11 – How to Delete Text

The document MYFIRST should now be displayed on the screen, as shown in Figure 1.6.

Inserting text is easy. Just move the cursor and type. But how do you delete text that you no longer want in the document? You already know that you can press the Backspace key to delete characters to the left of the cursor. Here are other ways of deleting.

Deleting Characters

Let's delete the words *floppy or hard* that you inserted in the last chapter.

1. Use the arrow keys to place the cursor on the letter *f* in *floppy*.

2. Press the Del key. When you do, the character above the cursor is erased and the remaining text moves to the left.

    Keep in mind the difference between Backspace and Del. Backspace deletes characters to the left; Del deletes the character at the cursor position.

3. Now press the Del key 14 more times until the rest of the words have been deleted and the text readjusts as shown in Figure 2.3

```
        WordPerfect allows the creation, editing, and printing of
all types of documents. They can be saved on a disk and recalled
at any time.

        Because WordPerfect is designed to use the full powers of
your computer, you can format and manipulate text in ways
unimaginable with a typewriter.




C:\WP5\MYFIRST                              Doc 1 Pg 1 Ln 1.16" Pos 5.7"
```

Figure 2.3: The document MYFIRST after deletions

When deleting other groups of words you might have to press an arrow key to readjust the text.

Just as there are advanced cursor movement commands, there are advanced deletion commands. These let you erase text faster than one character at a time.

*D*eleting Words

1. Place the cursor on the word *full* in the second paragraph. The cursor can be on any character of the word.

2. Press Ctrl-Backspace. The entire word is deleted.

3. Press an arrow key to adjust the text. It should now look like this:

> **WordPerfect allows the creation, editing, and printing of all types of documents. They can be saved on a disk and recalled at any time.**
>
> **Because WordPerfect is designed to use the powers of your computer, you can format and**

> **manipulate text in ways unimaginable with a typewriter.**

*D*eleting Lines

1. Place the cursor in the space before the word *on* in the first paragraph.

2. Press Ctrl-End. This command deletes every character on the line to the right of the cursor. Your screen should now read

> **WordPerfect allows the creation, editing, and printing of all types of documents. They can be saved at any time.**
>
> **Because WordPerfect is designed to use the powers of your computer, you can format and manipulate text in ways unimaginable with a typewriter.**

*M*ass Deletion

Finally, you can delete the entire last paragraph.

1. Place the cursor in the blank line following the first paragraph.

2. Press Ctrl-PgDn. The prompt

> **Delete Remainder of page? (Y/N) No**

appears. Press *N* for now because you'll be using this document later. Ctrl-PgDn deletes all of the text from the position of the cursor to the end of the page.

*D*eleting Parts of Words

You can quickly delete from the cursor position to either the beginning or the end of a word in which the cursor is placed. Look at the following example:

> **reperçussion**

Press Home Backspace (one after the other, not together) to delete from the cursor position to the start of the word. This would result in *cussion*.

Or press Home Del (one after the other, not together) to delete from the cursor position to the end of the word. In this example, *reper* would remain.

A Summary of Deletion Commands

COMMAND	WILL DELETE
Backspace	the character to the left of the cursor
Del	the character above the cursor
Ctrl-Backspace	the entire word under which the cursor is placed
Ctrl-End	from the cursor to the right margin
Ctrl-PgDn	from the cursor to the end of the document
Home Backspace	from the cursor to the beginning of the word
Home Del	from the cursor to the end of the word

Lesson 12 – How to Restore Deleted Text

Oops! By accident, you just deleted an entire paragraph. Press the F1 (Cancel) key to display the prompt

Undelete 1 Restore; 2 Show Previous Deletion: 0

The last characters you deleted, whether a single character, a word, or an entire page, will reappear highlighted at the position of the cursor. Press *1* to restore the character(s) at that location on the screen. Since WordPerfect "remembers" the last three deletions made, press F1 to show the last deletion, then *2* to reveal the one before, and *2* again for the deletion before that. Whatever text is highlighted will be restored when *1* is pressed at the Undelete prompt.

F1 can also be used as a quick way of moving words or phrases. Delete the text, move the cursor, then just press F1 1 whenever you want the text to appear.

Let's try using the Undelete key. If you quit WordPerfect after the last lesson, start the program and load the document MYFIRST.

1. Place the cursor at the start of the second paragraph.

2. Press Ctrl-PgDn Y to delete all the text starting at the position of the cursor.

3. Press F1, the Cancel key. The text you just deleted reappears highlighted on the screen with the Undelete prompt in the status line (Figure 2.4). The highlighted text is not yet restored, however.

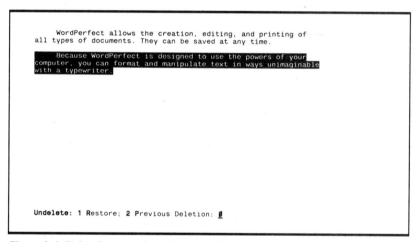

Figure 2.4: Deleted text ready to be restored

4. Press *1* to restore the deleted text.

Now let's see how F1 can move text from one position to another.

5. Place the cursor again at the start of the second paragraph.

6. Press Ctrl-PgDn Y to delete the paragraph.

7. Place the cursor at the start of the first paragraph.

8. Press F1. The deleted paragraph appears highlighted at the new position.

9. Press *1* to restore the paragraph.

You'll learn some even more efficient ways to move text in Chapter 10. First, let's see how you can save a new copy of this edited document.

*L*esson 13 – How to Save a Document after Revisions

In Lesson 7 you saved MYFIRST on your disk. Now let's save the edited version.

1. Press F7 to display the prompt

    Save Document? (Y/N) Yes

2. Press ←┘.

3. Since the document already has a name, it will appear in the next prompt:

    Document to be saved: B:\MYFIRST

    To keep the same name, press ←┘. If you want to change the document's name, just type another name and you will have both the old and the new versions of the document saved on disk.

    If you did not change the name, the prompt would change to

    Replace B:MYFIRST? (Y/N) No

    Press *Y* to replace the original version with the new text. If you press *N*, the *Document to be saved* prompt will again appear so you can give the revised document a new name.

    You cannot have two different documents with the same name on the same disk, so if you give a new document the name of an existing one and press *Y* to the Replace prompt, the original will be erased.

4. To quit WordPerfect, press *Y* at the prompt

    Exit WP? (Y/N) No

*S*aving and Continuing with the Same Document

As a precaution, get into the habit of saving your work every 15 minutes or so, even when you're not finished working on a document.

If anything goes wrong with your computer (such as a pulled plug or an accidental reset) you won't lose a great deal of work. Saving the current document in this way leaves you in the WordPerfect program.

1. Press F10, the Save key. The prompt

   Document To Be Saved

   will appear.

2. Type a name or press ◄— if the name already appears at the prompt. Type a new name if you want to change it. If the document is already on the disk, the screen will display

   Replace (your document-name)? (Y/N) No

   Press *Y* to "replace" the document—that is, to save all the changes you've made since you last saved the document.

*S*aving and Starting a New Document

To start a new document when one is already on the screen, save the current document first. Follow the same steps as when saving and quitting, but enter *N* to the prompt

Exit WP? (Y/N) No

The current document will be stored on the disk and the screen will clear.

*Q*uitting WordPerfect without Saving the Document

There are times when you write a document but do not want to save it. For example, you might type a brief note and print it immediately. Once printed it may not be important enough to save. Or you may make some changes to a document and then decide they should not have been made. In these cases, press F7 for the *Save Document?* prompt but press *N* for no. Then press *Y* to exit WordPerfect or *N* to clear the screen and remain in the program.

3
More Efficient Revision Techniques

*F*eaturing

Typeover
Revealing codes
Combining and
splitting paragraphs
Repeating commands
Multiple documents
Inserting the date

*L*esson 14 – How to Use Typeover

One way to change characters is to delete the incorrect ones and then insert new ones in their place.

But there is also a *Typeover* mode, entered by pressing Ins, that can be used to change characters quickly. With Typeover, the new characters you type replace existing ones. Each new character takes the place of one already there.

While Typeover is a fast way to change mistakes, it has limited value. Use Typeover when you are replacing characters with the same number of new ones. This way you will not erase words accidentally as you continue typing. I can't tell you how many times I've mistakenly deleted text by trying to insert while in Typeover mode.

You can use either Typeover or Insert to add characters to the end of a paragraph.

Let's try using Typeover.

1. Start WordPerfect.

2. Using the TAB key to indent the paragraphs, type the letter shown in Figure 3.1.

3. Press the Ins key so the word *Typeover* appears in the status line.

4. Place the cursor on the *t* in the word *two*.

5. Type

    ten

    The new characters simply took the place of the existing ones.

6. Place the cursor at the start of the word *class* in the first paragraph.

7. Type

    September class

    Even though you typed more new characters than were in the line, they did not affect the carriage return at the end of the line.

```
January 12, 1988

Mr. Robert Williams
53 Kinder Lane
Willow Grove, PA. 18985


Dear Mr. Williams:

     The admissions committee has reviewed your application and I
am pleased to offer you a place in our class of 1999.

     However, it is imperative that you notify this office within
two days  to reserve your  place. If we  do not hear  from you by
that  time, we  will award  your place  in  the class  to another
student.

     We are looking forward to hearing from you. We are confident
the next year will be an exciting one for you.

                         Sincerely,

                         Wilfred Magatel
                         Admissions Director
```

Figure 3.1: The sample letter

If you are not ready to continue, save your document under the name *LETTER*. Press F7, answer *Y* to the Save prompt, type *LETTER* (or *B:LETTER* if you have floppy drives), press ◄─┘, and then *Y* to leave WordPerfect.

If you're staying in WordPerfect, press Ins to return to Insert mode. The word Typeover will disappear from the status line.

*L*esson 15 – How to Work with Codes

Keys like Tab and ↵ do not display any characters on the screen although they affect the format of the text. They do, however, insert "invisible" codes that can be deleted just like any other character. While you don't have to see these codes to delete them, making them visible simplifies the editing of complex documents.

If you quit WordPerfect after the last lesson, start WordPerfect again and recall the document LETTER.

*R*evealing Codes

1. Place the cursor at the start of the second paragraph.

2. Press Alt-F3 to reveal the codes (see Figure 3.2).

   A *scale line* near the middle of the screen shows the positions of the tabs (with little triangles) and the left and right margins. Above the scale line are eleven lines of text, the one containing the cursor and ten lines before it. Beneath the scale

Figure 3.2: *WordPerfect screen with codes revealed and scale line*

line are also eleven lines of text, two above the cursor position and eight below, but with symbols showing the invisible codes. The position of the cursor is shown highlighted, or *in reverse video.*

Hard carriage returns (created by pressing the ←┘ key) are represented by [HRt], soft carriage returns (added by word-wrap) are shown as [SRt], and tabs are [TAB]. Figure 3.3 lists the most common codes. Don't try to memorize the codes or worry about them. As you use the program you'll become familiar with the important ones. In most cases, you can work with WordPerfect without even thinking about the codes themselves.

3. Use the arrow keys to move the cursor in all four directions. Notice that the cursor changes position both above and below the scale line.

    With the codes revealed, you can delete either text or the codes themselves by pressing Del or Backspace. The text both above and below the scale line will change accordingly.

4. Place the cursor to highlight the [TAB] code in the first paragraph.

CODE	MEANING
[Algn][C/A/Flrt]	Begin and end tab align or flush right
[BOLD][bold]	Begin and end boldface
[Cntr][C/A/Flrt]	Begin and end centering
[Center Pg]	Center page within top and bottom margins
[CndlEOP:*n*]	Conditional end of page (*n* lines to keep together)
[Col Def:]	Column definition
[Col On]	Column mode turned on
[Col Off]	Column mode turned off

Figure 3.3: Common WordPerfect codes

[Date:n]	Date/time function using format *n*
[Form: size,type]	Page size and form type
[Hdr/Ftr:*n*,*n*;text]	Header or footer definition
	n is type and occurrence number followed by the *text* of the header or footer
[HPg]	Hard page break inserted by operator
[HRt]	Hard return inserted with Enter key
[-> Indent]	Beginning of left indent
[-> Indent<-]	Beginning of left and right indent
[<- Mar Rel]	Margin released *n* positions
[L/R Mar:*n*,*n*]	Left and right margin settings
[Pg#:n]	Page number set to *n*
[Pg# Pos:*n*]	Position of page number
[Rt Just On]	Right justification on
[Rt Just Off]	Right justification off
[Ln Spacing:*n*]	Line spacing set at *n* lines
[SPg]	Soft page break inserted by program
[SRt]	Soft carriage return inserted by word-wrap
[SUBSCRPT]	Subscript
[SUPRSCRPT]	Superscript
[TAB]	Tab
[Tab Set:]	Tab stops
[T/B Mar:*n*",*n*"]	Top and bottom margin setting in *n* inches
[UNDRLN][undrln]	Begin and end underlining

Figure 3.3: Common WordPerfect codes (continued)

5. Press Del. The text will readjust on both sides of the scale line.

6. Press Alt-F3. The scale line and bottom display area disappear.

7. The cursor should still be at the beginning of the first paragraph. Press Tab to indent the paragraph again.

You'll learn more about deleting codes in later lessons. However, remember that you do not have to reveal codes to delete them. For example, you could also have deleted the tab by placing the cursor at the start of the line and pressing Del.

Take advantage of these codes when you're working. For instance, I recommend displaying the codes (by pressing Alt-F3) whenever the text on the screen just doesn't appear correct. Sometimes you may enter a format code by accidentally pressing the wrong function key. By revealing the codes, you can tell where these incorrect functions were added and easily delete them.

Working with Codes Revealed

Displaying the codes at the bottom of the screen simply gives you two views of the same document. You can leave the codes revealed and continue writing or editing in the upper portion. However, you'll only be able to see eleven lines of your text in the top window and seven lines under the scale line. Three of the lines below the scale line are also shown above.

So it's much easier to press Alt-F3 to reveal the codes when needed, then Alt-F3 again to return the screen to normal for writing and editing.

Lesson 16 – How to Split and Combine Paragraphs

You press the ⏎ key to begin a new paragraph. This inserts the Hard Carriage Return code [HRt] at the end of a line. It follows, then, that if you press ⏎ when the cursor is within a paragraph, an [HRt] code will be inserted, dividing the paragraph into two. And by deleting an [HRt] code between two paragraphs, they will be combined into one.

Combining Two Paragraphs

To combine two paragraphs into one, position the cursor immediately after the first paragraph you want to combine and press Del. The paragraph below will move up one line. (If one delete doesn't do the trick, there might be some extra spaces between the end of the sentence and the [HRt] code. Keep pressing Del until the paragraphs come together.) If you double-spaced between paragraphs by pressing ↵ twice, you must press Del twice.

If the codes are revealed, place the cursor on the [HRt] code before pressing Del. We'll use this technique to readjust the letter on the screen.

1. Place the cursor at the end of the first paragraph.

2. Press → to move past the last word in the sentence.

   The cursor didn't move into the blank spaces after the sentence, but down to the next line. That's because there are *no* blank spaces after the sentence, just the [HRt] code. Let's confirm this by looking at the codes again.

3. Press Alt-F3. Look at the end of the first paragraph. There's the [HRt] code. When you moved the cursor with the → key the cursor first moved past the [HRt] code and then to the next line.

4. Press Alt-F3 to clear the displayed codes.

5. Now, again place the cursor at the end of the first paragraph.

6. Press the Space bar. This inserts the space that will separate the two sentences.

7. Press Del three times. While no codes were revealed, you deleted first the [HRt] code after the sentence, then the [HRt] code that created the blank line between paragraphs, and finally the [TAB] code that indented the second paragraph (Figure 3.4).

Splitting a Paragraph into Two

To split one paragraph into two, position the cursor at the beginning of the sentence that will start the new paragraph and press ↵.

```
    Mr. Robert Williams
    53 Kinder Lane
    Willow Grove, PA. 18985

    Dear Mr. Williams:

        The admissions committee has reviewed your application and I
    am pleased to offer you a place in our September class. However,
    it is imperative that you notify this office within ten days to
    reserve your place. If we do not hear from you by that time, we
    will award your place in the class to another student.

        We are looking forward to hearing from you. We are confident
    the next year will be an exciting one for you.

                            Sincerely,

                            Wilfred Magatel
                            Admissions Director



    C:\WP5\LETTER                           Doc 1 Pg 1 Ln 2.33" Pos 6.6"
```

Figure 3.4: *Two [Hrt] codes and a tab deleted*

The text of that paragraph from the cursor position down will move down to the next line. Press ⏎ again if you want to double-space between paragraphs, then Tab to indent the first line.

1. Place the cursor on the word *If*, which begins the third sentence of the first paragraph.

2. Press ⏎ twice—the first time to separate the paragraphs, and again to insert the blank line between paragraphs.

3. Press Tab to indent the new paragraph.

4. Press an arrow key to adjust the text.

5. If you are not ready to continue with Lesson 17, resave the document.

Lesson 17 – How to Repeat Keystrokes

Sometimes you want to repeat a certain keystroke a specific number of times. For example, you might want to place a line of 64 dashes across the screen, or move the cursor a specific number of spaces or lines. You also might need to repeat a certain command more than once—to delete the next five words or seven lines, for instance.

In each of these examples, you would have to press the appropriate keystroke repeatedly, counting the strokes and watching the screen carefully. However, with WordPerfect you can use the Esc key to perform repeated actions easily and quickly.

In a moment we'll use Escape to edit the document LETTER. Here's how it works: Press Esc to show the

Repeat Value = 8

prompt on the status line. The default value of 8 indicates that the next nonnumeric keystroke that follows will be executed eight times. If you want a different number of repetitions, type a new number. Type the keystroke, or press the command, to be repeated. You can only press one keystroke or one command. Because the number of repetitions is specified, you don't have to count each one.

For example, to print a line of dashes across the screen, press Esc, type *64* (the number of characters in a line), then press –. To delete the next ten words, press Esc, type *10,* then press Ctrl-Backspace. To delete five lines, place the cursor at the start of the first line, press Esc, type *5,* then press Ctrl-End.

Now we'll use the Esc key with the document LETTER. If you quit WordPerfect after Lesson 16, start the program and recall LETTER.

1. Press Home Home ↑ to place the cursor at the start of the letter.

2. Press Esc 10 ↓. The cursor moves down ten lines.

3. Press Esc 4 Ctrl-Backspace to delete the first four words.

4. Type

   have the pleasure of offering

5. Press ↓ to adjust the text. Your screen should now look like Figure 3.5.

*A**djusting the Screen after Editing*

Several times now you've been instructed to press an arrow key to adjust the text after adding or deleting characters. This forces the document to realign itself.

In these instances, or when the text on the screen fails to conform to any changes you've made, you can also use the Rewrite command.

```
January 12, 1988

Mr. Robert Williams
53 Kinder Lane
Willow Grove, PA. 18985

Dear Mr. Williams:

     The admissions committee has reviewed your application and I
have the pleasure of offering you a place in our September class.
However, it is imperative that you_notify this office within ten
days to reserve your place.

     If we do not hear from you by that time, we will award your
place in the class to another student.

     We are looking forward to hearing from you. We are confident
the next year will be an exciting one for you.

                         Sincerely,

                         Wilfred Magatel
                         Admissions Director
C:\WP5\LETTER                               Doc 1 Pg 1 Ln 2.83" Pos 4.4"
```

Figure 3.5: *The sample letter revised using the Escape key*

Here's how:

1. Press Ctrl-F3 to display the prompt

   0 Rewrite; 1 Window; 2 Line Draw: 0

2. Press *R, 0,* or ↵ to rewrite the screen so it adjusts to recent editing or format changes.

In the next lesson, you'll learn how to use the Window option in this prompt line to display and edit more than one document at a time.

*L*esson 18 – How to Work with Multiple Documents

You're working feverishly on a document and want to refer to another on the same disk. You may have come up with an idea for a change to the other document, or it may have a section of text that can be used to make your work easier. But it will just take too long to save the current document and then load the other.

Fortunately for times like this, WordPerfect allows you to work with two documents at one time. You can recall the second document without saving or exiting the first. By pressing Shift-F3, you can switch back and forth between the two, even copying text from one to the other.

Try this with the document already on the screen:

1. Press Shift-F3, the Switch command. The screen will clear and the status line will change to

   Doc 2 Pg 1 Ln 1″ Pos 1″

   You are now in the second document window. Anything you type, or any commands used, will have no effect on the text displayed in document 1, which is safely stored in memory. Each document can be edited or saved separately.

   You could now start typing the second document, or retrieve an existing one from the disk. (With the Document 2 window displayed, load a saved document using the exact same techniques you've already learned—press Shift-F10 then type the name of the document, or use the F5 key to display the directory listing.) To switch back and forth between the two documents, just press Shift-F3. Think of this as a toggle between document 1 and document 2.

2. Type

   I am pleased to accept the position in the September class.

3. Press Shift-F3 to switch back to the first document. It's still there, unchanged.

4. Press Shift-F3 to return to document 2. Now let's save this document and return to the first.

5. Press F7, answer *Y* to the Save prompt, type *ACCEPT* (or *B: ACCEPT*), and press ⏎. In a few moments the prompt will change to

   Exit Doc 2? (Y/N) No

6. Press *Y.* The first document reappears.

*D*isplaying Two Documents

Working with two documents is easier if you can see them both on the screen at the same time. For this, use the WordPerfect Window command. Try this now with the document already on the screen.

1. Press Ctrl-F3.

2. Press *1* or *W* (Window) to show

   # Lines in this Window: 24

   The default 24 indicates that the current document will use all 24 lines of the screen (the status line uses the 25th).

3. Type *12,* then press ←⎯. The screen is divided at the twelfth line, as shown in Figure 3.6.

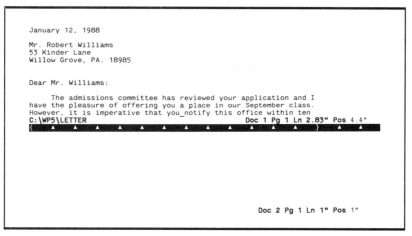

```
January 12, 1988

Mr. Robert Williams
53 Kinder Lane
Willow Grove, PA. 18985


Dear Mr. Williams:

    The admissions committee has reviewed your application and I
have the pleasure of offering you a place in our September class.
However, it is imperative that you notify this office within ten
C:\WP5\LETTER                              Doc 1 Pg 1 Ln 2.83" Pos 4.4"




                                            Doc 2 Pg 1 Ln 1" Pos 1"
```

Figure 3.6: *The screen divided into two document areas*

After pressing Ctrl-F3 1, you could also have pressed the ↑ or ↓ keys instead of typing a number. The scale line would have appeared and moved in the direction of the arrow key being pressed. Press ←⎯ when the scale line reaches the desired position.

4. Press Shift-F3. The cursor moves to the document in the bottom window and the triangular tab markers now point down.

5. Recall the document ACCEPT. Press Shift-F10, type *ACCEPT*, then press ←⎯. Parts of both documents are now displayed (Figure 3.7). Scrolling in one document window will not affect the other.

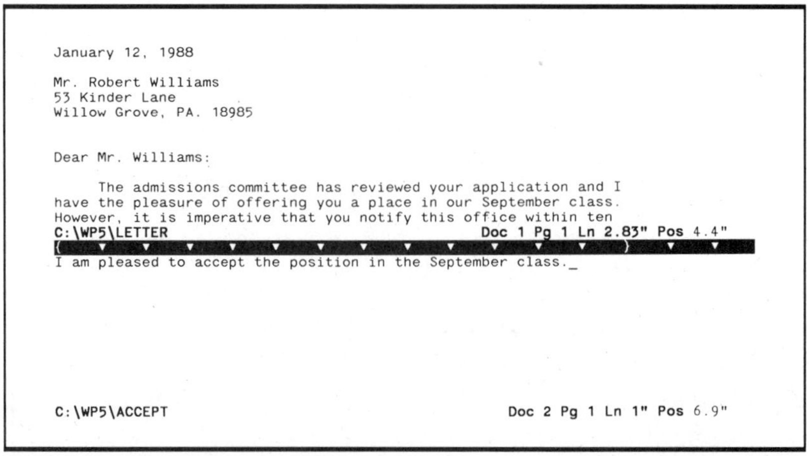

```
    January 12, 1988

    Mr. Robert Williams
    53 Kinder Lane
    Willow Grove, PA. 18985

    Dear Mr. Williams:

         The admissions committee has reviewed your application and I
    have the pleasure of offering you a place in our September class.
    However, it is imperative that you notify this office within ten
    C:\WP5\LETTER                               Doc 1 Pg 1 Ln 2.83" Pos 4.4"
    (      ▼     ▼    ▼   ▼     ▼    ▼     ▼    ▼      )    ▼     ▼
    I am pleased to accept the position in the September class._




    C:\WP5\ACCEPT                            Doc 2 Pg 1 Ln 1" Pos 6.9"
```

Figure 3.7: *Two documents on the screen with the cursor in the second document*

Clearing Windows

1. Still in the bottom window, press F7 N Y to exit document 2. In this case, even though you did exit from document 2, the screen is still divided into two windows. The cursor is in the first document, however.

   To remove the bottom window, make the other one fill the entire screen.

2. Press Ctrl-F3 1 to change the window size.

3. Type *24* and press ←. The second document window disappears.

Displaying the Scale Line

In some word processing programs, the scale line is always displayed as a point of reference for margins and tabs. WordPerfect gives you a choice. If you want the scale line displayed, follow these steps:

1. Press Ctrl-F3 1 for the Window option.

2. Type *23* and press ← to set the window at 23 lines.

When you size a window at 23 lines, the scale line dividing windows appears at the bottom of the screen. When you switch windows, the scale line stays at that position but changes to reflect the format of the other document, which now appears on the screen. To delete the scale line, resize the window to a full 24 lines by pressing Ctrl-F3 1 24 ⏎. The 25th screen line is used by the status line.

*L*esson 19 – How to Add the Date to Documents

The document LETTER contains the date you typed on the first line. If you don't print and mail the letter until some time later, the date will be incorrect. So you would have to delete the incorrect date and type the current one just before printing.

Instead, you can use WordPerfect's Date function to automatically insert the date when the letter is printed. To use this function you must enter the correct date when starting DOS, or have a built-in clock in your computer.

1. Delete the date at the top of the letter.

    a. Press Home Home ↑ to place the cursor at the start of the letter.

    b. Press Ctrl-End to delete the date.

2. Press Shift-F5, the Date key. This displays the prompt line

    1 Date text; 2 Date code; 3 Date format; 4 Outline; 5 Para num; 6 Define: 0

3. Press *2*. This inserts a Date code into the text, and the current date maintained by DOS will be displayed on the screen. When the document is printed, that day's date will appear on the finished copy. Thus, you can complete a letter on another day and have the date on which it is printed appear in the letter. But keep in mind that if you later recall the letter, the current date will appear, not the date it was written or printed. You cannot use the function to remind you when the letter was mailed.

    Option 1 on the prompt line would also insert the system date. However, this inserts the current date as text into the document. No matter when the document is printed or recalled, the date when the function was originally entered will appear. Use this if you type and print a letter the same day, since the date will serve as a reminder of when it was mailed. You can also use this when writing a diary or log. Press Shift-F5 1 to display the date, then type the entry for that day.

4. Press Alt-F3 to reveal the codes. The date appears in the top part of the screen, with the Date code in the bottom part (Figure 3.8). If you have selected option 1, the same date appears in both areas.

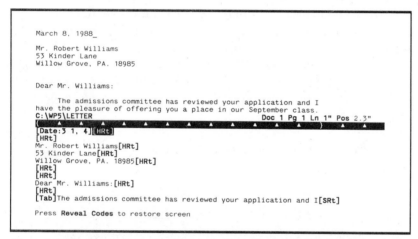

Figure 3.8: The Date code causing the current date to be displayed in the typing window

5. Press Alt-F3 to clear the displayed codes.

6. Resave the document and exit WordPerfect. Press F7, answer *Y,* and press ◄── to save the document with the same name. Press *Y* to confirm the replacement, and then *Y* again to exit the program.

One word of caution if you do not have a built-in clock: Unless you enter the date when you start your computer, the system date could be something like January 1, 1980. If you enter the date one day and use the Date function, be sure to enter the date again if you later restart the computer to print the document. Otherwise, *January 1, 1980* could appear on your letter.

*C*hanging Date Formats

Option 3 allows you to change the format in which the date and time appear. Follow these steps to change the format:

1. Start WordPerfect then press Shift-F5 3. The Date Format menu appears (Figure 3.9).

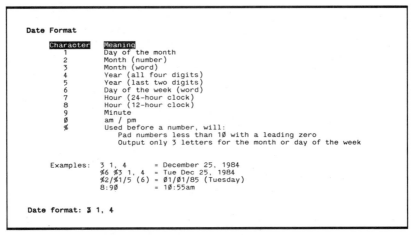

```
Date Format

        Character    Meaning
            1        Day of the month
            2        Month (number)
            3        Month (word)
            4        Year (all four digits)
            5        Year (last two digits)
            6        Day of the week (word)
            7        Hour (24-hour clock)
            8        Hour (12-hour clock)
            9        Minute
            Ø        am / pm
            %        Used before a number, will:
                         Pad numbers less than 1Ø with a leading zero
                         Output only 3 letters for the month or day of the week

        Examples:  3 1, 4       = December 25, 1984
                   %6 %3 1, 4   = Tue Dec 25, 1984
                   %2/%1/5 (6)  = Ø1/Ø1/85 (Tuesday)
                   8:9Ø         = 1Ø:55am

Date format: 3 1, 4
```

Figure 3.9: *Date Format menu*

2. Enter the numbers and any punctuation desired to correspond to the format you wish to appear. These examples will help you:

KEYSTROKES	RESULTING FORMAT
3 1, 4	December 25, 1988
2/1/5 (6)	3/5/84 (Tuesday)
8:9 0	2:55 am
6, 3 1, 4	Tuesday, December 25, 1988
7:9 (0)	23:30 (pm)

You can also insert leading zeros in front of date and time numbers or abbreviate the names of days and months by using the % key. For example:

KEYSTROKES	RESULTING FORMAT
%2/%1/5 (%6)	03/05/84 (Tue)
%8:9 0	02:55 am

3. Press ⏎ twice to return to the typing window.

4

Enhancing the Appearance of Your Documents

*F*eaturing

Default values
Left and right margins
Line spacing
Ending pages
Document comments
and summary

It's an unfortunate fact of life, but first appearances often mean the difference between success and failure. How your document looks can be as important as what it says. Just picture how you look through your own mail. If you're like me, you open the envelopes that look important first, leaving ones that appear to be junk mail until the end.

Arranging the appearance of your text on the page is called *formatting*. And an attractive format is almost a guarantee that your document will be read.

With a typewriter, formatting can be like jumping into a bottomless pit. But with WordPerfect, you can arrange and rearrange your document as often as you like until it's just right.

*L*esson 20 – Default Values and Format Changes

Each time you start WordPerfect, standard default settings are provided automatically to let you type and print documents without worrying about page size, line spacing, and other details of format. The default settings are

Page Size:	$8^{1}/_{2}$ by 11 inches
	66 lines per page
	54 typed lines
Top Margin:	1"
Bottom Margin:	1"
Left Margin:	1" (10 character positions from the left)
Right Margin:	1" (character position 74)
Page Numbering:	None
Line Spacing:	Single space, 6 lines per inch
Font:	Standard single-strike, 10 pitch (10 characters per inch)
Tabs:	Every 5 spaces ($^{1}/_{2}$ inch)
Right Justification:	On (when printed; not displayed)

These settings result in a page with 54 lines of text, each line 65 characters (or about $6^{1}/_{2}$ inches) wide. The text will appear neatly arranged when printed on standard business stationery, with text aligned on both the left and right margins.

You don't have to change a thing if you like these settings and want to use them for every page of your document. But you can change any of these settings easily if you want other formats.

Most often you'll make temporary format changes that affect only the document in which they are made. Every other document will follow the default values, or the format changes you make within that document. In fact, page format changes need not affect the entire document. They just control the text from the cursor position where the change was made to either the next format change or the end of the document, whichever comes first. Finally, format changes can be inserted within existing text, just like any other code. They then automatically change the original format with which the text was typed, so that the previously typed text now conforms to the new format. Say you have already typed a document single-spaced. If you place the cursor midway through the text and insert a Double-space code, all text from that position on will become double-spaced.

The ability to change the format of text at any time is one of the greatest features of word processing. You can type the document using the default settings, then adjust the margins, line spacing, and other dimensions until they appear the way you desire. In fact, you'll do just that in the next lesson.

Lesson 21 – How to Change Left and Right Margins

There are many ways to adjust the final format of a printed document. This lesson explains how to change the right and left margins— of either an entire document or just parts of it.

In determining the right and left borders of a page, margin settings also set the length of the printed line, adjust for different widths of paper, and affect the amount of text that will fit on a page. For example, to make a document appear longer, make the margins a little wider.

The default left margin is 1 inch, or 10 character positions. In this lesson you will learn how to change the margins. Follow these steps:

1. Start WordPerfect.

2. Press Shift-F8, the Format key, to show the menu in Figure 4.1.

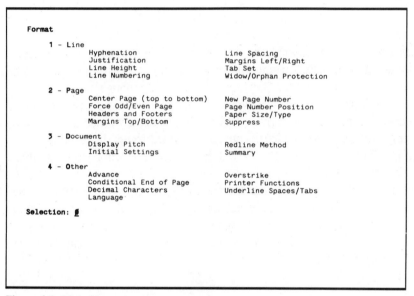

```
Format

    1 - Line
            Hyphenation                    Line Spacing
            Justification                  Margins Left/Right
            Line Height                    Tab Set
            Line Numbering                 Widow/Orphan Protection

    2 - Page
            Center Page (top to bottom)    New Page Number
            Force Odd/Even Page            Page Number Position
            Headers and Footers            Paper Size/Type
            Margins Top/Bottom             Suppress

    3 - Document
            Display Pitch                  Redline Method
            Initial Settings               Summary

    4 - Other
            Advance                        Overstrike
            Conditional End of Page        Printer Functions
            Decimal Characters             Underline Spaces/Tabs
            Language

    Selection: 0
```

Figure 4.1: Main Format menu

This is the main menu that you'll use to adjust the format of your document. Take a moment to review the options under each of the four major categories. When you want to adjust the format of your document, first press Shift-F8 to display this menu. Then look for the particular format you wish to change and press its option number to display another menu containing your choice. In this case, you're interested in setting the left and right margins, an option under choice 1, Line.

3. Press *1* to show the Format Line menu (Figure 4.2).

The current settings, the default formats being used by WordPerfect, are shown next to each type of format. You select which option

```
Format: Line

    1 - Hyphenation                        Off

    2 - Hyphenation Zone - Left            10%
                          Right            4%

    3 - Justification                      Yes

    4 - Line Height                        Auto

    5 - Line Numbering                     No

    6 - Line Spacing                       1

    7 - Margins - Left                     1"
                  Right                    1"

    8 - Tab Set                            0", every 0.5"

    9 - Widow/Orphan Protection            No


Selection: 0
```

Figure 4.2: Format Line menu

to change by typing either the number next to the option or the letter that is highlighted.

Notice that option 7 is used to change the left and right margins. So you can change margins by typing *7* or *m* (either uppercase or lowercase).

4. Press *7* or *m*. The cursor moves to the default 1" left margin setting.

5. Type *2*, then press ←⏎. Word Perfect automatically adds the inches sign *(")* after the entry and moves the cursor to the right margin setting.

6. Type *2*, then press ←⏎. The new settings are stored on the menu.

7. Press ←⏎ twice, once to return to the Format Line menu, again to display the typing screen.

8. Now type the following proposal. The lines will be about 45 characters wide.

> **Fox and Associates, Inc. is happy to bid on your proposal for data processing training. We have been professional trainers for over 15 years. Fox and Associates, Inc. has earned an outstanding reputation and we will be pleased to provide references upon request.**

> In consideration for the amount of $800.00, Fox and Associates will perform the following services:
>   Provide two days of training in word processing for two operators at 6543 Fifth Avenue, Boston.
>   Fox and Associates will guarantee this price only for the next 60 days. We maintain the authority to adjust the bid if contracts are not formalized in that period.
>   This bid is submitted pursuant to the laws of New York State and, if accepted, its terms shall be binding on both parties.
>   Fox and Associates greatly appreciates the opportunity to bid on this project.
>   This proposal represents an estimate of the cost of materials and labor. While every effort has been made to accurately compute all costs involved, the actual price of services, binding on both parties, will be stated in the final contract.

9. Save the document now under the name CONTRACT. You will use it in a later lesson.

   a. Press F10.

   b. Type *CONTRACT*.

   c. Press ◄┘.

   Saving the document in this way will not exit the WordPerfect program.

10. Press Home Home ↑ to reach the start of the text.

11. Press Alt-F3 to reveal the codes. The [L/R Mar:2",2"] code is in the text (Figure 4.3).

    Let's experiment with the margin setting to see what happens. First you will insert a new margin code to the right of the current one. The new code should reformat all of the text on the screen.

12. Press Alt-F3 to remove the code display.

13. Press Shift-F8 1 7 for the margin prompt. Now let's set 1/2" margins.

```
      _     Fox and Associates, Inc. is happy to bid
on your proposal for data processing
training. We have been professional trainers
for over 15 years. Fox and Associates, Inc.
has earned an outstanding reputation and we
will be pleased to provide references upon
request.
           In consideration for the amount of
$800.00,  Fox and Associates will perform the
following services:
           Provide two days of training in word
C:\WP5\CONTRACT                                    Doc 2 Pg 1 Ln 1" Pos 2"
▲▬▬▬▲▬▬(▬▲▬▬▬▲▬▬▬▲▬▬▬▲▬▬▬▲▬▬▬▲▬▬)▬▲▬▬▬▲▬▬▲▬▬▲
[L/R Mar:2",2"][Tab]Fox and Associates, Inc. is happy to bid[SRt]
on your proposal for data processing[SRt]
training. We have been professional trainers [HRt]
for over 15 years. Fox and Associates, Inc.[SRt]
has earned an outstanding reputation and we[SRt]
will be pleased to provide references upon[SRt]
request. [HRt]
[Tab]In consideration for the amount of[SRt]
$800.00,  Fox and Associates will perform the[SRt]
following services: [HRt]

Press Reveal Codes to restore screen
```

Figure 4.3: A Margin Set code in the text

14. Type *.5*, press ↵, type *.5*, then press ↵ three times to return to the document. Notice that the text still conforms to the original two inch margins.

15. Press Ctrl-F3 0 to select the Rewrite option, adjusting the text to the new margins. You could also adjust the text by moving the cursor down through the text. Use Ctrl-F3 0 if you want to adjust the text without moving the cursor, so you can edit or add text at the current location.

16. Reveal the codes again by pressing Alt-F3. Notice that both Margin Set codes are still in the text (Figure 4.4).

    Text is always formatted by the code immediately before it, so the second Margin Set code is now used to format the document. However, the first code does not disappear, so you can return to the previous margins by simply deleting the new code.

17. Press Alt-F3 to return to the typing window.

18. Place the cursor on the left side of the screen at the fifth paragraph.

19. Change both margins to 1½ inches.

    a. Press Shift-F8 1 7.

    b. Type *1.5*.

```
  _      Fox and Associates, Inc. is happy to bid on your proposal for data
processing training. We have been professional trainers
for over 15 years. Fox and Associates, Inc. has earned an outstanding
reputation and we will be pleased to provide references upon request.
        In consideration for the amount of $800.00,  Fox and Associates will
perform the following services:
        Provide two days of training in word processing for two operators at
6543 Fifth Avenue, Boston.
        Fox and Associates will guarantee this price only for the next 60
days. We maintain the authority to adjust the bid if contracts are not
formalized in that period.
C:\WP5\CONTRACT                                    Doc 2 Pg 1 Ln 1" Pos 0.5"
(     ▲        ▲      ▲        ▲     ▲      ▲     ▲    ▲      ▲          )
[L/R Mar:2",2"][L/R Mar:0.5",0.5"][Tab]Fox and Associates, Inc. is happy to bid
on your proposal for data[SRt]
processing training. We have been professional trainers [HRt]
for over 15 years. Fox and Associates, Inc. has earned an outstanding[SRt]
reputation and we will be pleased to provide references upon request. [HRt]
[Tab]In consideration for the amount of $800.00,  Fox and Associates will[SRt]
perform the following services: [HRt]
[Tab]Provide two days of training in word processing for two operators at[SRt]
6543 Fifth Avenue, Boston. [HRt]
[Tab]Fox and Associates will guarantee this price only for the next 60[SRt]

Press Reveal Codes to restore screen
```

Figure 4.4: Two Margin Set codes in the text

c. Press ⏎.

d. Type *1.5*.

e. Press ⏎ three times.

f. Press Ctrl-F3 0.

The text from the cursor position down adjusts to the new margins, but the text above the cursor remains unchanged (Figure 4.5). The margins of the text will appear in the appropriate relative positions on your screen. So the paragraphs

```
        Fox and Associates, Inc. is happy to bid on your proposal for data
processing training. We have been professional trainers
for over 15 years. Fox and Associates, Inc. has earned an outstanding
reputation and we will be pleased to provide references upon request.
        In consideration for the amount of $800.00,  Fox and Associates will
perform the following services:
        Provide two days of training in word processing for two operators at
6543 Fifth Avenue, Boston.
        Fox and Associates will guarantee this price only for the next 60
days. We maintain the authority to adjust the bid if contracts are not
formalized in that period.
  _           This bid is submitted pursuant to the laws of New
        York State and, if accepted, its terms shall be binding
        on both parties.
                Fox and Associates greatly appreciates the
        opportunity to bid on this project.
  ·             This proposal represents an estimate of the cost
        of materials and labor.  While  every effort has been
        made to accurately compute all costs involved, the
        actual price of services, binding on both parties,
        will be stated in the final contract.


C:\WP5\CONTRACT                           Doc 2 Pg 1 Ln 2.83" Pos 1.5"
```

Figure 4.5: Not all text may appear after a margin change

with 1¹/₂-inch margins are indented from those above having just ¹/₂-inch margins. If you set very small margins, the resulting lines will be too long to fit on the screen, so they'll scroll off the side. When this happens, use the → and ← keys to scroll the text into view.

All formatting codes affect only the text from the position where they are inserted to the end of the document—or to the next similar formatting code.

20. To delete the margin setting, press Backspace, then *Y* in response to the prompt.

Delete [L/R Mar: 1.5″, 1.5″]? (Y/N) No

21. Press F7 N N to clear the document from the screen without saving the changes.

*D*eleting Margin Set Codes

Margin Set codes can also be deleted from the text. With codes revealed, just place the cursor on the [L/R MAR] code and press Del. When the codes are not revealed, the message

Delete [L/R Mar:]? (Y/N) No

appears. Press *Y* to delete the code, *N* or ↵ to leave it as is.

Prompts like this appear asking you to confirm the deletion of most codes.

*L*esson 22 – How to Adjust Line Spacing

Like right and left margins, line spacing also changes the overall appearance of the document.

Like margins, line spacing can be changed for the entire document, or just for sections within it. Spacing is allowed in half-line increments, although text will appear on the screen in the nearest integer. For example, lines spaced at 1.5 will be double-spaced on the screen, although they will be printed at 1.5.

Because only 24 lines can be displayed on the screen at one time, it is wise to type documents single-spaced. This reduces the amount of scrolling you'll have to do during the editing process. Then, before printing, change the line spacing where desired and make any adjustments.

We will now use the Line Spacing function to adjust the appearance of the document that you called CONTRACT in the last lesson. If you exited WordPerfect after the last lesson, start the program.

1. Recall CONTRACT. The text has 2-inch margins.

2. Press Shift-F8 1 to display the Format Line menu, then *6* or *s* to select line spacing.

3. Press *2* for double-spacing, then press ◄— three times. The paragraphs, and the spaces between them, will become double-spaced.

4. Press Alt-F3 to reveal the codes and notice the [Ln Spacing:2] code in the text.
   Each time you press the ↑ or ↓ key, the Ln indicator will change in two-line increments.

5. Press F7 N N to clear the screen without saving the document. The original CONTRACT remains unchanged as you saved it in Lesson 21.

So far we have concentrated on documents of just one page. Longer documents will automatically be divided into pages by auto-pagination. The next lesson explains how to manually end a page before the ending point established by auto-pagination.

*L*esson 23 – *How to Control Page Breaks*

You already know that WordPerfect paginates documents as you type. Using the default settings, a new page starts after every 54 lines. A dashed line will appear across the screen and the Pg indicator will increase by one. These are called *soft page breaks* and are marked with the [SPg] code.

However, you might want to end a page before it is filled, as when typing a short cover memo or title page. This calls for a new page or *hard page break*—[HPg].

To insert a hard page break, press Ctrl-◄—. A double row of dashes (=) appears, so you can tell whether page breaks are soft or hard.

Like all codes, the hard page break can be inserted in existing text and deleted.

1. Type the following:

    MEMORANDUM

    TO: All Department Chairpersons
    FROM: Rose Savage
    SUBJECT: Reserved Equipment List

    Attached is a list of Class 2 equipment that must be reserved at least two weeks before needed.

2. Press ←⎯.

3. Press Ctrl-←⎯.

    A double line of dashes will appear on the screen, with the cursor underneath. The Pg indicator will read *2* (Figure 4.6).

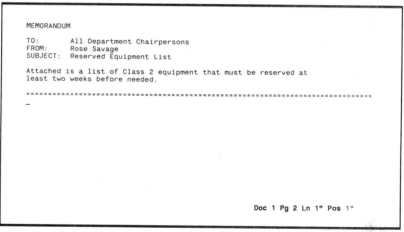

```
MEMORANDUM

TO:        All Department Chairpersons
FROM:      Rose Savage
SUBJECT:   Reserved Equipment List

Attached is a list of Class 2 equipment that must be reserved at
least two weeks before needed.

================================================================================
_




                                                   Doc 1 Pg 2 Ln 1" Pos 1"
```

Figure 4.6: A hard page break inserted

There are only eight lines above the page break line. But when printed, the first page will roll out and the second, if there is one, will begin printing.

4. Press Alt-F3 to reveal the codes. Instead of a page break line there is an [HPg] code.

5. Press Alt-F3 to return to the document, then type the text of the second page. In Chapter 6 you'll learn how to center text automatically. But for now, press Tab five times to center the title.

Class 2 Equipment

Electron Microscopes
Fluorescent Microscopes
Cryostat
Serum Glutamic Pyruvic Transaminase Analyzer
Flow Cytometer
Nuclear Magnetic Resonance Scanner

6. Press Shift-F7 1 to print the two-page document. The memorandum is printed at the top of the first page. When WordPerfect encountered the Hard Page Break code, it ejected the first page before printing the next.

Deleting Page Breaks

Soft page breaks can only be changed by adding or deleting text. But hard page breaks, which are manually inserted, can be deleted just like any other code.

7. Place the cursor on the line just above the page break line.

8. Press Del. The page break line will disappear.

When you delete a Hard Page code, any text that was on the page below will be added to the one above. Soft page breaks following will adjust automatically.

9. If you are not ready to continue with the next lesson, save the document and exit WordPerfect.

   a. Press F7 Y.

   b. Type *MEMO*, then press ⏎.

   c. Press *Y* to exit WordPerfect.

Margins, line spacing, and page endings are three of the most useful formatting techniques. In later lessons you will learn how to format individual characters, paragraphs, and pages. The next lesson is really not about document formats. But it will be an invaluable aid, not only when you are creating a document but also if you ever need to refer to that document again.

Lesson 24 – How to Add Document Comments and Summary

As you write, you're going to keep adding documents to your disk. It will get harder to remember what you've named each document and just as difficult to distinguish one from the other on the directory listing. After all, an 11-character name (eight characters plus the extension) can't fully identify every different document you write.

My own directory is so full of useless listings (such as *MEMO1* and *MEMO2*) that it's like reading a menu in some obscure foreign language.

Luckily, WordPerfect allows us to add a document summary to each document and to insert comments within the text itself. Neither the summary nor the comments are printed along with the text. But they can be displayed on the screen to help identify the document or to serve as reminders and messages.

You can have only one summary per document, and it is stored in a special area with the file.

Comments, however, can be inserted anywhere in the document, and you can have as many as you wish. Use them to write notes and reminders that you'll need when working on the document but that you do not want printed with it.

If you are not in WordPerfect, start the program and recall the document MEMO.

Document Summary

1. Press Shift-F8 to display the Format menu. Notice the Summary option under Document Formats, option 3.

2. Press *3* to select Document Formats and display the Format Document menu shown in Figure 4.7. Most of the options on

this menu are for more complex formatting tasks. But a document summary is created using option 5.

```
Format: Document

      1 - Display Pitch - Automatic       Yes
                          Width           Ø.1"

      2 - Initial Codes

      3 - Initial Font                    Courier 1Ø pitch (Roman-8)

      4 - Redline Method                  Printer Dependent

      5 - Summary




  Selection: Ø
```

Figure 4.7: Format Document menu

3. Press *5* or *s* to display the Document Summary screen shown in Figure 4.8.

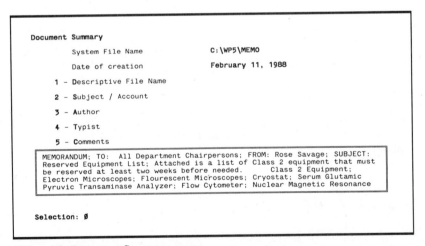

```
Document Summary

          System File Name           C:\WP5\MEMO

          Date of creation           February 11, 1988

      1 - Descriptive File Name

      2 - Subject / Account

      3 - Author

      4 - Typist

      5 - Comments
    ┌──────────────────────────────────────────────────────────────┐
    │ MEMORANDUM; TO:  All Department Chairpersons; FROM: Rose Savage; SUBJECT: │
    │ Reserved Equipment List; Attached is a list of Class 2 equipment that must │
    │ be reserved at least two weeks before needed.       Class 2 Equipment; │
    │ Electron Microscopes; Flourescent Microscopes; Cryostat; Serum Glutamic │
    │ Pyruvic Transaminase Analyzer; Flow Cytometer; Nuclear Magnetic Resonance │
    └──────────────────────────────────────────────────────────────┘

  Selection: Ø
```

Figure 4.8: Document Summary screen

The name of the document, if it has one, and the date it was created are already displayed. You can also add a descriptive file name and the subject, up to 40 characters each, and the author's and typist's names.

The first 400 characters of the document automatically appear in the comment area. You can add to or edit the text in the comment area without changing the text in the document itself. The comments can be up to 780 characters.

Let's delete the text in the Summary Comments window and enter your own.

4. Press *5* or *c* to place the cursor in the comment area.

5. Press Ctrl-End six times to delete the comment text. Remember, deleting the text in this box does not affect the text in the document itself.

6. Type

    Memo to be sent to all chairpersons, no response expected.

7. Press F7 to exit the comment area, then ⏎ three times (once to reach the Format Document menu, again to display the Format menu, and a third time to return to the typing area.)

You won't see the summary information on the screen and it won't be printed along with the document. However, it will appear when you look at a document from the directory listing using the F5 key, and you can always refer to it or edit it by pressing Shift-F8 3 5.

Comments

When you enter a document comment, first place the cursor where you want the comment to appear in the text. Comments usually relate to a specific section of text, unlike a summary, which refers to the entire document.

Follow these steps to add a comment to the text on the screen:

1. Place the cursor after the heading, just before the first paragraph.

2. Press Ctrl-F5 to display the prompt line

    1 DOS Text; 2 Password; 3 Save Generic; 4 Save WP 4.2; 5 Comment: 0

3. Press *5* or *c* to select the Comment option and display the prompt line

Comment: 1 Create; 2 Edit; 3 Convert to text: 0

4. Press *1* or *c* to create a comment and display the Comment window (Figure 4.9).

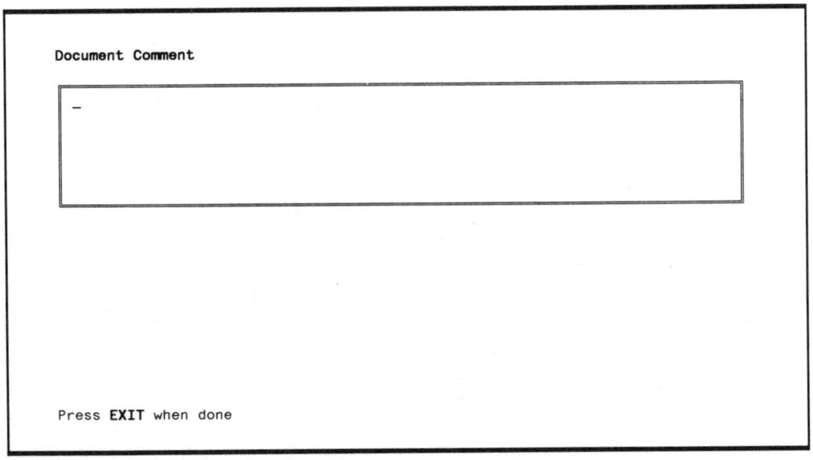

```
Document Comment

  ┌──────────────────────────────────────────┐
  │ –                                          │
  │                                            │
  │                                            │
  └──────────────────────────────────────────┘




Press EXIT when done
```

Figure 4.9: Document Comment window

You can enter up to 1,024 characters in the comment box.

5. Type

Make sure the complete list is enclosed for all departments

6. Press F7 to return to the document. The comment appears in the text, surrounded by a box, as shown in Figure 4.10.

*E*diting and Printing Comments

Although the comments appear on the screen, they will not be printed along with the document and you cannot edit them as you would edit normal text. To print them, you must first convert the comment to regular text. To edit them, you must redisplay the Comment screen.

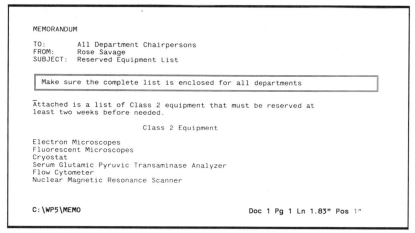

Figure 4.10: *Comment shown in the text*

Start by pressing Ctrl-F5 5 to reveal the Comment prompt line.

To edit a comment press *2* or *e*. WordPerfect will display the first comment above the cursor position. Edit the comment then press F7.

To convert a comment to regular text from the Comment prompt line, press *3* or *t*. The box surrounding the first comment above the cursor position will disappear but the text will remain. Since it is now regular text, it will be printed along with your document. Later you'll learn how to convert regular text into a non-printing comment.

Finally, to delete a comment, place the cursor just before it and press Del, or just following it and press Backspace. You'll see the prompt

Delete [Comment]? (Y/N) No

Press *Y* to delete the comment from the document.

Save the current document by pressing F7 Y, typing *MEMO*, and pressing ⏎. Press *Y* if you are not ready to continue with the next lesson. Otherwise, press *N* to clear the screen.

This chapter covered several fundamental formatting commands. In Chapter 5 you'll learn how to format characters in order to bring attention to important points.

5
Formatting Characters for Emphasis and Variety

*F*eaturing

Boldface and underline
Uppercase/lowercase
Superscripts and
subscripts
Type styles and sizes

WordPerfect 5 combines a full-featured word processing program with the most practical aspects of a desktop publisher and page composition system: an unbeatable combination that enables you to produce newsletters, combine graphics with text, and create publication-quality documents.

Before using this version, for example, I had to write and edit my text using one program—a word processor—then create page layouts using a graphics-oriented program. Sure, a desktop publisher has some word processing capabilities, but not the full power of WordPerfect. So I'd use two separate programs, then merge text and graphics together for printing.

I could have purchased one of those expensive and complicated desktop publishers that did it all. But I'm not publishing *Time* magazine—I just need the basics.

It's all here in version 5.

You can use WordPerfect yourself to create attractive and impressive documents. So using the ABC's approach, let's tackle the task in three steps.

Step A, formatting characters, is covered in this chapter. Here you'll learn how to use your printer's capabilities to produce text using different type styles and sizes.

Step B, arranging the text on the page, is discussed in several chapters that follow, including Chapter 12, where you'll learn how to create multicolumn documents.

Step C, adding graphics to your document, is discussed in Chapter 18. This is a complex subject, so we'll just cover the basics in this book.

Before going on, however, keep in mind that your printer may not be able to reproduce all of the features discussed in this chapter. So don't be surprised if your printouts don't look like the examples shown here. There's nothing wrong with your printer—it just doesn't have all of the capabilities discussed.

Also remember that you won't be able to see all of the features—even those that can be printed—on the screen. For instance, underlined characters may appear underlined, in reverse (highlighted), or even in a different color, depending on your computer. Monochrome monitors, for example, display normal, bold, underlined, reversed, and blinking characters. Most color systems will display the various type styles using colors instead.

*L*esson 25 – How to Boldface and Underline Text

Do you want to make a particular word or phrase stand out from the rest? Is there an important point that you want to make sure is not missed by the reader? You can emphasize text by printing it boldfaced, underlined, or both.

Boldfaced text will appear darker than surrounding characters because the printer actually strikes (prints) each character twice. This results in a darker, slightly thicker, image that catches the reader's eye. Underlining has the same eye-catching effect. You can boldface or underline text as you type it or afterward. Since the steps are similar for printing boldface and underlines, both are included in this one lesson.

*B*oldfacing and Underlining As You Type

To boldface characters as you type them:

1. Press F6.

2. Type the characters.

3. Press F6 again or press → once.

F6 is a toggle key. You press it once to turn boldface on, and again to turn boldface off. If you reveal the codes, boldface on appears as [BOLD], boldface off as [bold]. You can also turn boldfacing off when you're done by pressing the → key. This moves the cursor to the right of the [bold] code so the next characters entered will be normal. When boldface is turned on, the position indicator in the status line will also appear boldfaced. If you have a color or graphics monitor, boldfaced characters will appear either as a different color or as brighter than surrounding text.

To underline characters as you type them:

1. Press F8.

2. Type the characters.

3. Press F8 again or press → once.

Like F6, the F8 key is also a toggle. Underlining codes are [UNDRLN] and [undrln]. When F8 is on, the characters *Pos* will appear the same way underlined characters do on the screen. If you have a color or graphics monitor, underlined characters will appear either as a different color or in reverse (dark letters on a light background). On monochrome monitors, the characters will be underlined.

*B*oldfacing or Underlining Existing Characters

Once characters are typed, pressing F6 or F8 will have no effect on them; it would only insert the codes in the text with no characters between them. You can, however, easily add boldfacing or underlining to existing text. Try this now:

1. Start WordPerfect and type

   This text is boldfaced.
   This text is underlined.
   This text is both.

2. Place the cursor on the letter *b* of *boldfaced*.

3. Press Alt-F4. The words *Block on* will blink in the status line. Alt-F4 is the Block toggle key. It can be used to perform some powerful text manipulations, as you'll see in Chapter 10.

4. Press the → key to move the cursor to the end of the line. Notice that the characters become highlighted, or reversed, as the cursor moves over them (Figure 5.1).

5. Press F6. The highlighting disappears and the text is bold-faced.

6. Now underline the second sentence:

   a. Place the cursor on the *u* in *underline*.

   b. Press Alt-F4.

   c. Press the → key until the word is highlighted.

   d. Press F8.

```
This text is boldfaced.
This text is underlined.
This text is both.




Block on                                    Doc 1 Pg 1 Ln 1" Pos 3.2"
```

Figure 5.1: *The Block key highlighting characters*

7. Now underline and boldface the entire final sentence:

   a. Place the cursor at the start of the third sentence.

   b. Press Alt-F4 End.

   c. Press F6.

   d. Press Alt-F4 Home ←.

   e. Press F8.

8. Make sure your printer is ready, then press Shift-F7 1 to print the three formatted lines. If you are using hand fed paper, you'll have to press *4 G* for the printer to start.

Compare the printout with Figure 5.2. If your text does not appear boldfaced or underlined, make sure you have the proper printer definitions selected.

```
This text is boldfaced.

This text is underlined.

This text is both.
```

Figure 5.2: *Text with underline, boldface, and both*

Deleting Boldface and Underline

You can delete both styles with the codes either revealed or hidden. When codes are revealed, place the cursor on either the starting—[BOLD] [UNDRLN]—or ending—[bold] [undrln]—codes and press Del.

When codes are not revealed, place the cursor on the first character of the formatted text. If the Pos indicator is not boldfaced or underlined, the cursor is actually under the code, even though it appears to be under the first character. Press Del Y to delete the code.

However, if the Pos indicator is boldfaced or underlined, then the cursor is on the character, not the code. Press the ← key once. The cursor will remain in the same position but the Pos indicator will become normal. Then press Del Y.

Underline Styles

By default, WordPerfect uses a single continuous underline, which means that both words and the spaces between words are underlined. You can change the underline style to non-continuous, which is under words but not spaces, and to include the blank spaces inserted when you press Tab. Here's how:

1. Place the cursor at the location where you want to change the underline style. You can change the style for text already underlined or for new text you're about to type. To change existing underlining, place the cursor before the text. Like all codes, this affects only the text following it in the document.

2. Press Shift-F8 to display the Format menu, then *4* to reveal the Format: Other menu shown in Figure 5.3.

3. Press *7* to place the cursor on the Underline Spaces option. Press *N* for non-continuous underlining or *Y* for continuous. The cursor moves automatically to the Underline Tabs selection. When you select non-continuous underline, the code [Undrln:] is inserted—[Undrln: Spaces] will appear if you later select continuous underlining.

```
Format: Other
      1 - Advance
      2 - Conditional End of Page
      3 - Decimal Character            .
          Thousands' Separator         ,
      4 - Language                     EN
      5 - Overstrike
      6 - Printer Functions
      7 - Underline - Spaces           Yes
                      Tabs             No




Selection: 0
```

Figure 5.3: Format: Other menu

4. Press *Y* if you want to underline tab spaces, *N* if you don't. The possible codes are [Undrln: Spaces, Tabs], which underlines both tabs and spaces, or [Undrln:Tabs], which underlines just tabs.

5. Press ⏎ twice to return to the document.

6. Press F7 N N to clear the screen without saving the text.

When you underline text, spaces inserted with the Space bar are underlined (or appear in reverse or color) on screen unless you select non-continuous style. Tab spaces will also conform to the selected style on screen, underlined or not, depending on your selection on the Format: Other menu.

Just like other format commands, the change in underline style affects all text below the cursor position. So to change styles later in the document, repeat these steps and select the desired type of underlining. If you change your mind and want to return any underlined text to the default, delete the [Underln:] code.

While boldface and underline are the most used character formats, WordPerfect provides many others. These are covered in the upcoming lessons.

Lesson 26 – How to Control the Uppercase/Lowercase Option

Have you ever accidentally pressed the Caps Lock key, then discovered several lines later that everything is in uppercase? Or have you typed titles in lowercase letters and then decided they would have greater impact in all uppercase? With the Shift-F3 key you can quickly change the case of a series of characters.

To change all uppercase letters to lowercase, or vice versa, first highlight the text with the block (Alt-F4) and cursor keys, then press Shift-F3 to show the prompt

1 Uppercase; 2 Lowercase: 0

Press *1* to make the highlighted block all uppercase characters, *2* for lowercase. Note that Shift-F3 is used for case conversion when the Block function is on, and for switching between documents when Block is off.

Unlike other format commands, this inserts no codes into the text. It just changes the case of the characters. To reverse your action, highlight the same text and select the opposite case.

Lesson 27 – How to Change the Appearance of Characters

When you selected printers in Appendix C you specified to Word-Perfect the special codes needed for your printer to operate. If you found your exact printer name in the list of printers, then you'll be able to print in boldface and underlining, and perhaps in a number of different type sizes and styles. Many printers, for example, can produce italic type, proportional spacing, and various pitches. *Pitch* is the number of characters that can be printed in an inch of space.

We'll divide these styles into two sections. In Lesson 28 you'll learn how to change the size and position of characters. In this lesson, you'll learn how to adjust the appearance of characters, such as printing double underlines or italics.

As a test, however, let's try using all of the possible character appearances just to see what your printer can do.

Changing the Appearance of Characters As You Type

Follow these steps when you want to change the appearance of new characters:

1. Press Ctrl-F8 to display the prompt line

   **1 Size; 2 Appearance; 3 Normal; 4 Base Font;
   5 Print Color: 0**

   Let's review the basic functions of each option:

   - *Size* controls the size of the characters and is used in creating superscripts and subscripts. This option is discussed in Lesson 28.

   - *Appearance* determines some details of character shape and other factors. You'll soon learn all of the choices under this option.

   - *Normal* cancels any of the other selections, just like pressing F6 toggled boldface off.

   - *Base Font* determines the type style your printer will use.

   - *Color* changes the color of the printed character. Of course you must have a color printer for this to work.

2. Press *2* (or *a*) to select Appearance and display the prompt line

   **1 Bold 2 Undrln 3 Dbl Und 4 Italc 5 Outln 6 Shadw
   7 Sm Cap 8 Redln 9 Stkout: 0**

   Pressing *1* or *2* would boldface or underline your text, just like pressing F6 or F8. So you could press either F6 or Ctrl-F8 2 1 to boldface, F8 or Ctrl-F8 2 2 to underline. To stop boldfacing or underlining, press F6 or F8, press the → key, or select Ctrl-F8 3, Normal. You'll learn more about Normal soon.

   Option 3 prints a double underline; 4, italic printing; 5, outline letters; 6, shadow characters; and 7, small capital letters.

   Redline printing, option 8, designates text that you'd like to add to the document; Strikeout, option 9, is for text you'd like to delete. Use these options when making tentative changes to a document, or when working with another individual.

3. Press *3* (or *d*) to select Double Underlining. The position indicator will change color or appearance depending on your computer hardware.

4. Type *Double underline.*

5. Press Ctrl-F8 3 to select Normal, turning off the double underline style. You could have also just pressed the → key. Remember, the text may not appear underlined on the screen.

6. Press ⏎.

7. Press Ctrl-F8 2 4 (or *i*) to select Italic printing.

8. Type *Italic,* press the → key once, then press ⏎. Again, the text may change color or appear in reverse, depending on your system.

9. Press Ctrl-F8 2 5 (or *o*) to select Outline printing.

10. Type *Outline,* press → then ⏎.

11. Press Ctrl-F8 2 6 (or *h*) to select Shadow printing.

12. Type *Shadow,* press → then ⏎.

13. Press Ctrl-F8 2 7 (or *c*) to select Small Cap printing.

14. Type *Small caps,* press → then ⏎.

15. Press Ctrl-F8 2 8 (or *r*) to select Redline printing.

16. Type *Redline,* press → then ⏎.

17. Press Ctrl-F8 2 9 (or *s*) to select Strikeout printing.

18. Type *Strikeout,* press → then ⏎.

19. Press Shift-F7 1 to print a copy of the test document.

Figure 5.4 shows a sample printout made with a Hewlett Packard LaserJet printer. Notice that even this sophisticated printer doesn't produce outline letters.

Your own printout will show which types of appearances your printer can produce. Keep it handy when you're typing a real document.

Combining Styles

In each of the examples above, you returned the style back to normal before selecting the next. That way, each line was formatted in only one

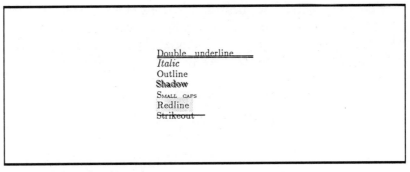

Figure 5.4: Sample print styles

way—either italic or underlined, for example. If you didn't revert back to normal, the styles would be combined. For example, to strike out italic characters, press Ctrl-F8 2 4 then Ctrl-F8 2 9. Depending on your printer, some combinations may not be possible, such as italic small capitals. You'll just have to experiment with possible combinations.

Changing the Appearance of Existing Characters

If you want to change the appearance of text you've already entered, you must first block it like you did for boldface and underlining in Lesson 25.

Place the cursor at the start of the text you wish to change, then press Alt-F4. Move the cursor to the end of the text then press Ctrl-F8. You'll see the prompt

Attribute: 1 Size; 2 Appearance: 0

Press *2* or *a* to show the Appearance prompt line, then select the style desired. All of the highlighted characters will be formatted.

To return formatted characters to normal, display the codes then delete the Appearance codes in the text.

Removing Redline and Strikeout

While you can remove the Redline and Strikeout codes in the same way, these serve special purposes. Remember, you strike out text to show that you'd like to delete it, and you redline text that you'd like to add. So if you really want to make these changes you can have WordPerfect do the final editing for you.

Before printing the document, follow these steps. You'll be using the Mark Text command, Alt-F5, a powerful command that's also used to create a table of contents, an index, and other reference sections. These uses, however, are beyond the scope of this book.

1. Press Alt-F5 to display the prompt

   1 Auto Ref; 2 Subdoc; 3 Index; 4 ToA Short Form; 5 Define; 6 Generate: 0

2. Press *6* to display the menu shown in Figure 5.5

```
Mark Text: Generate

    1 - Remove redline markings and strikeout text from document

    2 - Compare screen and disk documents for redline and strikeout

    3 - Expand master document

    4 - Condense master document

    5 - Generate tables, indexes, automatic references, etc.




    Selection: 0
```

Figure 5.5: Mark Text Generate menu

3. Press *1*. The prompt line changes to

   Delete redline markings and strikeout text? (Y/N) No

4. Press *Y.*

Any text that has been formatted as strikeout will be deleted, and the redline markings will be removed.

Summary

Because you've learned a number of options in this lesson, let's review the basic pattern.

1. Type until you want to set the appearance of characters, or use Alt-F4 to highlight existing text as a block.

2. Press Ctrl-F8 2.

3. Press the letter or character that stands for the appearance desired.

4. If you've been entering new characters rather than working with a block, press Ctrl-F8 3 or the → key when done.

L *esson 28 – How to Change the Size and Position of Characters*

In this lesson you'll take character formatting one step further into desktop publishing. You'll learn to print characters as subscripts and superscripts, and in sizes: fine, small, large, very large, and extra large (Figure 5.6). But except for superscripts and subscripts, which most printers can do, many printers will not be able to print in the different sizes and styles that we discuss here. And remember, you won't normally see any difference in the way characters appear on the screen.

H_2O
Footnote goes here[1]
Fine
Small
Normal
Large
Very Large
Extra large

Figure 5.6: Sample character positions and font sizes

But first a little background.

A *type style* refers to the general shape of a character. Some type styles have small cross-strokes at the ends of letters—called *serifs*—and some don't—*san-serif.*

If you take all of the letters, numbers and punctuation marks of one type style in one size, you have a *font*. Fonts are measured in *points*. There are approximately 72 points to an inch, so a 12-point typeface will fit six lines of type in 1 inch of space.

A 12-point font will contain all of the characters of a type style in that size. The 12-point bold font of the same type style contains the same characters but in boldface, just as 12-point italic contains all italic characters.

With WordPerfect you can print all of the type styles and sizes that your printer allows. For some printers, this may mean only one style and one size. But many dot matrix printers, for example, can print several sizes of characters. And laser printers can print a variety of shapes and sizes.

The main type style used is called the *base font*. This is the default character style used for normal characters. Other sizes and appearances are just variations on the base font. If your printer allows, you can change the base font to another style. That way you could have more than one style in the same document.

Let's see how to change font sizes, and test your printer at the same time. By the way, you can change font size and type style without worrying about the margins. WordPerfect will automatically adjust the margin and line spacing settings to accommodate your choice.

1. Press Ctrl-F8 4 to see the possible base fonts available on your printer. The one marked with an asterisk is the default font assigned to your printer. All of the font sizes are determined from the base font. For example, Figure 5.7 shows the base fonts available for a laser printer containing *downloaded* fonts. These are type styles that are stored on a disk and loaded into the printer when needed.

    In this case, the base font is called Century Schoolbook 12 pt. (for *point*). The large font in this typeface would be the next size, 14 pt., the very large would be 18 pt., and the extra large, 24 pt.

    However, if you changed the base font to 10 pt., everything would shift down—large would be 12 pt., very large 14 pt., and extra large 18 pt.

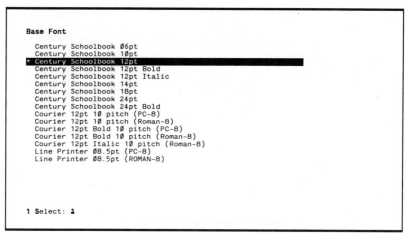

```
Base Font

    Century Schoolbook Ø6pt
    Century Schoolbook 1Øpt
  * Century Schoolbook 12pt
    Century Schoolbook 12pt Bold
    Century Schoolbook 12pt Italic
    Century Schoolbook 14pt
    Century Schoolbook 18pt
    Century Schoolbook 24pt
    Century Schoolbook 24pt Bold
    Courier 12pt 1Ø pitch (PC-8)
    Courier 12pt 1Ø pitch (Roman-8)
    Courier 12pt Bold 1Ø pitch (PC-8)
    Courier 12pt Bold 1Ø pitch (Roman-8)
    Courier 12pt Italic 1Ø pitch (Roman-8)
    Line Printer Ø8.5pt (PC-8)
    Line Printer Ø8.5pt (ROMAN-8)




  1 Select: 1
```

Figure 5.7: Base fonts for a Laserjet +

Look carefully at Figure 5.7. What sizes would be available if the base font were changed to Courier 12 pt.? None, because there are no other sizes in that typeface.

2. Press F7, then Ctrl-F8 again.

3. Press *1* or *s* to select Size. The prompt line changes to

> **1 Suprscpt; 2 Subscpt; 3 Fine; 4 Small; 5 Large; 6 Vry Large; 7 Ext Large:0**

Don't select anything now, but when you want to change size or position, type the number or letter corresponding to your choice, type the characters, then press Ctrl-F8 3 or the → key to return the characters to normal.

4. Press F1 for now.

If you select a new size, WordPerfect will automatically compute the proper margins and line spacing for you.

Let's see what positions and sizes your printer handles. Follow these steps to enter the text shown in Figure 5.6:

1. Type *H*.

2. Press Ctrl-F8 1 2 (or *b*) to select a subscript character.

3. Type *2*.

4. Press Ctrl-F8 3 to return the position to normal, then type *0.*

5. Press ← then type *Footnote goes here.*

6. Press Ctrl-F8 1 1 (or *p*) to select Superscript.

7. Type *1,* then → to move the cursor beyond the Superscript code.

8. Press ←.

9. Press Ctrl-F8 1 3 (or *f*) for Fine printing.

10. Type *Fine,* press →, then ←.

11. Press Ctrl-F8 1 4 (or *s*) to select Small printing.

12. Type *Small,* press → then ←.

13. Type *Normal,* then press ←.

14. Press Ctrl-F8 1 5 (or *l*) to select Large printing.

15. Type *Large,* press →, then ←.

16. Press Ctrl-F8 1 6 (or *v*) to select Very Large printing.

17. Type *Very large,* press → then ←.

18. Press Ctrl-F8 1 7 (or *e*) to select Extra Large printing.

19. Type *Extra large,* press → then ←.

20. Press Shift-F7 1 to print a copy of the test document. Compare your printout with Figure 5.6. Keep in mind that my figure was printed on a LaserJet + with several downloaded fonts.

You can have more than one size on a line and you can change the appearance of various sizes, to produce large bold characters, for example. Of course, you are always limited to the capabilities of your printer.

*C*hanging Font Families

You can have more than one type style in a document if your printer is capable. When you want to print a character other than in the base font, change to the base font containing the desired style.

To change the base font, press Ctrl-F8 4 to display the available fonts, use the arrow keys to move the highlighting to the font desired, then press ⏎ F7.

You can also change the default base font that WordPerfect uses every time you start the program. Here's how:

1. Press Shift-F7 S 3 to display the Printer Selection Edit menu, just as you did in Appendix B.

2. Press *6* or *i* for the Initial Font option. The list of possible fonts will appear on the screen.

3. Highlight the base font using the arrow keys, then press ⏎ three times to return to the document window. That base font will be used as the default whenever you start WordPerfect.

*C*hanging the Position or Size of Existing Characters

To change the position or size of text you've already entered, place the cursor at the start of the text you wish to change, then press Alt-F4. Move the cursor to the end of the text and press Ctrl-F8 to see the prompt

Attribute: 1 Size; 2 Appearance: 0

Press *1* or *s* to show the Size prompt line then select the style desired. All of the highlighted characters will be reformatted.

To return reformatted characters to normal, display the codes, then delete the Size codes in the text.

*F*ont Sizes and the Position Indicator

In Chapter 1 you learned that the position indicator in the status line shows the character position of the cursor. So using the default settings you'd normally see position 10 when the cursor was at the left margin. As you moved the cursor, the indicator would increase by one.

This changes when you're using font sizes that will not fit ten characters in each inch of space. Instead, with the cursor at the left margin the position indicator will show the number of character positions that make up the 1-inch margin at the type size you've selected. And as you move the cursor, the indicator changes in relation to the character size.

For instance, using Century Schoolbook 14 pt., the position indicator will read 9.09 at the left margin. With Century Schoolbook 16 pt. it will be 7.05.

If you're keeping the right margin consistent at 1 inch no matter what size type you're using, the character count will be different for each size. But don't worry, WordPerfect takes care of all this for you.

In the next chapter you'll take formatting one step further by learning how to control the position of lines. You'll learn how to center text, align it with the right margin, and set and use tab stops.

6

Centering, Flush Right, and Other Text Alignment

*F*eatining

Centering text
Flush right alignment
Tabs

*L*esson 29 – How to Center Text

You can center single lines of text as you type them, or as many lines of existing text as you want.

*C*entering New Text

Let's use the Center command to type a title page.

1. Start WordPerfect.

2. Press ◄─┘ six times.

3. Press Shift-F6. The cursor moves to the center of the screen.

4. Type

   The History of the World

   Characters will alternately move to the left and right, remaining centered.

5. Press ◄─┘ twice.

6. Press Shift-F6.

7. Type

   by

8. Press ◄─┘ twice.

9. Press Shift-F6.

10. Type your name.

11. Press ◄─┘.

    A Begin Center code [Cntr] will be placed at the start of the text, and End Center [C/A/Flrt] at the end. (That code represents the end of all centered, decimal-aligned, and flush right aligned text.) If the text wraps to the next line, only the first line will be centered. Since the cursor was at the far left margin when you pressed Shift-F6, the text was centered between the left and right margins. If you press Shift-F6 when the cursor is not at the margin, the cursor position becomes the centering point. This is covered in detail in Lesson 31.

12. Press F7 N N to clear the screen without saving the text.

Centering Existing Text

To center existing text:

- Place the cursor anywhere in the first line.
- Press Alt-F4, the Block key.
- Move the cursor to the end of the last line to be centered, highlighting the block.
- Press Shift-F6 to display

    [Cntr]? (Y/N) No

- Press *Y.*

Each line in the highlighted block will be centered on the screen and any soft returns [SRt] will be converted into hard returns [HRt]. Center codes will surround each line, so if you change your mind you'll have to delete the Center code in every line. Let's see how block centering works.

1. Type

    The History of the World
    by
    J. Paul Samsom

    A detailed study of the history of the world from 3000
    BC to the present time

2. Press ←⏎.

3. Press Home Home ↑ to place the cursor on the first line.

4. Press Alt-F4.

5. Press Home Home ↓ to highlight the entire text.

6. Press Shift-F6 Y. The text is centered on the screen.

7. Press Alt-F3 to reveal the codes. Notice that Center codes surround each line and the soft return was replaced with [HRt] (Figure 6.1).

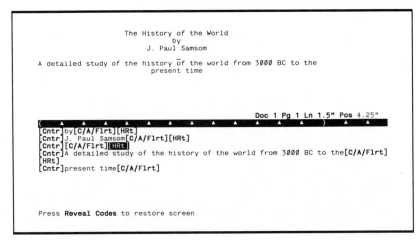

```
                     The History of the World
                              by
                        J. Paul Samsom

A detailed study of the history of the world from 3000 BC to the
                        present time




                                      Doc 1 Pg 1 Ln 1.5" Pos 4.25"
[Cntr]by[C/A/Flrt][HRt]
[Cntr]J. Paul Samsom[C/A/Flrt][HRt]
[Cntr][C/A/Flrt][HRt]
[Cntr]A detailed study of the history of the world from 3000 BC to the[C/A/Flrt]
[HRt]
[Cntr]present time[C/A/Flrt]




Press Reveal Codes to restore screen
```

Figure 6.1: Text centered as a block

8. Press Alt-F3 to remove the code display.

9. Press F7 N N to clear the screen and remain in WordPerfect.

Uncentering Text

To uncenter the text, delete either the [Cntr] or [C/A/Flrt] code. Without revealing codes, you can place the cursor at the left margin of the centered line and press Del Y.

Lesson 30 – How to Align Text Flush Right

Flush right text is aligned on the right margin with an uneven margin on the left—just the opposite from regular unjustified text.

This format is most commonly used in business announcements and programs:

Introduction   Ryan Hyde
                                                    President

Honor Awards	Jack Fanelli
	Vice President
Special Announcements	Margaret Shelby
	Treasurer
Closing Remarks	John Ryan
	Secretary

Aligning New Text on the Right

To align text on the right as you type it:

1. Press Alt-F6, the Align key. The cursor will move to the right margin.

2. Type the text. Characters entered will move to the left. If the text reaches the left margin, word-wrap will take effect and remaining lines will appear as normal.

3. Press ←⏎.

Begin [Flsh Rt] and End [C/A/Flrt] Align codes will surround the text. If the text word-wraps to the next line, only the first line will be aligned.

Aligning Existing Text on the Right

To align existing text on the right:

1. Place the cursor anywhere in the first line.

2. Press Alt-F4.

3. Move the cursor to the end of the last line to highlight the block.

4. Press Alt-F6 to display this prompt:

   [Flsh Rt]? (Y/N) No

5. Press *Y.*

Each line in the highlighted block will be aligned flush right and any soft returns [SRt] will be converted into hard returns [HRt]. Align codes will surround each line.

Returning Flush Right Text to Normal

To realign the text at the left margin, delete either the [Flsh Rt] or the [C/A/Flrt] code. Without revealing codes, you can place the cursor at the left margin of the aligned text and press Del Y.

Lesson 31 – How to Set Tabs

Tab stops are among those little things in life that can mean so much. Sometimes, like me, you might not use tabs for anything more than indenting the first line of a paragraph. But by setting tab stops, you can align columns on the page to create tables and lists, a table of contents, or forms.

A tab stop, for those of you not familiar with the old-fashioned typewriter, is a set position on the screen. When you press the Tab key, the cursor moves directly to the closest tab stop to the right. So rather than press the Space bar five times to indent the line, press the Tab key once. Press Tab again to move another five characters.

By default, WordPerfect sets tab stops every $1/2$ inch. But you can easily change these, and set your own, through the Format key, Shift-F8.

Column Alignment

How text aligns in columns when you press the Tab key depends on the type of tab stop you set. Text can be aligned on the left, right, or center. Columns of numbers can be aligned by the decimal point. And all tab stops can be set so a row of dots, called *dot leaders,* appears in the blank space before the text.

Left-aligned columns use regular tab stops:

William Morris

Sam Spady

Jane Pascalli

Other columns are centered, but not necessarily between the right and left margins:

William Morris

Sam Spady

Jane Pascalli

Decimal columns are aligned on the decimal point. Notice that numbers aligned on the decimal point are easier to read than left-aligned numeric columns:

345.34	345.34
.09	.09
23,456.00	23,456.00
1.12	1.12

Right-aligned columns resemble flush right text, but they are not at the far right margin.

William Morris

Sam Spady

Jane Pascalli

Finally, dot leader tabs can be of any of the above types, but periods fill the blank area preceding the text entered at the tab:

President ....William Morris

Vice President ....Sam Spady

Executive Director ....Jane Pascalli

Setting Tab Stops

The tab stops you set affect only the text from the cursor down. Follow these steps to enter several different types of tab stops:

1. Press Shift-F8 1 to reveal the Format menu, then the Format Line menu. Option 8 on that menu is Tab Set, and it shows the default setting of tab stops every $1/2$ inch.

2. Press *8* (or *t*) to select Tab Set and display the Tab Set form (Figure 6.2).

```
L....L....L....L....L....L....L....L....L....L....L....L....L....L....L...
  !    ^    !    ^    !    ^    !    ^    !    ^    !    ^    !    ^    !
  1"        2"        3"        4"        5"        6"        7"        8"
Delete EOL (clear tabs); Enter number (set tab); Del (clear tab);
Left; Center; Right; Decimal; .= Dot leader; Press EXIT when done.
```

Figure 6.2: Tab Set form

The ruler line represents positions starting at the left margin of the page, in this case the default 1 inch. Half inch positions are marked by the character ^ and each of the default left-aligned tabs is represented with an *L*. Below the ruler line are instructions for setting and clearing tab stops.

- To set a tab—use →, ←, or the Space bar to reach the desired tab position. The line will scroll if you move the cursor past the margins. You can set 40 tabs up to $54^1/_2$ inches. Once the cursor is at the desired position,

  - Press *L* for a left-aligned tab.

  - Press *C* for a centered tab.

  - Press *R* for a flush right tab.

  - Press *D* for a decimal tab.

After indicating the type of tab:

  - Press . if you want a dot leader. The letter representing the tab type will appear on the ruler line. Dot leader tabs appear in reverse.

You can also set a left-aligned tab by just typing its position number then pressing ←. Only left-aligned tab stops can be set this way.

- To delete a tab—position the cursor on the tab indicator and press Del.

- To delete all tabs—press Ctrl-End. This will delete all tab stops to the right of the cursor position. To delete all of the tab stops, place the cursor on position 0.

- To set evenly spaced left-aligned tabs—type the starting position number, a comma, then the spacing and ←. For example, type 1,1 to set tabs every 1 inch, starting 1 inch from the left side of the page.

  To set evenly spaced center, right-aligned, or decimal-aligned tab stops, move the cursor to the starting position and enter the tab stop. Then type the starting position number, a comma, then the spacing and ←.

3. Press Home ← to place the cursor on position 0.

4. Press Ctrl-End to delete all of the tabs.

5. Set a center tab at 2 inches:

   a. Move the cursor to the 2 inch position.

   b. Press *C*.

   When you type the column, the characters will center themselves around position 2". They will shift alternately left and right until you press ← or another tab.

6. Set a right-aligned dot leader tab at 6 inches:

   a. Move the cursor to the 6 inch position.

   b. Press *R*.

   c. Press . (the period key).

   When you press Tab to reach this tab stop, a series of periods will appear. Since this is a right-aligned tab, the characters will shift to the left to align evenly with position 6".

7. Set a decimal tab at 7 inches.

   a. Move the cursor to the 7 inch position.

b. Press *D*.

When you type at this tab stop, all characters will move to the left of position 7" until you type the decimal point. The decimal point will remain at 7" and following characters will move to the right as usual.

Figure 6.3 shows the completed tab stops.

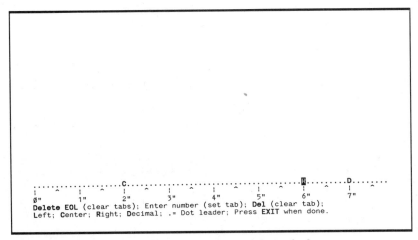

Figure 6.3: Centered, right-aligned dot leader, and decimal tabs set

8. Press F7 twice to return to the document.

9. Press Alt-F3 to reveal the codes (Figure 6.4). If you delete the code you will delete all of the tab stops, returning to the default. You can only delete individual tabs through the Tab Stop menu.

Using Tab Stops

All of the tab stops are reached with the Tab key. Text entered will conform to the type of tab that you set. Now enter the table shown in Figure 6.5.

1. Press Tab and type

   Director

2. Press Tab. Dot leaders will appear (Figure 6.6).

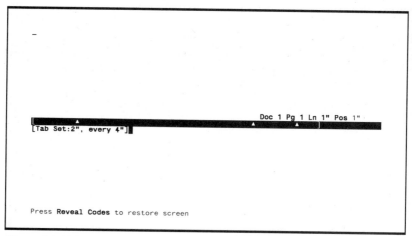

Doc 1 Pg 1 Ln 1" Pos 1"

[Tab Set:2", every 4"]

Press **Reveal Codes** to restore screen

Figure 6.4: *Tab Set code*

3. Type

   Jane Sugerman

   Since this is a right-aligned tab, text will move toward the left.

4. Press Tab, then type

   $65,087.00

   With decimal tabs, all text entered moves to the left until the period is pressed. The decimal point will remain at the tab stop position, then following characters will move to the right as normal.

5. Press ⏎.

6. Complete the text as shown in Figure 6.5.

7. Press Shift-F7 1 to print a copy of the text.

8. Exit the document without saving and start with a new document for the next section.

*A*ligning Columns As You Type

If you're typing tables or long columns, set tab stops so you don't have to worry about formatting individual entries. However, for short

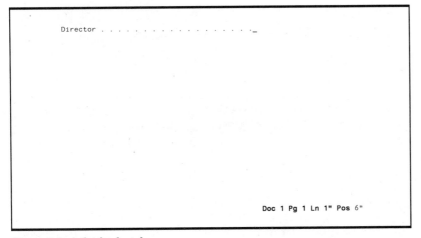

```
        Director . . . . . . . . . . Jane Sugerman    $65,087.00
Assistant Manager. . . . . . . .Dean Johnson          $58,500.00
     Supervisor. . . . . . . . John Earl Paulson      $40,500.00
          Guard. . . . . . . . . Harvey Smithson      $32,000.00_




                                        Doc 1 Pg 1 Ln 1.5" Pos 7.3"
```

Figure 6.5: A table using three tabs

```
        Director . . . . . . . . . . . . . . . . . ._




                                        Doc 1 Pg 1 Ln 1" Pos 6"
```

Figure 6.6: A dot leader tab

documents, you can quickly simulate centered, right-aligned, and decimal-aligned tabs using regular left-aligned tabs as you type. This way, the default tab stops are left untouched if you need them later in the same document.

Lets see how these formats are created by entering a short inventory table as shown in Figure 6.7.

```
        Hammers              200                     3.45
      Screwdrivers            50                     2.56
         Nails              1000                      .02
      Socket Sets             10                    15.56
```

Figure 6.7: Sample table

1. Press the Space bar or the Tab key to place the cursor at position 2".

2. Press Shift-F6.

3. Type

   Hammers

   When you press Shift-F6 at a position other than the left margin, the text is centered there, rather than between the margins.

4. Press Ctrl-F6 four times to reach position 4". Each time you press Ctrl-F6, the cursor shifted to the next tab stop and the status line read

   Align Char = .

   Ctrl-F6 is a special type of tab key. As with the regular Tab key, each time you press it the cursor moves to the next tab stop on the line. However, as you type, the characters shift to the left, instead of to the right as usual, until an Align character is entered. Characters after that move to the right as usual. The default Align character is the period, used to create columns of numbers aligned on the decimal point. But Tab and Ctrl-F6 also act as Align characters, as long as the text itself does not contain a period. We will use this feature to create a right-aligned column.

5. Type

   200

   Since this is a character-aligned tab, text moves toward the left.

6. Press Ctrl-F6 five times. The cursor shifts to the next tab stop.

7. Type

   3.45

   The numbers shift left until the decimal point, which stays at the tab stop position just like a decimal-aligned tab.

8. Press ⬅.

9. Complete the text as shown in Figure 6.7. Press Ctrl-F6 the proper number of times to reach position 4" for the second column—three times after typing *Screwdrivers* and *Socket Sets,* four times after *Nails.*

   While you can simulate center, right-aligned, and decimal tab stops in this way, you can't automatically add dot leaders.

10. Press Shift-F7 1 to print a copy of the text.

11. Press F7 N N to exit the document without saving the text.

Changing Tabs

If you change your mind about new tab stops, you can delete them individually or return quickly to the default tab stop every ¹/₂ inch.
To delete individual tab stops:

1. Press Alt-F3 to reveal the codes.

2. Place the cursor immediately after the [Tab Set] code.

3. Press Alt-F3 to remove the code display.

4. Press Shift-F8 1 8.

5. Position the cursor on the tab stop and press Del.

6. Press F7 twice to return to the document.

The original Tab Set code, including the tab you just deleted, will still be in the text. But the new Tab Set code, closest to the text, will be in force.
To return to the default tab stops:

1. Press Alt-F3 to reveal the codes.

2. Place the cursor on the [Tab Set] code.

3. Press Del.

4. Press Alt-F3. The default tab stops are automatically returned.

If you delete or change tab stops, any text already entered at those positions will adjust automatically to the new, or default, tab stop position.

So far you have learned how to format characters (in Chapter 5) and lines. The next chapter deals with paragraph formats.

7

Right and Left Indents and Other Paragraph Formats

Featuring

Indenting paragraphs
Hanging indentations
Hyphenation and justification
Previewing documents

*L*esson 32 – How to Indent Paragraphs

The default paragraph format used by WordPerfect is the block style. Every line, including the first one in a paragraph, starts at the left margin. If you want to indent the first line of a paragraph, just press the Tab key.

> But you might want to indent a whole paragraph, like this one, from the left margin. This helps to make a specific point stand out.

> You might also want to indent a paragraph
> from both the right and left margins.
> This is frequently required for long quotations.

*I*ndenting from the Left Margin

You can indent a paragraph by changing the left margin, but this method is cumbersome if you only want to indent one paragraph for a special effect and then switch back to the normal left margin for the remaining text.

WordPerfect's Indent commands create indented paragraphs using temporary margin changes. Word-wrap returns the cursor to the indented position, not the original margin, until the ⏎ key is pressed to cancel the indented margin. You can use these commands to format individual paragraphs quickly without affecting other text.

Pressing the F4 key creates a temporary left margin. Each time you press the key, the left margin moves to the next tab stop to the right and an [->Indent] code is inserted into the text. Press F4 once to indent a paragraph $1/2$ inch (the first tab by default), twice for a 1-inch indentation, and so on.

To see how easy it is to indent paragraphs with WordPerfect, we'll create a document with several levels of indentation. Follow the steps below.

1. Start WordPerfect.

2. Press Shift-F6 to center the cursor.

3. Type

   Classifications of Computers

4. Press ◄─┘ twice.

5. Type the following paragraph, starting at the left margin:

   The largest computer systems are called mainframes. These are large centralized computer systems that can be accessed by a great many users at one time, performing many different tasks.

6. Press ◄─┘ twice, press F4 to indent the next paragraph ½ inch, and type the following text:

   The next size computers are called minicomputers. These are still centralized systems that can be used by a number of persons. However, they have less processing capability than mainframes and can accommodate fewer users.

7. Press ◄─┘ twice, press F4 twice to indent the next paragraph 1 inch, and type the following text:

   Supermicros are smaller than minicomputers. These are smaller computer systems, based on microcomputers, which serve a number of persons at a time. These are called multi-user, multi-tasking microcomputers.

8. Press ◄─┘ twice, press F4 three times, and type the following text:

   A microcomputer, also called a personal or desktop computer, can be used by only one individual at a time. Compared to the other types of computers, the microcomputer has limited processing capabilities.

9. Press ⏎ twice, press F4 four times, then type the following text:

> **The special purpose computer is designed to perform a very specific task. It can be large or small, but it is "dedicated" to the one job for which it was made. Special purpose computers can be found in automobiles, industrial equipment, and even home appliances.**

10. Press ⏎.

11. Press Alt-F3 to reveal the codes. Move the cursor up through the document to see the [->Indent] codes in the text.

12. Press Alt-F3, then press Shift-F7 1 to print the document (Figure 7.1).

```
Classifications of Computers

The largest computer systems are called mainframes. These are
large centralized computer systems that can be accessed by a
great many users at one time, performing many different tasks.

    The next size computers are called minicomputers. These are
    still centralized systems that can be used by a number of
    persons. However, they have less processing capability than
    mainframes and can accommodate fewer users.

        Supermicros are smaller than minicomputers. These are
        smaller computer systems, based on microcomputers,
        which serve a number of persons at a time. These are
        called multi-user, multi-tasking microcomputers.

            A microcomputer, also called a personal or desktop
            computer, can be used by only one individual at a
            time. Compared to the other types of computers,
            the  microcomputer  has  limited  processing
            capabilities.

                The special purpose computer is designed to
                perform a very specific task. It can be large
                or small, but it is "dedicated" to the one
                job for which it was made. Special purpose
                computers can be found in automobiles,
                industrial  equipment,  and  even  home
                appliances.
```

Figure 7.1: Paragraphs indented on the left

13. Save the document under the name CLASSES for use in several other chapters.

The F4 key gives you the flexibility to vary the paragraph format quickly.

*I*ndenting from Both the Left and Right Margins

The F4 key can only indent the left margin of paragraphs. If you want both margins indented, say for a long quotation, you must use the Shift-F4 combination. Each time you press Shift-F4, both margins move ½ inch toward the center of the screen and an [-> Indent <-] code is inserted.

Like F4, Shift-F4 stays in effect only until you press ◄┘. So if you want the right and left margins indented for an entire document, or even for a number of paragraphs, you should change the margins with Shift-F8 as you learned in Lesson 21.

Let's use Shift-F4 to produce the document shown in Figure 7.2.

1. Start WordPerfect if you exited after the last lesson.

```
The first level of classification is kingdom.  This group is
divided into plants and animals.  It is the largest division of
living things.

    The second level is phylum. A phylum is the largest
    division of a kingdom. It is based on specific traits
    from the appearance of the living thing.

        The third level is class. A class is the
        largest division of a phylum.

            The fourth level is order. The
            members of this division possess
            body parts and structures that are
            very much alike.
```

Figure 7.2: Paragraphs indented on both sides

2. Type the paragraph below, starting at the left margin.

     **The first level of classification is kingdom. This group
     is divided into plants and animals. It is the largest
     division of living things.**

3. Press ⏎ twice, press Shift-F4, and type the following text:

     **The second level is phylum. A phylum is the largest
     division of a kingdom.**

4. Press ⏎ twice, press Shift-F4 twice, and type the next para-
     graph. You do not have to press the Shift key each time—hold
     the Shift key down while you press F4 twice.

     **The third level is class. A class is the largest division
     of a phylum.**

5. Press ⏎ twice, press Shift-F4 three times, and type the final
     paragraph.

     **The fourth level is order. The members of this
     division possess body parts and structures that are
     very much alike.**

6. Press Shift-F7 1 to print the document. If WordPerfect is set
     for justified printing, each paragraph will appear neatly cen-
     tered below the one above.

7. Press Alt-F3 to reveal the codes. Even though the paragraphs
     are indented on both sides, the [->Indent<-] codes are only
     at the start of each.

8. Press Alt-F3, then F7 N N to clear the screen.

The Indent codes can be deleted or inserted to modify the appearance of the text at any time. It is always easier to delete codes when
they are revealed on the screen (by pressing Alt-F3). Just place the cursor on the code and press Del. The text both below and above the scale
line will adjust.

If the codes aren't revealed, place the cursor at the far left edge
of the screen on the first line and press Del. In the next lesson, you'll
use the F4 key to create another type of indented paragraph—the
hanging indentation.

*L*esson 33 – How to Create *Hanging Indentations*

Standard paragraphs have only the first line indented with remaining text flush on the left. *Hanging indentations* are just the opposite; the first line starts to the left of the rest of the paragraph. Use hanging indentations when you want paragraphs to stand out from each other, as with numbered paragraphs and outlines.

1. These lines are an example of a numbered paragraph with a hanging indentation. The main text is indented to the right of the level number. In this case the level number *(1.)* is at the far left margin. Because the level number stands out from the text, it is easy to see and can be differentiated from other paragraphs and levels.

By moving the left margin and indentation positions, you can create several levels of hanging indentations to make an outline.

*N*umbered Paragraphs

WordPerfect provides an automatic outlining feature for larger documents, but for shorter ones, you can use the F4 and Tab keys. As an example, we'll create the portion of a topical outline shown in Figure 7.3.

1. Type *1.* to begin the outline. It is not necessary to type any spaces after the level number, since these will be added automatically when you press F4 in the next step.

2. Press F4, then type

    The choice of media used for data communications depends upon the speed of the transmission and the distance it must travel. There are three general classifications of media.

3. Press ◄┘. The text indents to the first tab position while the level number "hangs" at the left margin.

```
    1.    The choice of media used for data communications depends upon
          the speed of the transmission and the distance it must travel.
          There are three general classifications of media.
          a.    Wire media include open copper wire, twisted pair, and
                coaxial cable.
          b.    Airborne media include broadcast and microwave
                transmission.
          c.    New technology includes fiber optic and laser beam
                transmission._




                                        Doc 1 Pg 1 Ln 2.34" Pos 3.3"
```

Figure 7.3: An outline using hanging indentation

4. Press Tab, then type *a.*

5. Press F4, then type

    Wire media include open copper wire, twisted pair, and coaxial cable.

6. Press ⏎.

    The F4 key creates a temporary left margin at the next tab stop position from where it was pressed. You used the Tab key to reach the position for the hanging letter, then F4 to create the indentation.

7. Press Tab, then type *b.*

8. Press F4, then type

    Airborne media include broadcast and microwave transmission.

9. Press ⏎.

10. Press Tab, then type *c.*

11. Press F4, then type

    New technology includes fiber optics and laser beam transmission.

12. Press Shift-F7 1 to print the text.

13. Save the document under the name MEDIA for use later, then clear the screen.

Changing the Format of Existing Text

If you've already typed some text using one paragraph style, you can easily change it to another. To change the format:

1. Press Alt-F3 to reveal the codes.

2. Delete the codes for the format you want to change.

3. Press Alt-F3 to return to the document.

4. Finally, place the cursor where you want the new format to start and press the appropriate format keys. The existing text will adjust to the new format.

Lesson 34 – How to Set Justification

Justified text has even margins on both the left and the right. Although WordPerfect does not display the text justified on the screen, it will print it justified by default. (However, you can see how the text will look justified in the View mode, explained in Lesson 36.)

During printing, extra spaces are inserted between words to spread out the line to the right margin. Only lines that end in the [SRt] codes from word-wrap are affected. These extra spaces often leave large gaps. If you find these gaps unsightly and do not want to hyphenate, turn off justification. Here's how:

1. Place the cursor at the start of the document.

2. Press Shift-F8 1 to show the Format menu then the Format Line menu.

3. Press *3* or *j* to select the Justification option.

4. Press *N* to turn off justification. *No* appears at the prompt.

5. Press ⏎ twice to return to the document. A [Just Off] code is inserted into the text.

If you change your mind, press Alt-F3 to display the codes, place the cursor on the [Just Off] code, then press Del.

*L*esson 35 – How to Hyphenate Text

Word-wrap lets you type without pressing ⏎ at the end of each line. But at times, such as when long words are carried to the next line, a justified paragraph can have too many extra spaces between words. Hyphenation is particularly useful when you're typing justified columns, as you will do in Chapter 12. For example, the following text, without hyphenation, has many noticeable gaps:

Word-wrap

automatically

returns   the

carriage   to

the left.

To avoid such problems, the text should be hyphenated. There are three methods of hyphenation in WordPerfect: entering hyphens yourself without help from WordPerfect, entering them manually but with assistance from WordPerfect, and having them entered fully automatically.

*E*ntering Hyphens Yourself

As you type, you can hyphenate words at the end of a line yourself. But what happens if you later add or delete text, and the hyphenated word moves to another line—bringing the hyphen with it? WordPerfect needs some way to distinguish those hyphens from symbols which belong in the text wherever it is placed, such as dashes and minus signs. So there are three different ways to enter the " – " character:

- Press the - key by itself in words that require hyphens, such as mother-in-law and son-in-law. If the paragraph is later reformatted, the hyphen could be used by word-wrap to divide the word between lines. A [-] code is inserted into the text.

- Press Home - to insert a minus sign for formulas, such as N = G-E. Word-wrap will never break a formula at the minus. To enter a dash, first press Home followed by - then - by itself.

- Press Ctrl- (the Ctrl key and the - key together) to enter a "soft" hyphen when you want hyphenation to limit extra spaces. No hyphen will appear on the screen until word-wrap uses it to hyphenate the word between lines. The hyphen will be displayed if you reveal codes. Use this when typing long words that are close to the end of a line but not yet affected by word-wrap. If later editing forces the word to be wrapped, it will be hyphenated instead, resulting in fewer extra spaces.

If you find it troublesome to add hyphenation manually, you can have WordPerfect help you or even hyphenate automatically. Let's see how.

*M*anual Hyphenation with Assistance

Ordinary manual hyphenation slows down your typing by making you pause at the end of lines to make hyphenation decisions. Instead, you can use manual assisted hyphenation, which suggests to you which words need hyphenation for an attractive document.

1. Before typing, press Shift-F8 1 to display the Format menu, then the Format Line menu.

2. Press *1* or *h* to choose the Hyphenation option. The prompt line changes to

   1 Off; 2 Manual; 3 Auto: 0

3. Press *2* or *m* to turn on manual assisted hyphenation. The word *Manual* replaces the word *No* at the Hyphenation option, and the [Hypn On] code is inserted in the text.

4. Press ⏎ twice to return to the document window.

As you type, WordPerfect will sense when word-wrap will leave too many spaces between words. Before carrying the word to the next line, the message

   Position Hyphen; Press ESC

will appear, followed by the word shown with a suggested hyphenation site (Figure 7.4).

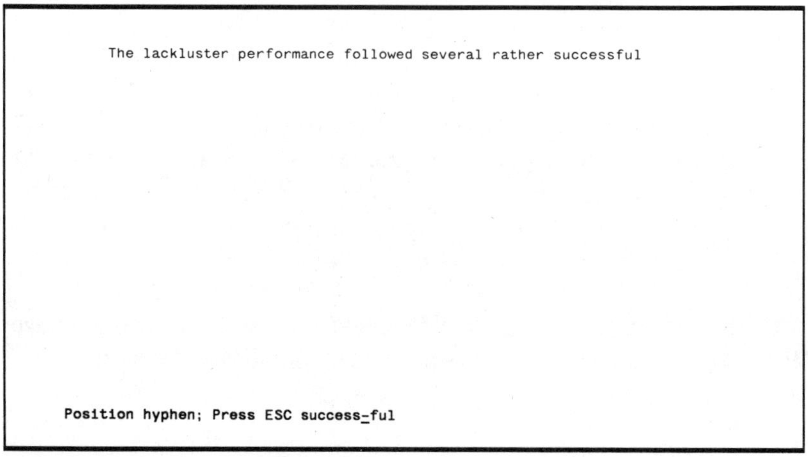

```
            The lackluster performance followed several rather successful

















        Position hyphen; Press ESC success_ful
```

Figure 7.4: Suggested hyphenation

   Use the → and ← keys to move the hyphen to an appropriate place, then press Esc to insert a soft hyphen into the text.
   Turn off manual assisted hyphenation by pressing Shift-F8 1 1 1, then press ↵ twice to return to your text.

*A*utomatic Hyphenation

   This feature goes one step further by actually dividing words for you and adding the hyphen. Before typing or editing, follow these steps to turn on automatic hyphenation:

1. Press Shift-F8 1 1 to display the Format Line menu and the Hyphenation selection line.

2. Press *3* or *a* to turn on automatic hyphenation. The word Auto appears as the Hyphenation option and the [Hyph On] code is inserted in the text.

3. Press ↵ twice to return to the document.

As you type, WordPerfect will automatically insert a soft hyphen where appropriate, without stopping for you to position the cursor. If WordPerfect's rules of hyphenation don't apply to the word, you will be placed in the Aided Hyphenation mode for that word only.

If you later want to delete or change the hyphen, delete the − character and edit accordingly.

Lesson 36 – How to View Documents

A document appears on the screen just as it will when printed, with a few exceptions. For example, the displayed text will be one size and not justified. Page numbers, headers, footers, and footnotes (all to be discussed later) will not appear on the screen, just on the final copy. However, you may want to see exactly how formatting commands such as character size and justification will affect the final appearance.

That's when you use the View mode.

Use this command to see on screen exactly how the document will appear on paper. I view all complex documents before printing. This way I can confirm that the final copy will appear like I imagined it when setting formats. This is particularly useful when using different size fonts or using WordPerfect's Graphics commands for page composition. For example, Figure 7.5 shows a page containing both text and graphics in View mode. This page also demonstrates the desktop publishing abilities of WordPerfect.

How your documents appear in View mode is dependent on your computer hardware—the type of graphic board you have installed and the resolution of the monitor. But even without high resolution, View mode is a powerful tool.

Load the document MEDIA to see how it will appear both justified and unjustified.

1. Recall MEDIA.

2. Press Shift-F7 to display the Print menu.

3. Press *6* or *v* to choose the View option.

The screen changes to View mode with the current page displayed on the screen (Figure 7.6). You can't edit or format the text while viewing it.

The characters may not be totally legible in this mode, but you can see how the lines are justified at the right.

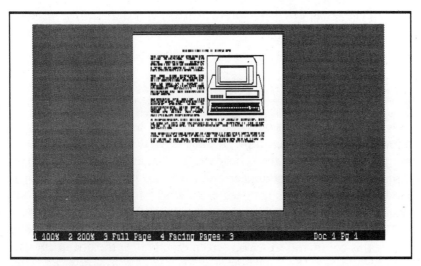

Figure 7.5: Viewing a page with text and graphics

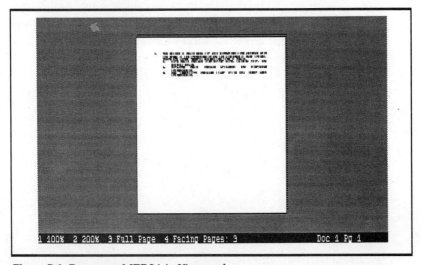

Figure 7.6: Document MEDIA in View mode.

The options at the bottom of the screen let you enlarge or reduce the displayed page. By default your screen shows the full page, option 3. But you can enlarge the display to show the page the same size (option 1—*100%*) as the actual printed sheet or twice the size (option 2—*200%*). You can also see how two adjacent pages will appear. In book form, page 1 is always on top. So adjacent pages can only be displayed for facing pages such as 2 and 3, 4 and 5, etc.

4. Press *2* to display the page at 200% (Figure 7.7).

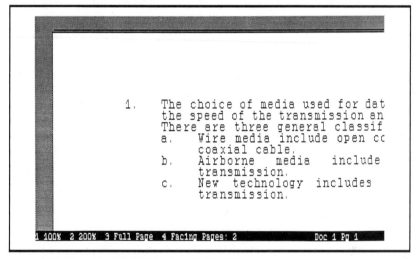

Figure 7.7: Document MEDIA viewed at 200%

At this enlargement the characters are fully readable. But the document is too large to be seen on the screen at one time.

5. Press → to scroll the screen. You can use any of the directional arrows to scroll through the displayed document.

 Now let's see how different the document appears when not justified.

6. Press F7 twice to return to the document.

7. Format the text as unjustified.

 a. With the cursor at the top of the document, press Shift-F8 1.

   b. Press *3* or *j* to select the Justification option.

   c. Press *N* to turn off justification.

   d. Press ⏎ twice to return to the document.

8. Press Shift-F7 6 3 to view the full page of the document again. The lines no longer appear justified.

9. Press F7 twice to return to the document.

10. Press F7 N N to exit WordPerfect without resaving the text.

By now you should see WordPerfect's great potential. So now let's work on even more formatting skills.

8

Page Formatting for a Professional Look

*F*eaturing

Top and bottom margins

Page size, forms, and envelopes

Widow and orphan lines

Centering title pages

*L*esson 37–How to Set Top and Bottom Margins

The top and bottom margins, along with the font size, determine the number of lines you'll be able to fit on each page. Using the default font that prints six lines of typing per inch, the standard 8½" by 11" page is 66 lines long. So if you subtract the default 1-inch top and bottom margins, you'll have 54 actual lines of typing per page.

When you change the size of the top or bottom margin, WordPerfect automatically computes the number of lines per page, so the soft page break line will appear at the proper place.

Before changing margins, place the cursor at the start of the document if you want every page formatted the same way. To format a specific page, place the cursor at the start of that page.

Let's see how this is done by changing the top and bottom margins to 1½ inches.

1. Start WordPerfect.

2. Press Shift-F8 2 to display the Format Page menu (Figure 8.1).

```
Format: Page

        1 - Center Page (top to bottom)        No

        2 - Force Odd/Even Page

        3 - Headers

        4 - Footers

        5 - Margins - Top                       1"
                      Bottom                    1"

        6 - New Page Number                     1
            (example: 3 or iii)

        7 - Page Number Position                No  page numbering

        8 - Paper Size                          8.5" x 11"
            Type                                Standard

        9 - Suppress (this page only)

    Selection: 0
```

Figure 8.1: Format Page menu

These options control the arrangement of text and other elements on the page. You'll learn about most of these settings in other chapters. But now notice that option 5 sets top and bottom margins.

3. Press *5* or *m* to move the cursor to the top margin setting.

4. Type *1.5,* the size of the top margin in inches, then press ◄┘. WordPerfect adds the inches sign (") for you. If you only wanted to change the bottom margin, you would just press ◄┘ at this prompt.

5. Type *1.5,* the size of the bottom margin, then press ◄┘. If you just wanted to set the top margin and accept the default bottom, you would press ◄┘ instead.

6. Press ◄┘ twice to return to the document. The [T/B Mar:1.5", 1.5"] code is inserted in the text.

As you type, WordPerfect will end each page at the appropriate place. So with 1½-inch top and bottom margins you'll get only 48 lines before the page break is inserted.

To return to the original default margins, press Alt-F3 to display the codes and delete the Top and Bottom Margin code.

Changing margins, however, does not affect the overall size of the page. So it's time to look at a special WordPerfect feature—forms.

*L*esson 38 – How to Set Page Size and Shape with Forms

You determine the length and width of the page by selecting the *form* type.

A form represents the size and type of material you'll be printing on. The most common size is 8½ by 11 inches (called *Standard*). However, you might have several types of material in that size—plain paper, letterhead, large envelopes, label stock, etc. So in selecting a form you have to specify both the size and the type.

The default page size is 8½ by 11 inches and the type is Standard. While there are nine preset form sizes (you can always set your own), some printers only have the standard size and type *defined,* or ready to use. Some printers also have a form called All Others.

So to use another form size and type, you must first add it to the list of those available to your printer. Once you add the form to the list it will be available whenever you use WordPerfect. So you can use that form anytime without defining it again.

You only have to define a form if it is either longer or wider than the All Others form. You'll soon learn how to set smaller page sizes without creating a new form.

This may all seem very complicated. And it *can* be, depending on how may special form characteristics you want to add. But let's start by seeing what forms are available for your printer and, if necessary, adding a legal size form—8½ by 14 inches—to your printer's list. Because this is longer than the standard 11 inches, you must make sure it is defined before using it.

Most of the instructions in this lesson should be familiar to you. That's because you used many of the same menus when you selected your printer and paper feed type in Appendix C. So refer to the figures in that appendix if you have any questions.

Here's how to change your paper size to legal:

1. Press Shift-F7 S to choose the Select Printer function. The list of available printers is displayed.

   Make sure your printer is selected. If there isn't an asterisk next to it, highlight the name and press ⏎ then *S* to return to this listing.

2. Press *3* or *e* to edit the printer definition. The Printer Selection Edit menu appears.

3. Press *4* or *f* for the Forms option and display a list of defined forms for your printer.

   Is there a listing for a legal size form on your display? It would look someting like this:

   Legal 8.5" x 14"

If you have a legal form defined then you don't have to continue with steps 4 through 10—just press F7 four times. But review the steps anyway in case you want to define some other custom form size later on.

4. Press *1* or *a* (Add) to see the list shown below, then *1* to select the Standard type (normally used for plain paper). The Printer Selection Forms menu is displayed.

Select Printer: Paper Type

Form Type

1 - Standard
2 - Bond
3 - Letterhead
4 - Labels
5 - Envelope
6 - Transparency
7 - Cardstock
8 - [ALL OTHERS]
9 - Other

5. Press *1* or *s* to set the form size. You'll see the Form Size Selection menu, Figure 8.2.

```
Printer Selection: Form Size
                                    Inserted
                                    Edge

        1 - Standard                8.5"   ×   11"

        2 - Standard Wide           11"    ×   8.5"

        3 - Legal                   8.5"   ×   14"

        4 - Legal Wide              14"    ×   8.5"

        5 - Envelope                9.5"   ×   4"

        6 - Half Sheet              5.5"   ×   8.5"

        7 - US Government           8"     ×   11"

        8 - A4                      210mm  ×   297mm

        9 - A4 Wide                 297mm  ×   210mm

        0 - Other

Selection: 1
```

Figure 8.2: Form Size Selection menu

6. Press *3* or *L* for Legal. The Forms menu will be redisplayed.

7. Press *4* or *L* if the paper location (feed) is incorrect. The prompt line changes to

Location: 1 Continuous; 2 Bin Number; 3 Manual: 0

8. Press the number corresponding to the paper source. If you press *2* for Bin Number, you'll see the prompt

Bin Number:

Enter the number of the paper tray or bin containing the legal size paper.

Now look at option 3, Initially Present. Yes at this option means that the form is available for use. If it is not Yes, press *3* then *Y* to change the setting.

9. Press ←⎯. You'll see the list of defined forms with your new form inserted.

The other options on the last menu are used infrequently.

Orientation — used primarily for laser printers. *Portrait* orientation is normal printing with characters across the width; in *landscape* orientation, characters print down the length of the page.

Page Offset — sets any additional margin space at the top or left of the form. For example, multi-part 8½" by 11" forms often have a narrow area before the perforation at the top margin. The total form length is actually 8½ by 11½ inches. A top page offset of ½ inch and a top margin of 1 inch would advance the form 1½ inches before printing. Left offsets can be used with continuous form paper to accommodate the tractor holes.

10. Press F7 four times to return to the typing window.

This form definition is now added to those available. It can be easily selected when you want to print on legal paper. Here's how:

1. Make sure the cursor is at the start of the document, then

press Shift-F8 2 to display the Format Page menu. The default 8½" by 11" page size is at the Form option.

2. Press *8* or *f* to select Paper Size and display the Paper Size options.

3. Press *3* to select legal size. You'll then see the paper types listed.

4. Press *1* to select Standard.

    If you select a form size and/or type that hasn't been defined, WordPerfect will use Standard in its place and display the message *requested form is unavailable* in the menu.

5. Press ⟵ twice to accept the page size change. The code [Paper Sz/Typ: 8.5" x 14", Standard] is inserted into the text. Because the form is now 14 inches (84 lines) long, you'll be able to enter 72 lines between the top and bottom margins.

Entering Smaller Sizes without Defining Forms

Remember the *Other* option on the Form Size menu? This means that you can enter your own sizes. Maybe you're wondering why you couldn't just enter 8½ by 14 inches on this menu in the first place without defining the form. Actually, using this option you can enter other sizes that are not defined as forms, but they can be no larger than the standard or All Others form for your printer, whichever is larger. So if you select Legal Envelope, for example, the size is recorded as 8½ by 4 inches instead of the 9½ by 4 inches as shown on the menu.

But you can take advantage of this setting when working with smaller forms, such as 3" by 5" index cards. Let's do this now. You'll be selecting a width of 5 inches and a height of 3.

1. Press Shift-F8 2 to display the Format Page menu.

2. Press *8* or *s* to select the Paper Size option and display the Form Size options.

3. Press *O* to select Other. The prompt changes to

   Width: 8.5"

4. Type *5,* then press ◄—┘ to see the prompt

   Height: 11

5. Type *3,* then press ◄—┘ to display the Paper Type list.

6. Press *1* for Standard. (Card stock isn't defined.)

7. Press ◄—┘ twice to return to the document.
   Now let's confirm that the 3" by 5" form size is being used.

8. Type the numbers 1 through 7 down the side of the screen,
   such as

   1
   2
   3
   4
   5
   6
   7

The page break line appeared after the sixth line. Isn't that after just 1 inch of typing? Well, keep in mind that changing the page size does not change the top and bottom margins. So with the default 1-inch margin still in force, you only have 1 inch, or 6 lines, of typing per page. To fit more on the page, change the top and bottom margins as you learned in Lesson 37. Set the top and bottom margins to $1/2$ inch so all of the lines fit on the card. Figure 8.3 shows the card in View mode.

*F*orms and Page Feed

As you saw, you set the paper feed to manual, continuous, or sheet feeder when you define the location of the form. So, for example, you can feed envelopes manually into the printer or use continuous feed for tractor paper—sheets of paper connected with perforations.

But let's consider some special situations.

If you have a laser printer, use continuous feed for paper that's loaded in the tray. Even though they are individual sheets of paper, laser printers treat them as continuous feed.

Figure 8.3: Index card in View mode

What about printers that handle both single sheets and continuous paper? You might use plain continuous paper for some jobs but change to single sheets for letterhead or special paper. Each defined form can have only one location. Yet the solution is simple: Define two forms. Define and use the standard size and standard type as continuous paper. But also define a standard size and letterhead or bond type as manual. When you're ready to print, place the cursor at the top of the document and select the form type desired. The standard form type will use continuous paper, the letterhead or bond type will use manual.

*L*esson 39 – How to Eliminate *Orphan and Widow Lines*

The page settings determine how many text lines will be printed on a page. But because pagination simply counts lines before breaking pages without considering how the page looks, some paragraphs may be divided inappropriately.

An *orphan* is the last line of a paragraph that is printed by itself on the top of a page. A *widow* is the first line of a paragraph appearing by itself on the bottom of a page. Both can be avoided using the Page Format menu.

1. Press Home Home ↑ to place the cursor at the start of the document.

2. Press Shift-F8 1 for the Format Line menu.

3. Press *9* or *w* to select the Widow/Orphan Protection option.

4. Press *Y.* You will see *Yes* at the prompt.

5. Press ↵ twice to return to the document.

6. Press F7 N N to clear the screen.

When changing pages, WordPerfect will now shift lines up or down, sometimes printing fewer than the set number of lines per page, to avoid widow and orphan lines.

*L*esson 40 – How to Create Title Pages

Title pages usually contain several lines of text centered both horizontally and vertically on the page. To get this effect, you can use the Center Page Top to Bottom option on the Page Format menu. You will also have to press Shift-F6 to center text between the right and left margins. Follow these steps to create a title page:

1. Press Home Home ↑ to place the cursor at the left margin of line 1.

2. Press Shift-F8 2 for the Format Page menu.

3. Press *1* to select the Center Page Top to Bottom option. *Yes* appears at the prompt.

4. Press ↵ twice to return to the document. The [Center Pg] code is inserted into the text.

5. Press Shift-F6 and type

Tae Kwon Do in the Martial Arts

6. Press ◀─┘ twice, Shift-F6, then type

   by

7. Press ◀─┘ twice, Shift-F6, then type

   Liz Bressi-Stoppe

8. Press Ctrl-◀─┘ to insert a page break.

9. Press Home Home ↑ to reach the top page, then press Alt-F3 to reveal the codes (Figure 8.4).

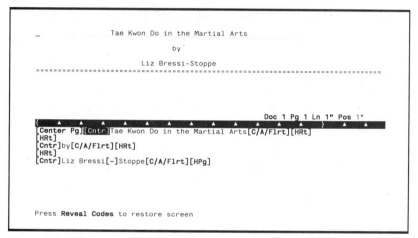

Figure 8.4: *Title page with codes revealed*

The [Center Pg] code will automatically add the necessary blank lines to center the text between the top and bottom margins.

If you want the text slightly higher than center, just add a few blank lines with the ◀─┘ key after typing the text. To print it slightly lower than center, add the lines above the text, but after the [Center Pg] code.

10. Press Alt-F3 to return to the typing area.

11. Press Shift-F7 V to see how the page will appear when printed (Figure 8.5). Press F7 twice when you have finished looking at the preview.

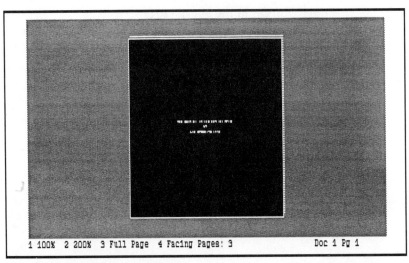

Figure 8.5: Title page in View mode

12. Save the title page under the name TITLE for use in an
    upcoming chapter.

If you later add or delete lines on the title page, WordPerfect will
automatically adjust the page when printing. To return the page to
normal, delete the [Center Pg] code. Changing the setting in the menu
has no effect.

Lesson 41 – How to Print Envelopes

So far you've printed everything on either business or legal sized
paper. Wouldn't it be nice if life were always so simple?

Well, it's not. Take envelopes for example.

Some people believe that if you don't print envelopes often, you
may find it easier to revert back to the typewriter for these. If you have
a laser printer, this might be particularly true because of special formatting problems.

But if you have either a daisy wheel printer or a dot matrix printer
with friction feed, envelopes are just another page of a different size.

Printing envelopes is a very useful skill, particularly if you do it a
lot. By combining the formatting skills you'll learn in this lesson with
form letter techniques you'll learn later on, you can print envelopes
for an entire mailing list easily and quickly.

If your printer already has an envelope form defined, then you can just select it as explained in the section "Selecting the Envelope Form."

Otherwise, let's create the envelope form right now and print a sample envelope. Using WordPerfect's Forms feature, you'll have to do this in three steps. First, you'll define the envelope form for a standard business envelope, 9½ by 4 inches. Then, you'll select the form from the Format Page menu. Finally, you will have to adjust the margins to print the address in the correct location.

Defining the Envelope Form

1. Press Shift-F7 S to choose the Select Printer function.
2. Press *3* or *e* to edit the printer definition.
3. Press *4* or *f* for the Forms option and display the Printer Selection Forms menu.
4. Press *1* or *a* to add a new form definition and display the Form Type menu.
5. Press *5* or *e* to select the envelope type.
6. Press *1* or *s* to set the paper size.
7. Press *5* or *e* for the envelope size.
8. Press *4* or *L*, then *3* to select Manual Feed.
9. Press *3* or *i,* then *N* for Initially Present.
10. Press F7. The new form type is inserted.
11. Press F7 four times to return to the typing window.

Selecting the Envelope Form

When you're ready to address and print an envelope, follow these steps:

1. Press Shift-F8 2 to display the Format Page menu.
2. Press *8* or *s* to select Paper Size and display the Form Size options.

3. Press *5* or *e* to select the envelope size.

4. Press *5* or *e* to select the envelope type.

5. Press F7 to accept the page size change. The code [Paper Sz/ Typ:9.5" x 4", Envelope] is inserted into the text.

*S*etting Envelope Margins

If you're in business, you probably have your return address already printed in the left corner of your envelopes. So you should set the margins to quickly print the recipient's address in the correct location. Let's do this first. Then I'll show you how to set the margins if you're using blank envelopes.

Business Envelopes

When you're ready to format and print an envelope, first select the form as you did above. Then set all of the margins—top, bottom, left, and right—in order to streamline envelope printing.

1. Press Shift-F8 2 to display the Format Page menu.

2. Press *5* or *m* to set the top and bottom margins.

3. Type *2* for a 2-inch top margin, then press ←.

4. Type *.5* for the bottom margin, then press ←. This will give you nine lines for the address.

5. Press ← to display the Format menu.

6. Press *1* for the Format Line menu.

7. Press *7* or *m* to set the margins.

8. Type *4* for the left margin.

9. Press ← four times to accept the default 1-inch right margin and return to the document.

With the margins set this way, you can type the address without worrying about formatting. Just type the address starting at the first line.

1. Type

   Barbara E. Cohen
   9642 Friendship Street
   Philadelphia, PA 19111

2. Insert an envelope into the printer. Line it up vertically so the top edge of the envelope is aligned with the print head, just where you'd start a regular piece of paper.

3. Press Shift F7 1 to print the envelope, then Shift-F7 4 G to issue the Go command. Figure 8.6 shows the envelope in View mode.

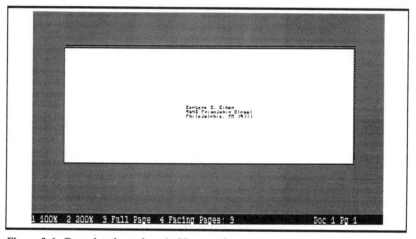

Figure 8.6: Completed envelope in View mode

The envelope will move up past the 2-inch top margin and the address will start printing 4 inches from the left.

Blank Envelopes

If you want to print your return address on the left corner, set the top, bottom, and left margins at ½ inch. Then type your address starting at the top of the screen.

Press ⬅ to reach line 18, and tab to position 40. Enter the recipient's address at this location and print the envelope as explained in instructions 2 and 3 above.

You have now learned all of the fundamental ways to format your documents. In the next chapter you'll learn about headers, footers, and page numbers.

9

Adding Headers, Footers, and Page Numbers

*F*eaturing

Creating and editing
headers and footers

Printing page numbers

Suppressing headers
and footers

New page number

*L*esson 42 – How to Create Headers and Footers

A *header* prints specified lines of text at the top of every page. *Footers* do the same at the bottom.

The most useful headers are those that identify the document to which the page belongs. That way, if individual pages get separated from the document, the reader will have little trouble locating their source.

In most cases, footers contain a page number and perhaps a continuation message, such as *(Continued on the next page)* or *(Please turn the page)*. Page numbers can be printed in headers or footers, or by themselves as explained in Lesson 43.

Before computers, the problem with typing headers was to remember to type them on the page; with footers it was to leave enough room for them at the bottom of the page. WordPerfect's automatic Header/ Footer function overcomes these problems.

Using this option, you first decide on the general placement of the header or footer. Do you want it to appear on every page including the first, only on odd-numbered pages, or only on even ones? Do you want the same headers and footers throughout the entire document, or different ones on specific pages? All of these options are available in WordPerfect.

After deciding on placement, you enter and save the text in a special typing area. Headers and footers will not appear on the screen when you are typing, but they will be added automatically to the printed text.

The header starts printing at the first line of text (not in the margin) with an extra blank line between it and the text. Footers begin printing on the last text line (54 by default) and may extend into the bottom margin. An extra blank line is inserted before the first footer line.

Because of their placement, headers and footers reduce the number of text lines on the page. A one-line header, for example, takes up two text lines, one for the header itself and one for the blank line following it—leaving only 52 text lines. If you add a one-line footer, only 50 lines of text will be printed on the page. So avoid cluttering documents with unnecessary headers or footers.

Let's create a document in which every page has a one-line header and a one-line footer containing the page number.

1. Start WordPerfect.

2. Press Shift-F8 2 to display the Format Page menu.

3. Press *3* or *h* for the Header option. The prompt line changes to

   1 Header A; 2 Header B: 0

   At any time you can have two different headers and two different footers, known as *A* and *B*. You can have all four types of headers and footers in the same document, even more than one of each type if they are on different pages. Both headers A and B can appear on every page, on odd or even pages only, or just on specified pages. You can put both A and B on the same page. The same is true for footers.

4. Press *1* to create header A. The status line changes to

   1 Discontinue; 2 Every page; 3 Odd pages; 4 Even pages; 5 Edit:0

1 Discontinue	Stops printing of the header or footer beginning on the page where the command is issued. To place a header or footer on just one page, create it on the desired page and then select the Discontinue option on the following page.
2 Every page	Prints the text on each page of the document, unless discontinued.
3 Odd pages	Prints the text only on odd-numbered pages.
4 Even pages	Prints the text only on even-numbered pages.
5 Edit	Allows you to edit the text of the selected header or footer.

5. Press *2* for *Every page.* The screen clears to display the Header/Footer Creation window, which is blank except for the status line:

   Press EXIT when done   **Ln 1 Pos 10**

Here is where you type the text of the header or footer. You can use all of the normal editing and cursor movement keys, and you can boldface, underline, or otherwise format the text.

6. Type the following header, but do not press ⏎ when you are done:

   1988 Computer Seminar

   If you had pressed ⏎, an extra blank line would have been included in the header, in addition to the blank line inserted to separate the header from the text.

7. Press F7 to save the header and redisplay the Format: Page menu. The header is saved within the document, not as a separate file.

8. Press *4 1 2* to create Footer A on every page.

9. Press Shift-F6 to center the cursor.

10. Type *Page.*

11. Press the Space bar.

12. Press Ctrl-B. The ˆB code, which stands for the page number, will be displayed (Figure 9.1).

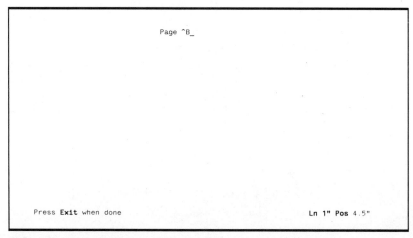

Figure 9.1: Footer with page number

WordPerfect will display the current page number at the location of the ^ B code in the text, in this case next to the word *Page*. The ^ B code can be in either the header or the footer.

In Lessons 43 and 45 you'll learn how to change the printed page number and how to include a page number without entering a header or footer.

13. Press F7 to accept the footer. The Format: Page menu appears, showing the selected position of the header and footer you just set.

14. Press ◄— twice to return to the typing window.

15. Press Alt-F3 to reveal the codes. The first 50 characters of each header or footer will be displayed along with the codes (Figure 9.2).

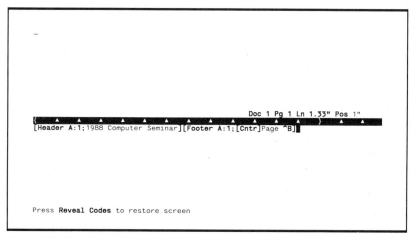

Figure 9.2: Header and Footer codes

16. Press Alt-F3 to return to the document, then type

    To All Seminar Participants:

    The enclosed materials will be discussed during the seminar. Please bring them with you to every session.

17. Press Shift-F7 V to view the document as it will appear when printed (Figure 9.3).

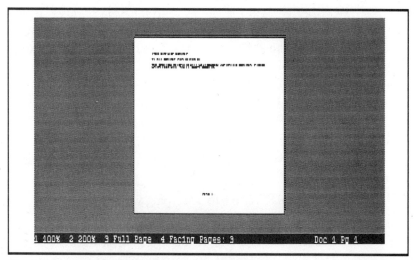

Figure 9.3: Document showing header and footer

18. Press F7 twice to return to the document.

Leave the text on the screen for use in the next section.

*H*eader/Footer Suggestions

The header should always be created at the top of a page. If the Header code follows text on a page, the header will not start printing until the next page. This can be used to your advantage in suppressing the header on an initial title page.

Headers and footers A and B should be coordinated carefully. The main advantage of having two headers or footers is to print them on alternating pages. One can print on the left side of even-numbered pages, the other on the right side of odd pages. You can also create both A and B at the start of the document and switch back and forth when needed.

But if you set their occurrences the same so they print on the same page, both headers or both footers may print on the same line, destroying the line format used to create them. One alternative is to enter header A on the left side of the first header line, and header B flush right. Then they will not interfere with each other. Otherwise, enter the headers on different lines, such as header A on line 1 and header B on line 2.

*E*diting Headers and Footers

To change the text of a header or footer, press Shift-F8 2 then *3* for a header or *4* for a footer. Press the key corresponding to the header or footer you want to edit. Then press *5* for Edit.

WordPerfect searches back through the document to the most recent header or footer of the type selected, then displays it in the editing window. Make the changes desired and press F7.

Delete a header by deleting its code, or just discontinue it with the Discontinue option (1).

In the next lesson you will learn a quick way to print page numbers without including them in a header or footer. So delete the footer in the current document. Follow these steps:

1. Press Home Home ↑ to go to the beginning of the document.

2. Press Alt-F3 to reveal the codes. The cursor is to the right of the Header and Footer codes.

3. Press Backspace to delete the Footer code.

4. Press Alt-F3.

5. If you are not ready to continue with Lesson 43, save the text under the name ENCL for use later on.

*L*esson 43 – How to Insert Page Numbers

A page number can be printed by itself on every page even without including a ^ B code in a header or footer. You cannot include any text (such as *Page 30*) but you can select the exact location where the number will appear. You can even change the number that will be printed on the page. Like headers and footers, the page number will not appear on the screen (unless previewed in View mode), but it will be printed.

In this lesson, you will add page numbers to the text created in Lesson 42 and merge it with the document CLASSES entered in Chapter 7. If you exited WordPerfect after the last lesson, start the program and recall the document ENCL. Then continue with the steps below.

1. Press Home Home ↓ to reach the end of the document.

2. Press Ctrl-← to insert a page break. Now recall the document CLASSES.

3. Press Shift-F10, type *CLASSES,* then press ← to recall the document, adding it to the end of the text already on the screen.

4. Press Home Home ↑ to make sure the cursor is at the top of the document. Now let's add a page number at the bottom center of the page. While this will number your pages consecutively starting from page 1, you'll learn how to handle title pages in Lesson 44.

5. Press Shift-F8 2 to display the Format Page menu.

6. Press *7* or *p* to reveal the Page Number Position menu (Figure 9.4).

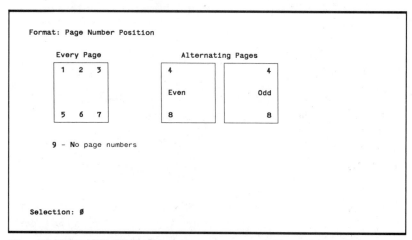

Figure 9.4: Page Number Position menu

Selecting a number from 1 to 8 will cause the page number to print at the position indicated on the menu. Number 9 turns off page numbering.

7. Press *7* to print the page number at the bottom right of every page. The Format Page menu will reappear.

8. Press ↵ twice to return to the document.

9. Press Shift-F7 V to view the first page of the document as it will appear when printed (Figure 9.5). The page number is in the bottom right corner.

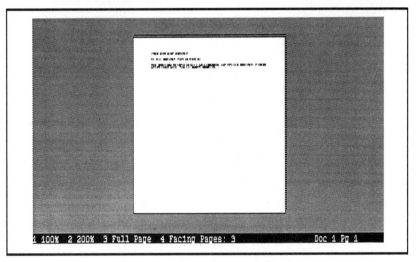

Figure 9.5: *Document showing header and page number*

10. Press F7 to return to the document.

Leave the document on the screen for use in the upcoming lessons. The document now contains two pages, a short cover page and one listing the various classes of computers. The header will be printed on the top of both pages, and each will be numbered at the bottom right.

Lesson 44 – How to Suppress Headers, Footers, and Page Numbers

If page numbering or headers and footers are selected, they are printed on every page. But in the case of the text now on the screen, the first page is just a cover letter; it is not really part of the document, and should not contain the header or be numbered. So let's keep the header and page number from appearing on it.

1. Press Shift-F8 2 to display the Format Page menu.

2. Press *9* to display the *Suppress (this page only)* menu (Figure 9.6).

```
Format: Suppress (this page only)
     1 - Suppress All Page Numbering, Headers and Footers
     2 - Suppress Headers and Footers
     3 - Print Page Number at Bottom Center    No
     4 - Suppress Page Numbering               No
     5 - Suppress Header A                      No
     6 - Suppress Header B                      No
     7 - Suppress Footer A                      No
     8 - Suppress Footer B                      No




Selection: 0
```

Figure 9.6: Suppress (this page only) menu

Through this menu, you can temporarily suspend any headers, footers, or page numbers from printing on the current page. Other pages are not affected.

You can individually suppress headers, footers, or page numbering by selecting options 4 to 8. If you select *2,* all headers and footers are suppressed, and options 5 through 8 change to Yes. Option 1 also suppresses headers and footers, as well as any page numbering you set with the Page Number Position option. Prompts 4 to 8 change to Yes.

Option 3 is used to print just a page number at the bottom center even if headers, footers, and other page numbering have been suppressed.

3. Press *1* to suppress the header and page number.

4. Press ↵ three times to return to the document. The code [Suppress:PgNum, HA, HB, FA, FB] is inserted into the text.

*L*esson 45 – How to Set New Page Numbers

Now only one problem remains. While a page number will not appear on the first page, it is still counted as page 1 as far as numbering is concerned. So what we want to count as the first page of the text, the classifications of computers, will be numbered as page 2. The New Page Number option will solve this problem.

1. Press PgDn to place the cursor at the top of the second page.

2. Press Shift-F8 2 to display the Format Page menu.

3. Press *6* or *n* for New Page Number. The cursor moves to that prompt on the menu.

4. Type *1* and press ◄─┘ three times to return to the document.

    Page numbering will now begin with the number you selected with this option for the current page. Following page numbers will continue from there, unless you enter a new page number on another page.

    Look at the page indicator in the status line. Even though you are in the second page of the text on the screen, it is marked as *Pg 1*. Press PgUp to reach the first page. It too is marked as *Pg 1* in the status line.

    If you want to number pages in lowercase Roman numerals, enter the new page number as i, ii, iii, iv, etc. The page indicator on the status line will show Arabic numbers, but Roman numerals will appear when printed.

5. Press Shift-F7 1 to print a copy of the document.

6. Save the document and exit WordPerfect.

Use the New Page Number option, as you did here, to start a document as page 1 even if it is preceded by a title page or cover letter. This option is also practical when you're composing and printing long documents in sections. Say you have typed, saved, and printed the first section of a long report, numbered 1 through 10. You then decide to add another section and type the next ten pages as a separate document. Before printing, place the cursor at the start of this second section and use the New Page Number option to start numbering at 11.

The next chapter revisits an old subject—blocks. You'll learn how to make major changes to your documents in just a few keystrokes.

10
Editing Entire Blocks

*F*eaturing

Deleting, moving, and copying blocks

Printing, saving, and appending blocks

*L*esson 46 – How to Delete, Move, and Copy Blocks

You've already learned how to boldface, underline, and otherwise format existing characters: press the Alt-F4 key and move the cursor until the text is highlighted, then press the appropriate format key. This is called a *Block* command because it affects an entire section, or block, of text.

Using similar techniques, you can delete a section of text, make a copy of it at another location, or even move it from one location or document to another. Let's say that you just completed a letter and noticed that one paragraph should be moved elsewhere. Rather than delete and retype it, use the Block command to move it.

Now let's use these commands. Imagine that after a document was completed you realized that the text needed to be rearranged. Rather than start from scratch, you'll use the Block commands to rearrange the text, making major changes with just a few keystrokes. Follow these steps:

1. Start WordPerfect.

2. Type the following:

> **There are a number of programming languages in use today. Here are the most common in order of popularity:**
>
> **FORTRAN stands for Formula Translator and was the first natural language compiler.**
>
> **COBOL comes from Common Business Oriented Language and is designed for large business and commercial applications.**
>
> **BASIC stands for Beginners All-purpose Symbolic Instruction Code. This language was initially developed for non–computer science majors but has grown in popularity with the use of microcomputers.**

PASCAL was named for Blaise Pascal. It was created primarily as a tool for teaching programming and algorithms.

To update this review of computer languages, you want to delete the paragraph about FORTRAN and place the paragraphs about Pascal and BASIC before COBOL.

First perform a block deletion.

3. Place the cursor on the letter F in FORTRAN.

4. Press Alt-F4, then move the cursor to the letter C in COBOL to highlight the paragraph you want to delete. If you move it too far, just move the cursor back again (Figure 10.1).

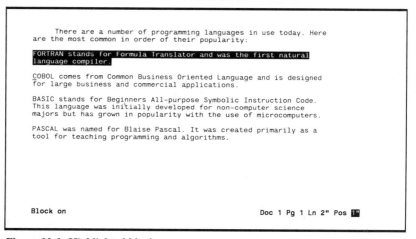

```
        There are a number of programming languages in use today. Here
are the most common in order of their popularity:

FORTRAN stands for Formula Translator and was the first natural
language compiler.

COBOL comes from Common Business Oriented Language and is designed
for large business and commercial applications.

BASIC stands for Beginners All-purpose Symbolic Instruction Code.
This language was initially developed for non-computer science
majors but has grown in popularity with the use of microcomputers.

PASCAL was named for Blaise Pascal. It was created primarily as a
tool for teaching programming and algorithms.




Block on                                        Doc 1 Pg 1 Ln 2" Pos 1"
```

Figure 10.1: Highlighted block

5. Press Ctrl-F4 to display the prompt

   Move: 1 Block; 2 Tabular Column; 3 Rectangle: 0

6. Press *1* to select Block. The prompt line changes to

   1 Move; 2 Copy; 3 Delete; 4 Append: 0

7. Press *3* to delete the block.

   Placing the cursor under the letter C in COBOL also caused the [HRt] codes between the sentences to be deleted, so the remaining text moved up to replace the deleted paragraph.

   Now let's move a block from one location to another.

8. Place the cursor on the letter B in BASIC.

9. Press Alt-F4.

10. Move the cursor to the letter P in PASCAL (Figure 10.2).

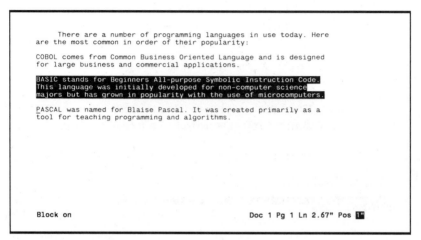

```
        There are a number of programming languages in use today. Here
are the most common in order of their popularity:

COBOL comes from Common Business Oriented Language and is designed
for large business and commercial applications.

BASIC stands for Beginners All-purpose Symbolic Instruction Code.
This language was initially developed for non-computer science
majors but has grown in popularity with the use of microcomputers.

PASCAL was named for Blaise Pascal. It was created primarily as a
tool for teaching programming and algorithms.




   Block on                          Doc 1 Pg 1 Ln 2.67" Pos
```

Figure 10.2: Highlighted block ready to be moved

11. Press Ctrl-F4 1 1 to select Block Move. The text disappears from the screen and the status line changes to

   Move cursor; press Enter to retrieve

12. Place the cursor on the letter C in COBOL.

13. Press ← to reinsert the cut text from the retrieval area.
   Finally, let's copy a block from one location to another. This time, however, you will perform a "speed block" function. If you want to cut or copy just one sentence, paragraph, or page, you do not have to highlight it first.

14. Place the cursor anywhere in the second sentence of the last paragraph.

15. Press Ctrl-F4 to display the prompt

   Move: 1 Sentence; 2 Paragraph; 3 Page; 4 Retrieve: 0

16. Press *1* to highlight the entire sentence and display the same prompt line seen in step 6.

17. Press *2* to make a copy of the sentence. Notice that the block is not erased from its original position. The Move command removes the highlighted text; Copy makes a duplicate of it.

18. Now place the cursor at the end of the paragraph describing BASIC.

19. Press the Space bar to insert a space.

20. Press ⏎ to retrieve the copy of the block and insert it into the text at this new location (Figure 10.3).

```
        There are a number of programming languages in use today. Here
are the most common in order of their popularity:

BASIC stands for Beginners All-purpose Symbolic Instruction Code.
This language was initially developed for non-computer science
majors but has grown in popularity with the use of microcomputers.
It was created primarily as a tool for teaching programming and
algorithms.

COBOL comes from Common Business Oriented Language and is designed
for large business and commercial applications.

PASCAL was named for Blaise Pascal. It was created primarily as a
tool for teaching programming and algorithms.




                                          Doc 1 Pg 1 Ln 2" Pos 1"
```

Figure 10.3: Completed document

21. Save the document under the name LANGUAGE.

You can also move or copy text without inserting it immediately at its new location. Just press F1 when you see the prompt

Move cursor; press Enter to retrieve

The prompt will disappear. Now when you want to insert the text, press Ctrl-F4 4—the Retrieve option—to display

Retrieve: 1 Block; 2 Tabular Column; 3 Rectangle: 0

Press *1*. Unlike the Undo command, which can remember three deletions, you can only store one copied or moved block of text in the Retrieve area. But as long as it is in the Retrieve area, you can insert it as many times as you want by pressing Ctrl-F4 4 1.

Converting Text into a Comment

You can also use block techniques to convert regular text into a comment. But because comments will not be printed along with the document, this has the effect of cutting it from the text.

To convert text, highlight it as a block with Alt-F4, then press Ctrl-F5. The prompt changes to

Create a comment? (Y/N) No

Press *Y* to place a comment box around the blocked text.

Lesson 47 – How to Move Text between Documents

Cut or copied text remains in the retrieval area until you either exit WordPerfect or cut or copy another block. Saving a document, or switching to another, will not affect the stored text.

You can take advantage of this fact to move text between two or more documents. For instance, I have several research papers that contain paragraphs I can use in other documents. Rather than retype the paragraphs, I copy them from one document to the other. Keep in mind that there are two basic ways to store text for moving. Besides using the Cut and Copy commands, you can delete highlighted text by pressing Del Y.

- Using Del, the text is stored in an "undelete" area that can hold the last three deletions. Deleted text is recalled with F1. Text deleted with the "speed block" deletion option (choosing from the Ctrl-F4 selection line without first highlighting text) is also reinstated with the F1 key.

- Text moved or copied with the Ctrl-F4 key is stored in a separate retrieval area, which can only hold one deletion. Block-cut text is recalled with Ctrl-F4 4 1.

Since the two storage areas are independent, you can have four deleted blocks safely stored away for retrieval. Three will be in the undelete area (recalled with F1), the other in the block retrieval area (recalled with Ctrl-F4 4 1).

Pressing F1 will not retrieve text cut with Ctrl-F4. Pressing Ctrl-F4 4 1 will not retrieve the text deleted with the Del key.

Let's review the basic procedures for both methods and for moving text between documents.

*M*ultiple Documents

Let's say you have text in both the Doc 1 and Doc 2 windows. You see a line, a paragraph, or other text in one document that you can use in the other. Here's how to move it between typing windows:

1. Switch to the window that has the text you want to move.

2. Move the text into the retrieval area.

   a. Highlight the text with the Block (Alt-F4) and cursor keys.

   b. Press either Ctrl-F4 1 1 to move the block or Ctrl-F4 1 2 to copy it.

3. Press Shift-F3 to switch to the other document.

4. Place the cursor where you want to insert the text.

5. Press ◄⎯ to insert the text.

6. Save the document.

*A*fter Exiting a Document

In this case, you are only working with one document at a time. You want to save, or just exit, the current document and insert some text from it into another. Here's how:

1. Move the desired text into the retrieval area.

   a. Highlight the text with the Block (Alt-F4) and cursor keys.

   b. Press either Ctrl-F4 1 1 to move the block from the document or Ctrl-F4 1 2 to make a copy of it.

2. Clear the current document from the screen. If you do not want to save it, press F7 N N.

3. Recall the other document, the one in which you want to insert the text, to the screen.

4. Place the cursor where you want to insert the text.

5. Press ⏎ to insert the text.

6. Save the document.

Using these techniques, you can copy the same block to as many documents as you wish.

*L*esson 48 – How to Print Blocks

Another reason to highlight a block with the Alt-F4 key is to print a selected portion of the text. You might want a quick printed record of a certain list of names or a particular paragraph without printing the entire document. Here's how:

1. Place the cursor at one end of the block you want to print.

2. Press Alt-F4.

3. Move the cursor to the other end of the block you want to print.

4. Press Shift-F7 to show the prompt

   Print Block? (Y/N) No

5. Press *Y* to print just the highlighted block.

6. Press Alt-F4 to turn off the Block function.

The block will be printed with any headers, footers, page numbers, or other formatting marked in the document—even if the format codes are not in the highlighted section. If the block spans a page boundary, the text will appear on two pages. If you don't want to include the formatting codes from outside the section, use the method described in the next lesson to save the block, then print the text.

Lesson 49 – How to Save and Append Blocks

Yet another reason for blocking text is to save smaller portions of a larger document. Once text is marked as a block it can be either saved or appended.

Saving Blocks

Sometimes as you write you create a phrase or paragraph that you know you can use somewhere else. Rather than leave it lost in the current document, you can save just that text as a separate file on the disk. The saved block should be stored with a new name. If you give it the name of an existing document, the original will be replaced.

Here are the general procedures:

1. Place the cursor at one end of the block.

2. Press Alt-F4.

3. Move the cursor to the other end of the block.

4. Press F10 to show the prompt

   Block Name:

5. Type the name you wish to save the highlighted block under.

6. Press ←⎯. The text will be saved on the disk. If there already is a document with that name, you will be prompted with

   Replace (document-name)? (Y/N) No

   Press *Y* to erase the existing document, or *N* to enter another name. Press F1 if you change your mind about saving the block.

7. Press Alt-F4 to turn off the Block function.

Unlike when you print blocks, when you save a block only the text and codes within the highlighted block are saved. The formatting codes outside of the block, even those that would affect it when printed, are not included in the saved document.

Now that the block is saved, you treat it as any document. You can edit it, print it, or even add it to another document—just place the cursor where you want to insert it in the text and recall the block from the disk.

However, if you just want to add the block to the end of another document, read on.

*A*ppending Blocks

An *appended* block is added to the end of an existing document. This might be a collection of commonly used paragraphs, or an addition to a document that you are editing separately. It might be a small section of a long document that you want to work on without worrying about accidentally changing existing text; in this case, you can work on new sections individually and append them to the "master" document when they are edited and complete. Appending a block is easy because you don't have to recall and resave the other document.

When you append a block, the document to which it will be added must already exist on the disk. Follow these steps:

1. Place the cursor at one end of the block.

2. Press Alt-F4.

3. Move the cursor to the other end of the block.

4. Press Ctrl-F4 1 4 to show the prompt

   Append to:

5. Type the name of the document you wish to add the highlighted text to.

6. Press ←. The text will be added to the end of that document. If there is no document with that name, the message

   ERROR: file not found

   will appear for a moment.

7. Repeat the process or press Alt-F4 to turn off the Block function.

Block commands provide fast and convenient ways to manipulate sections of text. In the next chapter you'll learn ways to delete or change words or phrases throughout the entire document.

11

Streamlining Your Editing with Search and Replace

*F*eaturing

Forward search
Backward search
Search and replace

*L*esson 50 – How to Search for Text

Much of your time editing a document is spent scrolling through it to locate a particular reference or passage of text. Often you are looking for a specific word or phrase. You're sure it is somewhere in the document, but you don't know the exact page number. You can save time with WordPerfect's Search command. Just type the text you are looking for and WordPerfect searches for it, either backward or forward through the document, placing the cursor directly on the specific word or phrase.

- A forward search locates the first occurrence of the search characters from the position of the cursor toward the end of the document. To search the entire text, begin with the cursor at the start of the document.

- A backward search locates the first occurrence of the search characters from the position of the cursor toward the beginning of the document. To search the entire text, begin with the cursor at the end of the document.

The text to be searched for can be from 1 to 58 characters, including letters, numbers, spaces, punctuation marks, and even codes, such as a hard return or a format change.

Now let's see how Search works. You will recall the document LANGUAGE and use the Search command to locate specific text.

1. Start WordPerfect.

2. Recall the document LANGUAGE. With the document now on the screen, let's first search for the word *language*.

3. Press F2 to see the prompt

    —> **Srch:**

    The forward-pointing "arrow" (—>) indicates a forward search.

4. Type

    language

Do not press ⟵ after typing the word. If you did, WordPerfect would search only for the word *language* followed by a Hard Return code.

5. Press F2 to begin the search.

   The cursor will move to the word *languages* in the first paragraph. Why did the cursor stop there, and not at the first occurrence of the singular *language*? Actually, WordPerfect is not searching for a word at all. Instead, it is looking for the first occurrence of the characters *l a n g u a g e* in the text, even if they are part of another word. (So a search for *the* would place the cursor on words such as *their* and *other*.)

   Now let's find the next occurrence of the same word.

6. Press F2 to display the Search prompt again. The current search word is already at the prompt.

7. Press F2 again to locate the next occurrence.

8. Press F2 twice. The search will repeat and the cursor will be placed on the word *Language*. Now let's search for another word.

9. Press F2, type *PASCAL* (all uppercase), then press F2. The cursor finds the word in the last paragraph.

10. Press F2 twice. The prompt displays **Not Found** in the status line for a few seconds, even though *Pascal* appears later in the same paragraph. The cursor remains at the current location when the search characters are not found.

    Lowercase letters entered at the Search prompt will be matched with either lowercase or uppercase characters in the document. So a search for *language* found *Language*. Uppercase letters entered in the Search prompt will match only uppercase letters in the text. So *PASCAL* will not locate *Pascal*, and *Language* would not be matched with *language*.

11. Press Shift-F2 for a backward search. The prompt shows

    <— PASCAL

    The backward-pointing "arrow" (<—) indicates a backward search.

12. Type the text you want to search for next:

    teach

13. Press F2 to begin the search. The cursor moves backward through the document from the cursor position toward the start of the text, to the word *teaching* in the second paragraph. Remember that if you want to search the entire document you must first move the cursor to the either end by pressing Home Home ↑ or Home Home ↓.

    Now let's search for a code, in this case [TAB].

14. Press Shift-F2 for the Search prompt.

15. Press the Tab key. Notice that the [Tab] code is entered in place of the text in the Search prompt.

16. Press F2. The cursor moves to the start of the first sentence, where the Tab key was used.

17. Leave the text on the screen for use with the next lesson.

Searching For Codes

To search for codes that are inserted with single keystrokes, such as tab, boldface, or underlining, you just pressed the same keystroke at the Search prompt.

If the code requires more than one keystroke, start with the first keystroke. A second prompt line will appear. Make your selection and press F2.

For instance, to search for large type size, press F2, then Ctrl-F8. The prompt changes to

1 Size; 2 Appearance; 3 Normal; 4 Base Font; 5 Print Color: 0

Press *1* to select Size and display the prompt

1 Suprscpt; 2 Subscpt; 3 Fine; 4 Small; 5 Large; 6 Vry Large; 7 Ext Large: 0

Press *5* for Large. The Search prompt will appear:

—> Srch: [LARGE]

Press F2 to start the search.

The Search function can be an invaluable aid during editing. Rather than scan an entire document for a specific reference, just search for it.

I also use the Search function to move quickly to specific locations in a document. I'll insert a place holder at appropriate reference points in the document. The place holder is usually something like *xxxx*—text that I know won't be appearing anywhere else. Then when I have to refer back to that section of text, I search for the place holder.

*L*esson 51 – How to Replace Text

Have you ever misspelled the same word several times in one document or realized that you entered the wrong information in several places? Or do you have a certain document that could easily be modified for another use if the same word were changed several times—for example, a letter that could be used another time if you just changed "he" to "she"?

Using the Replace command, you can automatically locate any text and replace it with something else, no matter how many times it appears. Repeated mistakes can be corrected in a few keystrokes.

To see how Replace works, let's make some changes to the document LANGUAGE.

In that document, you used the word *popularity* twice. Let's use the Replace function to change the first of these occurrences to the word *use*.

Recall the document if it is not still on the screen from Lesson 50.

1. Press Home Home ↑ to place the cursor at the start of the document. Like a forward search, Replace works from the position of the cursor to the end of the document. So to replace every occurrence of the text, place the cursor at the start of the document.

2. Press Alt-F2 to start the Replace procedure. The prompt changes to

   w/Confirm? (Y/N) No

   If you enter *Y,* you will be given the opportunity to confirm each possible replacement. If you enter *N,* the replacements will occur automatically. The Confirm option is useful if you are unsure whether you want to replace all occurrences of the text.

3. Press *Y* for a confirmed replacement. The — > Srch prompt appears, followed by the last search phrase used, if any.

4. Type the term you want to replace:

    popularity

   Any search phrase or code already at the prompt is deleted as soon as you type another.

5. Press F2. The prompt changes to

    Replace with:

6. Type the word you want to insert:

    use

7. Press F2 to begin the replacement.
   WordPerfect first does a forward search for the word *popularity*, using the same uppercase-lowercase rules as a regular search.
   Since this is a confirmed search (because you entered *Y* in Step 3), the cursor stops at the first occurrence of the word and the prompt changes to

    Confirm? (Y/N) No

8. Press *Y* to replace the word *popularity* with the word *use*. The search will continue until it finds the next occurrence of the word.

9. Press F7 to stop the function since you only wanted to replace that one occurrence.
   Now let's try an automatic replacement.

10. Press Home Home ↑.

11. Press Alt-F2 N for an automatic (non-confirmed) search.

12. Type *teaching* (the word you want to replace), then press F2.

13. Type *learning* and press F2. The word *teaching* will be replaced with *learning* in the two instances where it was used.

If you type the search and replace words in all lowercase letters and the original word in the text is capitalized, the replacement will be capitalized. For example, say the text contains the words *Computer* and *computer*. If you enter *computer* as the search phrase and *machine* as its replacement, both occurrences will be replaced, by *Machine* and *machine* respectively.

However, if you enter *Computer* as the search phrase and *machine* as its replacement, only the capitalized *Computer* will be replaced—by *machine* in all lowercase letters.

Type the search phrase in all lowercase letters if you want to replace every occurrence of the word while maintaining the same capitalization as the original.

When the replacement is complete, the cursor remains at the last location where a replacement was made and the message *∗Not Found∗* appears for a second to indicate that there are no more examples in the document.

Automatic replacement is a powerful tool when editing documents. But because it changes the text, it can also result in unexpected, and unwanted, results. As an example, two sentences in the current document use the word *It* to refer to a computer language. So let's automatically replace the word *it* with *the computer language.*

14. Press Home Home ↑.

15. Press Alt-F2 N for an automatic search.

16. Type *it* and press F2.

17. Type *the computer language* and press F2. The two sentences that began *It was* now read *The computer language was*—just as we wanted.

    But look at the second paragraph. The *it* in *initially* was also replaced, resulting in *This language was inthe computer language ially developed.* The same problem occurs at other places in the text where the characters *it* were replaced.

    Use automatic replacement carefully.

18. Press F7 N Y to exit WordPerfect without saving the changed document.

As you've seen, WordPerfect is a comprehensive yet easy-to-learn word processing program. In the first eleven chapters, you learned how to edit, format, and print text. Beginning with Chapter 12 you'll learn some special "power-user" features of WordPerfect.

12

Creating Multicolumn Layouts

*F*eaturing

Newspaper columns
Parallel columns

*L*esson 52 – How to Create Newspaper Columns

Desktop publishing seems to be a magic phrase these days. If you're responsible for producing a newsletter or other multicolumn document, you can take advantage of WordPerfect's built-in Newspaper Column feature.

Newspaper columns (Figure 12.1) automatically run from one column to the next on the page, from left to right. When the far right column is filled, text moves to the left column on the next page.

Figure 12.1: Newspaper columns

Since there can be so much variation in the number and size of columns, you must first *define* the format of the page; that is, you must set the number and spacing of columns on the page.

In this lesson you will create a two-column newsletter with a title across the top of the page.

*D*efining Column Layouts

You must first define the number of columns and their spacing on the page. While it is possible to have columns of different sizes on the same page, equal width is more common. If you want equal-sized columns, WordPerfect will calculate the spacing for you.

Once you define a column layout it stays in effect throughout the document. You do not have to define it again, unless you want a different number or size of columns. Just turn on the Column mode when you want to type columns and turn it off for regular typing.

You can define up to 24 text columns on a page. Right now let's define a format for two even-sized columns, five spaces apart.

1. Start WordPerfect.

2. Press Alt-F7 to see the Math/Column prompt line.

   1 Math on; 2 Math Def; 3 Column On/Off; 4 Column Def;

3. Press *4* to see the Text Column Definition menu (Figure 12.2).

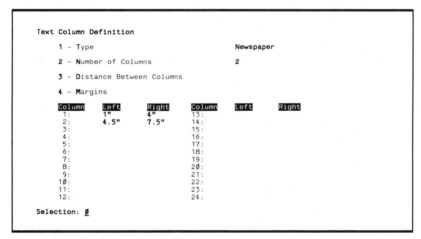

```
Text Column Definition

    1 - Type                          Newspaper

    2 - Number of Columns             2

    3 - Distance Between Columns

    4 - Margins

  Column    Left      Right     Column    Left      Right
    1:       1"        4"         13:
    2:       4.5"      7.5"       14:
    3:                            15:
    4:                            16:
    5:                            17:
    6:                            18:
    7:                            19:
    8:                            20:
    9:                            21:
   10:                            22:
   11:                            23:
   12:                            24:

  Selection: 0
```

Figure 12.2: Text Column Definition menu

The default column style is two newspaper columns spaced $1/2$ inch apart. Each column is 3 inches wide, and the first column begins at the left margin.

4. Press ← to accept all of the default settings.

If you wanted to change the number of columns or the spacing, you would select the appropriate option. For instance, to select three columns, press *2*—Number of Columns—then enter *3*. The measurements would automatically appear. Change intercolumn spacing by entering the measurement at option 3—Distance Between Columns. Change column width by selecting option 4—Margins. You'll see how to do this in the next lesson.

5. Press ← to clear the Column prompt line.

*T*yping Columns

Once the layout has been defined, it is easier if you turn Columns on before typing the columns themselves. This way you'll see how the columns will appear as you type them. You will first type any desired single-column text, such as a title or introductory paragraph, then turn on Columns and type the rest of the text. Follow these steps to create a newsletter:

1. Press Shift-F6 to center the cursor.

2. Type the title of our newsletter:

   Faculty Research Projects

3. Press ← three times to add space between the title and the text of the newsletter.

4. Press Shift-F8 1 3 N F7 to turn off justification. Because of the short line length, too many extra spaces would be inserted in justified columns.

5. Now turn on the Column mode by pressing Alt-F7 3. You must have a column layout defined before turning Columns on.

   With the Column mode now on, the word *Col* appears on the status line followed by the column number in which the cursor is placed.

6. Type the following, noticing how the text conforms to the two-column layout:

Factors Involved in French Language Word Processing Utilizing The Standard English Language Keyboard, Dr. Renee Voltaire, French Department

Dr. Voltaire analyzed several popular word processing programs for their capacity to display and print French language characters. Dr. Voltaire then studied the difficulties encountered in typing French documents using the standard QWERTY keyboard.

The Possible Contributions of Computers to the Creative Writing Process, Dr. Leslie Van Mot, English Department

Dr. Van Mot tested the effects of using word processing programs on the creative output of students. The writing of student volunteers was measured using several criteria. These included sentence complexity, character development, and grammatical accuracy. The students were divided into test and control groups. The test group was trained in using a word processing program, while the control group was given standard writing practice exercises. This report studies the results of the training.

The Economic Impact of Computer Technology on the Gross National Product, Dr. William Duke, Economics Department

Dr. Duke abstracted data from the past ten years supplied by the National Economics Institute. He concludes that starting in 1984 there has been a direct relationship between the GNP and the fortunes of the computer industry.

Art Education and the Computer, Dr. Wilma Stephens, Art Department

Dr. Stephens has been researching the use of computer technology in the design process. Her

primary interest is in the use of simulated graphics to project light patterns on angular objects and the effects of the projections on color density as observed by the human eye.

7. Press Alt-F7 3 to exit Columns mode.

8. Press Shift-F7 1 to print the newsletter (Figure 12.3).

9. Save the document under the name NEWS, and stay in Word-Perfect for the next lesson.

No matter how long the document, text will flow from column to column and from page to page. To type single-column text again, press Ctrl-← to end the last column, then press Alt-F7 3 to turn off the Column mode.

When editing you can move from column to column with the Ctrl-Home (GoTo) command. Press Ctrl-Home → to move to the column on the right, Ctrl-Home ← to the column on the left.

Lesson 53 – How to Create Parallel Columns

In some cases you don't want text to flow freely from column to column because text on the left refers directly to text on the right. For example, in Figure 12.4 the text in the right column explains what's in the left. They go together as a set and you want to make sure that the corresponding text is kept together.

This format is used often in job resumes, where the left column contains employment dates, and the right column includes the employer and job responsibilities.

These are called *parallel columns* and they must be defined and typed differently from newspaper columns. For instance, in newspaper columns you just continued typing and let WordPerfect run the text from column to column. With parallel columns, however, you enter the text in blocks: the first text on the left, then its corresponding text on the right; the second text on the left, then its corresponding text on the right, etc. You use the Ctrl-← key to end a block and move to the other column.

Use these techniques when the text in each column will not fit on one line. When creating numeric columns or tables use Tab, as shown

```
                    Faculty Research Projects


Factors Involved in French        been a direct relationship
Language Word Processing          between the GNP and the
Utilizing The Standard English    fortunes of the computer
Language Keyboard, Dr. Renee      industry.
Voltaire, French Department
                                  Art Education and the
Dr. Voltaire analyzed several     Computer, Dr. Wilma Stephens,
popular word processing           Art Department
programs for their capacity to
display and print French          Dr. Stephens has been
language characters. Dr.          researching the use of
Voltaire then studied the         computer technology in the
difficulties encountered in       design process. Her primary
typing French documents using     interest is in the use of
the standard QWERTY keyboard.     simulated graphics to project
                                  light patterns on angular
The Possible Contributions of     objects and the effects of the
Computers to the Creative         projections on color density
Writing Process, Dr. Leslie       as observed by the human eye.
Van Mot, English Department

Dr. Van Mot tested the effects
of using word processing
programs on the creative
output of students. The
writing of student volunteers
was measured using several
criteria. These included
sentence complexity, character
development, and grammatical
accuracy. The students were
divided into test and control
groups. The test group was
trained in using a word
processing program, while the
control group given standard
writing practice exercises.
This report studies the
results of the training.

The Economic Impact of
Computer Technology on the
Gross National Product, Dr.
William Duke, Economics
Department

Dr. Duke abstracted data from
the past ten years supplied by
the National Economics
Institute. He concludes that
starting in 1984 there has
```

Figure 12.3: Sample newsletter

in Chapter 6. But when typing paragraphs, use parallel columns.

Parallel columns can be regular or block-protected. Block-protected parallel columns are kept next to each other even if it means

```
                    Popular Computer Software Packages

       Word Processing,          These are applications software
       data management,          packages. They are designed to perform a
       graphics,                 specific useful functions. For most
       spreadsheet, project      users in business and academic areas,
       planning                  applications software is the most
                                 important to master.

       COBOL, FORTRAN,           These are programming languages. They
       BASIC, Pascal, C,         are used to write specific applications
       PL/1, Assembly            for which appropriate or adequate
                                 applications software is no available.

       PC/DOS, MS/DOS,           These are disk operating systems. The
       TRS/DOS, UNIX             operating systems is a very
                                 sophisticated software package that
                                 handles the interface between the
                                 computer, devices that are attached to
                                 it, and the user.
```

Figure 12.4: Parallel columns

moving them all to a new page. Regular parallel columns, on the other hand, will span a page break.

In this lesson, you will create the text shown in Figure 12.4, two uneven parallel columns with 5 spaces between them. One column is 20 characters wide, the other 40.

For your own documents, plan how wide you want each column to be, making sure they are wide enough to contain the text. Columns that are too narrow are difficult to read.

*D*efining Parallel Columns

The procedures for parallel columns are almost exactly the same as for newspaper columns—define the layout, turn Column mode on, and enter the text.

The number and width of parallel columns must be defined, including the spacing between columns. Since the text in the right column refers to the text on the left, WordPerfect will use Block Protect to keep corresponding paragraphs on the same page.

Follow these steps to define two parallel columns:

1. Press Alt-F7 to show the Math/Column prompt line.

2. Press *4* to get to the Text Column Definition menu.

3. Press *1* to select the column type. The prompt line changes to

   Column Type: 1 Newspaper; 2 Parallel; 3 Parallel with Block Protect:0

4. Press *2* for regular parallel columns. The number of columns and the column spacing remain at the default 2. So now let's change the width of the two columns by using the Margin option.

5. Press *4* or *m* for Margins. The cursor moves to the left margin setting for the first column.

6. Press ← to accept the default 1 inch setting. The cursor moves to the right margin setting for that column.

7. Type *3* for its right margin, then press ←. This creates a column 20 characters wide.

8. Type *3.5* for the second column's left margin, then press ←.

9. Press ← to accept the default right margin of 7.5 inches and return to the prompt line.

10. Press ← to return to the typing area.

11. Press ← once more to clear the Column prompt.

*T*yping Parallel Columns

Now that the columns have been defined, you can turn on Column mode when you are ready to enter the text.

1. Press Shift-F6 and type

   Popular Computer Software Packages

2. Press ← three times to add space between the heading and the columns.

3. Press Shift-F8 1 3 N F7 to turn off justification.

4. Press Alt-F7 3 to turn on Column mode. *Col 1* will appear on the status line.

5. Now type the text of the first column:

   Word processing, data management, graphics, spreadsheet, project planning

   The text will conform to the column margins.

6. Press Ctrl-←. The cursor will move to the left margin of the next column. When the Column mode is on, Ctrl-← ends one column and moves to the next. (With Column mode off, Ctrl-← ends the page.)

   Use Ctrl-← only when you are done typing the parallel text in one of the columns and you want to move to another to type corresponding text. Do not try to use it as a cursor movement command when editing, to move from column to column. As with newspaper columns, move from column to column with the Ctrl-Home → and Ctrl-Home ← commands.

   With regular parallel columns, WordPerfect uses the Ctrl-← codes to move from column to column. However with block-protected parallel columns, special codes—[BlockPro:On] and [BlockPro:Off]—surround each column. WordPerfect uses these to determine which blocks will be kept on the same page. If the text in one column extends into the new page, both blocks will be carried over so they start on that page. If you select regular parallel columns, the longer column will span the page break.

7. Type

   These are *applications software packages.* They are designed to perform a specific useful function. For most users in business and academic areas, applications software is the most important to master.

8. Press Ctrl-← to end that column and move back to the first column.

9. Type the following:

   COBOL, FORTRAN, BASIC, Pascal, C, PL/1, Assembly

10. Press Ctrl-← , then type

    These are *programming languages.* They are used to write specific applications for which appropriate or adequate applications software is not available.

11. Press Ctrl-↵ , then type

     PC/DOS, MS/DOS, TRS/DOS, UNIX

12. Press Ctrl-↵, then type

     **These are *disk operating systems.* The operating
     system is a very sophisticated software package that
     handles the interface between the computer, devices
     that are attached to it, and the user.**

13. Press Alt-F7 3 to turn Columns off.

14. Press Shift-F7 1 to print the parallel columns or Shift-F7 V to
     view them.

15. Press F7 N N to clear the screen and remain in WordPerfect.

WordPerfect's automatic on-screen Column feature can save you
hours of formatting. If you're unsure how to use it, first type
your document using the default single column format and save it
to your disk. Then place the cursor where you want the columns to begin
and experiment with various column definitions. Remember, you can
always delete the Column Definition code and try another format.

In the next chapter you'll learn another powerful yet simple word
processing feature—how to create form letters.

13
Creating Personalized Form Letters

*F*eaturing

Form letters
Merging to the screen
Merging to the printer

*L*esson 54 – How to Write the Form Letter

Form letters and junk mail just seem to go together, but that's because many form letters are obviously mass-produced and are as "personal" as the phone directory.

That doesn't have to be the case. You can use form letters yourself whenever you want to send the same message, or a similar one, to more than one person. For example, you might want to send a form letter as a response to an employment ad, a letter of complaint, a request for information, or an invitation to a party.

While there are many personal uses for form letters, there are many more business uses. They can serve as notices to customers, requests for proposals, or announcements. In fact, WordPerfect provides form document commands that can convert the word processor into a sophisticated data management system.

Every use of form letters requires certain basic steps:

- A form letter must be written that contains the text common to all copies of the document. This letter is written only once, no matter how many copies will be printed.

- A data file must be prepared, or be already available, that contains the variable information to be inserted into each letter. Once the data file is created, it can be used with other form documents.

- The two files must be merged for printing. They can be merged onto the screen, saved in a file and printed later on, or printed as they are merged.

This lesson will explain the first step, writing the form letter. Constructing the data file will be covered in Lesson 55, and the final step of merging and printing is in Lesson 56.

*T*he Primary Document

The form letter is also called the *primary document*. In addition to the words or phrases that will be used in every copy of the letter, it includes special *Field* codes that will insert variable information during the "personalization" process.

Each field stands for one item of personal information, such as a last name, an address, a telephone number, or a credit rating. When a letter is printed, the field will be replaced by an item of information. For instance, the Name field might be replaced by *Frederick Rogers.* The fields can be used in any order and the same field could even be used more than once in the same primary file. There are also special Merge codes in the primary document that tell WordPerfect how to merge the documents.

Unlike other codes used by WordPerfect, the Field and Merge codes are displayed on the screen along with other text. You do not have to press Alt-F3 to display them. As long as you print the documents through the special Merge feature, as explained in Lesson 56, the variable information, not the codes, will be printed.

In this lesson, you will create a form letter containing codes for seven fields: name, company, address, city, state, zip code, and salutation (Figure 13.1).

```
^D

^F1^
^F2^
^F3^
^F4^,  ^F5^        ^F6^

Dear ^F7^:

        As a school project in financial management, we are
analyzing the annual reports from the nation's largest companies.
        We would like to include the annual report for ^F2^ in our
study. Since your firm is known for sound fiscal policies and
strategic planning, we feel its report would contribute greatly
to our work.

                        Sincerely,

                        Alvin A. Aardvark
                        M.B.A. Candidate
```

Figure 13.1: The completed primary document

Follow these steps:

1. Start WordPerfect.

2. Press Shift-F9 to display the Merge Codes prompt:

   ^ C; ^ D; ^ E; ^ F; ^ G; ^ N; ^ O; ^ P; ^ Q; ^ S; ^ T;
   ^ U; ^ V:

These are all of the Merge codes that can be included in primary documents. Many of the codes are used for advanced merging and database functions that go beyond basic form letters. In this chapter, you will learn how to use the D, E, F, T, N, and P codes.

3. Press *D* to insert the ⌃D (Date) code. During merging, the system date will be inserted at this location.

4. Press ⏎ twice to space between the date and the inside address.

5. Press Shift-F9 to get the Merge Codes prompt, then press *F.* The prompt shows

    Field:

    Remember, each field stands for an item of information that will be merged into the document. Because you can have many fields, each must be given a number.

6. Press *1* (the first field number) then ⏎. The characters ⌃ *F1* ⌃ will appear in the text. In this case, field 1 will represent the name of the recipient, which will be inserted at the position of the ⌃F1⌃ code in the text.

7. Press ⏎.

8. Press Shift-F9 F 2 ⏎ to insert the ⌃F2⌃ code. This will represent the name of the company. It will be used twice in the letter.

9. Press ⏎, then Shift-F9 F 3 ⏎ to insert the ⌃F3⌃ code for the street address.

10. Press ⏎. The last address line will be a combination of three fields (city, state, and zip code) and will look like this:

    ⌃**F4**⌃ , ⌃**F5**⌃   ⌃**F6**⌃

11. Press Shift-F9 F 4 ⏎ to insert the fourth field.

12. Type a comma (,) then press the Space bar.

13. Press Shift-F9 F 5 ⏎ for the state field.

14. Press Tab, then Shift-F9 F 6 ⏎ for the zip code field.

15. Press ⏎ twice to space between the inside address and salutation.

16. Type *Dear.*

17. Press the Space bar.

18. Press Shift-F9 F 7 ←⏎.

19. Type a colon (:), then press ←⏎ twice before typing the body of the letter.

20. Type

    As a school project in financial management, we are analyzing the annual reports from the nation's largest companies.

    We would like to include the annual report for

21. Press the Space bar once after typing the word *for.*

22. Press Shift-F9 F 2 ←⏎, the code for the company name. A code can be used more than once in a document if you want the same information repeated. Since you want the name of the company to appear again here, you enter the same Field code again.

23. Press the Space bar, then continue typing:

    in our study. Since your firm is known for sound fiscal policies and strategic planning, we feel its report would contribute greatly to our work.

    Sincerely,

    Alvin A. Aardvark
    M.B.A. Candidate

24. Press ←⏎.

    The form letter is now complete and the variable information that you enter in the next lesson will be inserted into each copy of the primary document. Everything will appear correctly as long as you have seven bits of information to match the seven fields.

25. Press F7 Y, type *FORM* and press ←⏎ to save the primary file.

26. Press *N* to continue with the next lesson, or *Y* to exit Word-Perfect.

The primary form document is now complete.

*L*esson 55 – How to Assemble the Variable Information File

The variable information file, called the *secondary merge file* by WordPerfect, is entered as a series of *records*. Each record contains all of the individual items of information that can be merged into a letter. The order of the items must correspond to the field numbers representing them in the primary document. For instance, the recipient's name, which was assigned to field 1 in our letter, must be the first item in the record. The item represented by field 2 must be second, and so on. Thus if you are sending letters to 20 companies, there will be 20 records, each containing seven fields.

When the data file is entered, some means must be used to mark the end of each field and of each record. With WordPerfect, the end of each field is marked by the Merge R (^R) code, entered by pressing F9. The end of each record is shown by the Merge E (^E) code, entered by using Shift-F9 E. The placement of these codes is important, so let's practice by following these steps.

1. Start WordPerfect or make sure the screen is clear by pressing F7 N N.

2. Type (but do not press ← when done)

   Frederick Rogers

3. Press F9. WordPerfect will display the code ^*R* next to the name and move the cursor to the next line.

4. Type *Rogers Motor Company* and press F9.

5. Type *431 Broad Street* and press F9.

   As you should see by now, you must press the F9 key immediately after each field. Do not press the ← key or you'll get extra lines in your letters.

6. Type *Philadelphia* and press F9.

7. Type *PA* and press F9.

8. Type *19101* and press F9.

9. Type *Mr. Rogers* and press F9. This is the last field for the first letter, so another code must be entered now to end the record.

10. Press Shift-F9 E. The ^E code is placed at the end of the record and a hard page break is inserted. Do not press ↵ after inserting the ^E code or you will get an extra line at the beginning of the next record.

11. In the same manner, enter the next three records. Insert the ^E code after the last record.

> **Milford Wilson ^R**
> **Wilson Widget Company ^R**
> **42 East Broad Street ^R**
> **Beuford ^R**
> **PA ^R**
> **19011 ^R**
> **Mr. Wilson ^R**
> **^E**
> **Jean Kohl ^R**
> **Kohl Scientific ^R**
> **45th Street and Osage Avenue ^R**
> **El Paso ^R**
> **TX ^R**
> **23123 ^R**
> **Mrs. Kohl ^R**
> **^E**
> **Dr. Adam Chesin ^R**
> **Northwest Drugs, Inc. ^R**
> **401 Ocean Ave. ^R**
> **Margate ^R**
> **NJ ^R**
> **71652 ^R**
> **Dr. Chesin ^R**
> **^E**

The completed file should appear as in Figure 13.2.

```
        Frederick Rogers^R
        Rogers Motor Company^R
        431 Broad Street^R
        Philadelphia^R
        PA^R
        19101^R
        Mr. Rogers^R
        ^E
        Milford Wilson^R
        Wilson Widget Company^R
        42 East Broad Street^R
        Beuford^R
        PA^R
        19011^R
        Mr. Wilson^R
        ^E
        Jean Kohl^R
        Kohl Scientific^R
        45th Street and Osage Avenue^R
        El Paso^R
        TX^R
        23123^R
        Mrs. Kohl^R
        ^E
        Dr. Adam Chesin^R
        Northwest Drugs, Inc.^R
        401 Ocean Ave.^R
        Margate^R
        NJ^R
        71652^R
        Dr. Chesin^R
        ^E
```

Figure 13.2: The completed sample data file with page break lines dividing each record

12. Press F7   Y, type *LIST*, and press ⏎ to save the secondary document.

13. Press *N* to continue with the next lesson, or *Y* to exit Word-Perfect.

You can add or delete names from the secondary file as needed. Just remember to maintain the proper format with ^ *R* after each field, ^ *E* after each record, and seven fields per record in the same order. Note that there is nothing in either file that links them. The primary file can be merged with any secondary file that has seven fields in each record. Likewise, the secondary file can be used with any form document needing name and address information.

So, for example, you can use the same secondary file to print envelopes for the form letters. Format a new primary document for printing envelopes (as explained in Lesson 41) and enter the following:

```
^ F1 ^
^ F2 ^
^ F3 ^
^ F4 ^ , ^ F5 ^          ^ F6 ^
```

Using the techniques explained in the next lesson to merge and print the form letters, you can then print the envelopes.

*H*andling Missing Information

In the form letter and data file you just created, you coded seven fields (variables) in the form letter and seven in the data file. Each record in the data file must contain at least the same number of fields as in the form letter (it could contain more, with some just not being used).

But what if you don't have all of the same information for every letter? Say, for example, that you're writing to someone at a large company in a small town. Because the firm is so well known, they don't use any street address, such as

Mr. Word Perfect
WordPerfect Corporation
Orem, Utah 84057

Remember, the address in the form letter looks like this:

```
^ F1 ^
^ F2 ^
^ F3 ^
^ F4 ^ , ^ F5 ^          ^ F6 ^
```

Since the record must have at least the same number of fields, it would look like this, with an empty field line for the missing address:

Mr. Word Perfect ^ R
Word Perfect Corporation ^ R
^ R
Orem ^ R
Utah ^ R
84057 ^ R

Mr. Perfect ^ R
^ E

Because of the missing data, the merged address would have an extra blank line:

Mr. Word Perfect
WordPerfect Corporation

Orem, Utah 84057

To avoid this if you think a certain field will be missing from some records, insert a question mark after the field number, but before the closing caret— ^ F3? ^ . WordPerfect will not leave a blank line if the field is empty.

*L*esson 56 – How to Merge Files

By default, the results of merging primary and secondary files are displayed on the screen. The variable information from a record is inserted in the appropriate place in a form letter. A page break is inserted and another letter is created, until all of the records have been used.

Newly merged documents can be printed immediately, saved on disk, or edited. By merging them on the screen, you can add a large group of form letters to the queue and print them while you work on another document. You can also delete blank lines resulting from missing data.

If your mailing list is large, however, the resulting merged document may be too large for your computer's memory and available disk space. In this case you have two alternatives before you run out to the computer store for more memory.

First, you can break the large mailing list down into smaller ones. Then merge and save each set individually.

Second, you can direct the output of the merge to the printer, instead of to the screen. Each letter is printed as it is generated without saving it on the disk. Special codes have to be added to the end of the primary document for this type of output.

In this lesson you will merge the letters to both the screen and the printer.

*M*erging Form Documents to the Screen

Once both the primary and secondary files are completed, you can merge them. In this chapter the primary file is called FORM and the secondary file LIST.

You should still be in WordPerfect. If not, start the program before following these steps.

1. Press Ctrl-F9 (the Merge/Sort key) to display the prompt

   1 Merge; 2 Sort; 3 Sorting Order: 0

2. Press *1* to select the Merge option and display the prompt

   Primary file:

3. Type *FORM*.

4. Press ◄— to display the prompt

   Secondary file:

5. Type *LIST*.

6. Press ◄—. The word *Merging* will appear on the status line as the letters are generated. The letters will be displayed on the screen only after all of the merging is completed. Press Home Home ↑ to see your merged letters (Figure 13.3). You can now

```
October 12, 1988

Dr. Adam Chesin
Northwest Drugs, Inc.
401 Ocean Ave.
Margate, NJ  71652

Dear Dr. Chesin:

     As a school project in financial management, we are
analyzing the annual reports from the nation's largest companies.
     We would like to include the annual report for Northwest
Drugs, Inc. in our study. Since your firm is known for sound
fiscal policies and strategic planning, we feel it's report would
contribute greatly to our work.

                    Sincerely,

                    Alvin A. Aardvark
                    M.B.A. Candidate



                                        Doc 1 Pg 1 Ln 3" Pos 2.2"
```

Figure 13.3: A completed form letter

save the merged letters as a new document or print them with Shift-F7 1.

7. For now, press F7 N N to clear the screen.

*M*erging Form Documents to the Printer

Let's merge the letters once more, but this time we'll print them at the same time. First you'll have to recall the primary file and add several new codes. Follow these steps:

1. Press Shift-F10, type *FORM*, and press ←┘.

2. Press Home Home ↓ to reach the end of the document.

3. Press Shift-F9 T Shift-F9 N Shift-F9 P Shift-F9 P. This inserts the codes ^ T ^ N ^ P ^ P, which do the following:

   ^ T   Sends the text to the printer as letters are merged.

   ^ N   Gets the next record after printing a letter. This is not needed when merging to the screen.

   ^ P ^ P Uses the same primary document for each record in the secondary document. You can use a new primary file by inserting its name between the ^ P codes. With no name between the codes, the same letter is repeated.

4. Press F7 Y ←┘ Y N to save the edited form letter and clear the screen.

5. Press Ctrl-F9 1 to select the Merge option.

6. Type *FORM* at the Primary File prompt, then press ←┘.

7. Type *LIST* at the Secondary File prompt, then press ←┘. The records will be merged into the form letter and printed.

8. Press F7 N Y to exit WordPerfect.

You now know two ways to merge form letters: to the screen and directly to the printer. Each method has its advantages and disadvantages.

- Merging to the screen allows you to edit or save the merged letters; when you merge to the printer, no new document is created.

- Merging to the printer is appropriate when many copies of the letter must be generated. Otherwise you'd need enough disk space to hold all of the letters, and you'd still have to print them later.

Whichever method you select, merging can save a great deal of time and effort.

14
Adding Footnotes and Endnotes

*F*eaturing

Entering footnotes
Changing note options
Entering endnotes

*L*esson 57–How to Enter Footnotes

If you write academic or technical reports, you no doubt have been faced with the problem of footnotes. Placing footnotes on the bottom of appropriate pages can be a drudge using a typewriter or some word processing programs. If you later add or delete lines, the citation numbers may move to another page, forcing you to move a footnote.

WordPerfect, however, provides a feature known as *floating footnotes*. The program automatically places footnotes at the bottom of the appropriate page. If you delete or insert a footnote, the others will be renumbered automatically. The note is entered in a separate typing window, much like headers and footers, by pressing Ctrl-F7.1. While the footnote is stored in its own area, the Note code associated with it is inserted in the text of the document. When printing, WordPerfect will place the footnote on the same page as the code, automatically adding superscripted note references and adjusting the text. If the Note code moves to another page because text is added or deleted, the note will be printed on the new page.

In this lesson, you will enter several footnotes into the document SYSTEM.

1. Start WordPerfect.

2. Type the document shown in Figure 14.1.

3. Place the cursor at the end of the first paragraph, the location of the first footnote citation.

4. Press Ctrl-F7 (the Footnote key) to display the prompt line

     1 Footnote; 2 Endnote; 3 Endnote Placement:0

5. Press *1* or *f* to select Footnote and display the prompt

     Footnote: 1 Create; 2 Edit; 3 New number; 4 Options: 0

6. Press *1* or *c* to create a footnote. The footnote screen, as shown in Figure 14.2, will appear with the first footnote number already displayed and indented ½ inch.

7. Type the text of the first footnote.

     Short-term goals are those aimed at objectives within four years.

```
Decision Support Needed

     With changing economic conditions the quality of management
is becoming crucial to the existence of clinical laboratories. No
longer should laboratory managers do without the decision support
systems necessary for setting and obtaining both short- and long-
term goals.

The Systems Approach

     The clinical laboratory is no different than any production
environment. Therefore the systems approach can be used to divide
this process into three basic steps: input, transformation, and
output.

     Input

     Resources of all types become the input to the system. In
the clinical laboratory, these resources include personnel,
equipment, supplies, and samples for testing.

     Transformation

     These resources are put through a conversion process in
which tests are performed, hardware maintained, and staff
interacts.

     Output

     The results of this process are the output: results are
communicated to other systems in the organization and personnel
gains satisfaction and other rewards from participation in the
process.

The Flow of Resources

     To the informed manager, this flow of resources is critical,
since every action that takes place uses some resource. Each of
these "transactions" depletes the total pool of resources
available and should contribute to the output. When problems
occur in any organization, they can usually be traced to some
problem in this flow.
```

Figure 14.1: A sample document

8. Press F7. This "saves" the footnote and redisplays the document. The footnote number is next to the main text (Figure 14.3).

9. Place the cursor at the end of the last paragraph.

10. Press Ctrl-F7 1 1. The footnote window appears, but with *2* for the second note.

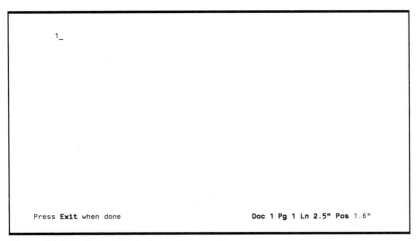

Figure 14.2: A footnote window

11. Type the footnote.

Some analysts consider all staff interactions as "transactions," even social ones that have no direct relationship to the job.

12. Press F7. The number *2* is now in the text.

```
Decision Support Needed

     With changing economic conditions the quality of management
is becoming crucial to the existence of clinical laboratories. Mo
longer should laboratory managers do without the decision support
systems necessary for setting and obtaining both short- and long-
term goals.1_

The Systems Approach

     The clinical laboratory is no different than any production
environment. Therefore the systems approach can be used to divide
this process into three basic steps: input, transformation, and
output.

     Input

     Resources of all types become the input to the system. In
the clinical laboratory, these resources include personnel,
equipment, supplies, and samples for testing.

     Transformation

     These resources are put through a conversion process in
                                   Doc 1 Pg 1 Ln 2" Pos 2.2"
```

Figure 14.3: A footnote citation number in the text

13. Press Shift-F7 1 to print the document (Figure 14.4).

```
Decision Support Needed

    With changing economic conditions the quality of management
is becoming crucial to the existence of clinical laboratories. No
longer should laboratory managers do without the decision support
systems necessary for setting and obtaining both short- and long-
term goals.¹

The Systems Approach

    The clinical laboratory is no different than any production
environment. Therefore, the systems approach can be used to
divide  this  process  into  three  basic  steps:  input,
transformation, and output.

    Input

    Resources of all types become the input to the system. In
the clinical laboratory, these resources include personnel,
equipment, supplies, and samples for testing.

    Transformation

    These resources are put through a conversion process in
which tests are performed, hardware maintained, and staff
interacts.

    Output

    The results of this process are the output: results are
communicated to other systems in the organization and personnel
gains satisfaction and other rewards from participation in the
process.

The Flow of Resources

    To the informed manager, this flow of resources is critical,
since every action that takes place uses some resource. Each of
these "transactions" depletes the total pool of resources
available and should contribute to the output. When problems
occur in any organization, they can usually be traced to some
problem in this flow. ²

    _____

    ¹Short-term goals are those aimed at objectives within four
years.

    ²Some analysts consider all staff interactions as
"transactions," even social ones that have no direct relationship
to the job.
```

Figure 14.4: The printed page with footnotes

The footnotes will be printed at the bottom of the appropriate page, using the following default format:

- Notes are single-spaced.
- Citation numbers run consecutively from page to page.
- A 2-inch line separates the notes from the text.
- Footnote and citation numbers are superscripted.

Like all default values, these can be changed to suit your own needs.

With the footnotes added, the pagination automatically adjusts. The size of the footnotes will be taken into account and the page break line will reflect the end of the footnote text for that page.

Adding, Editing, and Deleting Footnotes

As documents are edited, footnotes often must be added or deleted from the text, moved around, or edited in some way. The process is a simple one with WordPerfect.

To edit a footnote, press Ctrl-F7 1 2, then the footnote number you want to edit, and press ←┘. The text of the note will be displayed. Make the desired changes and press F7.

Delete a footnote by deleting its citation number from the text. Add a footnote by positioning the cursor and inserting the note as usual. The subsequent notes will be renumbered automatically.

If you move a block of text containing a Note code, the citation numbers will change appropriately. In fact, to move a note, just move its code. You can do this by highlighting and moving the citation number that appears in the text.

Lesson 58 – How to Change Footnote Options

If you are pleased with the default formats used for notes, you can just follow the steps in the last lesson. But if you want to change these formats, then you'll have to use the Footnote Options menu displayed by pressing Ctrl-F7 1 4. Figure 14.5 shows this menu.

```
Footnote Options

      1 - Spacing Within Footnotes              1
                    Between Footnotes           Ø.16"

      2 - Amount of Note to Keep Together       Ø.5"

      3 - Style for Number in Text              [SUPRSCPT][Note Num]

      4 - Style for Number in Note                    [SUPRSCPT][Note

      5 - Footnote Numbering Method             Numbers

      6 - Start Footnote Numbers each Page      No

      7 - Line Separating Text and Footnotes    2-inch Line

      8 - Print Continued Message               No

      9 - Footnotes at Bottom of Page           Yes


   Selection: Ø
```

Figure 14.5: The Footnote Options menu

One reason to change formats is to print footnotes at the end of the document, a common academic style. But if you want both footnotes and endnotes in the document, you should also change default values. By default, both the footnote and endnote citations in the text are numbers. So with both in the document, there may be two number 1's, two 2's, etc. How will the reader know if a number 1 refers to a footnote or an endnote?

Using the Options menu, you can change the citations to either letters or special characters (such as asterisks). So instead of *1, 2, 3,* footnotes can be numbered *a, b, c* or **, **, ***.*

In this lesson, you will change the numbering style of footnotes to asterisks. Follow these steps:

1. Press Home Home ↑.

2. Press Ctrl-F7 1 4 to display the Footnote Options menu.

    The options determine the location of footnotes and the format of the notes and citation numbers. Change an option by pressing the corresponding letter or number and entering the desired setting. For example, to restart footnote numbering on each page, rather than consecutively throughout the document, press *6,* then *Y.*

3. Press *5* to change the footnote numbering method. The prompt line changes to

1 Numbers; 2 Letters; 3 Characters:0

4. Press *3* or *c* to select numbering by characters. The cursor moves to the prompt line in the menu.

5. Press *. Now footnotes will be "numbered" with asterisks. The first footnote is marked by one asterisk, the second footnote by two, and so on.

6. Press ← twice to return to the document.

7. Press Home Home ↓ to move the cursor to the end of the document. Notice that footnote citation numbers 1 and 2 changed to * and ** respectively.

If you want to make other format changes later, place the cursor after the [FtnOpt] code in the text and press Ctrl-F7 1 4. Return the notes to the default format by deleting the [Ftn Opt] code.

Now that the numbering scheme for footnotes has been changed, you can enter the endnotes in the next lesson.

*L*esson 59 – How to Enter Endnotes

If you are putting expository comments or other informal notes in footnotes, you can use endnotes to include formal references. Rather than taking up text space, the endnotes appear as a group at the end of the document.

In this lesson, you will add two endnotes to the document on the screen. Since your footnotes are expository, the endnotes will be bibliographical. Follow these steps to enter the endnotes into the text:

1. Place the cursor at the end of the second paragraph.

2. Press Ctrl-F7 2 to see

   Endnote: 1 Create; 2 Edit; 3 New number; 4 Options: 0

3. Press *1* to create an endnote. The screen will clear and display only

   1.

By default, numbers in the endnotes themselves are not superscripted and are followed by a period. The endnote citation in the text is superscripted, as it was in footnote citations.

4. Press Tab, then type the endnote.

   Barbara Neibauer, <u>The Systems Approach in Clinical</u>
   <u>Settings</u>, Lockhart, California, 1981, p. 45.

5. Press F7. The number *1* appears in the text.

6. Place the cursor at the end of the paragraph subtitled *output,* the location of the second endnote.

7. Press Ctrl-F7 2 1.

8. Press Tab, then type the second endnote.

   Personnel Policy, October 1986, p. 2.

9. Press F7.

   When you print a document, the endnotes will start immediately after the text. If there is a footnote on the last page, however, WordPerfect will insert a page break and print endnotes on their own page.

   But to make sure endnotes appear on a separate page, let's insert our own page break.

10. Press Home Home ↓ to move to the end of the document.

11. Press Ctrl-⏎ to insert the page break.

12. Press Shift-F7 1 to print the document and see how both footnotes and endnotes appear in the text. (In Figure 14.6, the location of the page break is indicated by a broken line.)

Unlike footnote numbers, endnote numbers or letters are not indented. For that reason you pressed Tab in both endnotes to make the text of the note stand out from the note numbers. Of course, you can use the Endnote Options menu to format the citation numbers any way you like.

For instance, to add spaces after the endnote number so you don't have to press Tab every time, follow these steps:

1. Place the cursor at the start of the document.

2. Press Ctrl-F7 2 4 to display the Endnote Options menu (Figure 14.7).

```
Decision Support Needed

     With changing economic conditions the quality of management
is becoming crucial to the existence of clinical laboratories. No
longer should laboratory managers do without the decision support
systems necessary for setting and obtaining both short- and long-
term goals.*

The Systems Approach

     The clinical laboratory is no different than any production
environment. Therefore, the systems approach can be used to
divide  this  process  into  three  basic  steps:  input,
transformation, and output.¹      `

     Input

     Resources of all types become the input to the system. In
the clinical laboratory, these resources include personnel,
equipment, supplies, and samples for testing.

     Transformation

     These resources are put through a conversion process in
which tests are performed, hardware maintained, and staff
interacts.

     Output

     The results of this process are the output: results are
communicated to other systems in the organization and personnel
gains satisfaction and other rewards from participation in the
process.²

The Flow of Resources

     To the informed manager, this flow of resources is critical,
since every action that takes place uses some resource. Each of
these  "transactions"  depletes  the  total  pool  of  resources
available and should contribute to the output. When problems
occur in any organization, they can usually be traced to some
problem in this flow. **
     _____

     *Short-term goals are those aimed at objectives within four
years.

     **Some  analysts  consider  all  staff  interactions  as
"transactions," even social ones that have no direct relationship
to the job.
─ ── ── ── ── ── ── ── ── ── ── ── ── ── ── ─
1.    Barbara Neibauer, The Systems Approach in Clinical Settings,
Lockhart, California, 1981, p. 45.

2.    Personnel Policy, October 1986, p.2.
```

Figure 14.6: The completed document with footnotes and endnotes

```
Endnote Options

      1 - Spacing Within Endnotes         1
              Between Endnotes            0.16"

      2 - Amount of Endnote to Keep Together  0.5"

      3 - Style for Numbers in Text       [SUPRSCPT][Note Num][

      4 - Style for Numbers in Note       [Note Num].

      5 - Endnote Numbering Method        Numbers




   Selection: 0
```

Figure 14.7: Endnote Options menu

3. Press *4* or *n* to select the Style for Numbers in Note option. This allows you to change the format of the endnote number as it appears in the note. The status line displays

   Replace with: [Note Num].

4. Press End to place the cursor at the end of the prompt, where you want to insert spaces.

5. Press the Space bar five times. (Tab has no effect here.)

6. Press ⏎ to accept the change. You'll see no change in option D. But now the text of the endnotes will start five spaces after the citation number.

7. Press ⏎ to return to the document.

This change inserts the [Ftn Opt] code into the text, changing the endnote format only for this document, not the WordPerfect default.

To edit an endnote, press Ctrl-F7 2 2, then the endnote number (or letter) and press ⏎. The note will appear in its window. Make the changes needed, then press F7 to return to the document.

15

Advanced Printing and Setup

*F*eaturing

*Customizing
WordPerfect
Printing options
Print queue control*

*L*esson 60 – *How to Customize WordPerfect*

WordPerfect's default values let you start typing without having to worry about formatting. Well, there are other default values that determine how WordPerfect works. You can change these through the Setup menu displayed by pressing Shift-F1 (Figure 15.1).

```
Setup

      1 - Backup

      2 - Cursor Speed              3Ø cps

      3 - Display

      4 - Fast Save (unformatted)   Yes

      5 - Initial Settings

      6 - Keyboard Layout

      7 - Location of Files

      8 - Units of Measure




  Selection: Ø
```

Figure 15.1: Setup menu

This menu contains a number of standard WordPerfect settings that you can modify. Some of these options are beyond the scope of this book, and changing them can be rather complicated. But several of them provide very useful and important features. Figure 15.2 summarizes all of the setup options. But let's take a look in detail at the Backup and Fast Save options.

*B*ackup

A *backup* is an extra copy of your document—the best insurance against disaster. You should make a backup of all important documents on another disk. This way all won't be lost if your disk becomes damaged. This type of backup, which has nothing to do with the Setup menu, is made using the Copy command, either from the DOS prompt or using the F5 directory listing. I'll show you how soon.

Summary of Setup Options

1. Backup

Allows you to make automatic backup copies of the document you're editing.

2. Cursor Speed

Determines the speed at which the cursor moves if you hold down a directional or character key.

3. Display

Sets the monitor and graphics board type, the colors displayed on the screen, and other aspects of text display.

4. Fast Save

Allows you to save text formatted or unformatted. Formatted text takes longer to save but can be printed from the disk.

5. Initial Settings

Determines the default settings for the format of the date and table of authorities, warning beeps, automatic code display, the number of repeats used for the ESC key, and automatic creation of summaries. With the 1/3/89 release of WordPerfect, it also sets the defaults for print options: binding width, number of copies, and text and graphics quality.

6. Keyboard Layout

Lets you redefine the purpose of function keys.

7. Location of Files

Determines where WordPerfect expects to find the dictionary and thesaurus, keyboard and macro files, backups, printer files, and hyphenation modules.

8. Units of Measure

Determines how certain measurements are entered—either as the default inches, or as centimeters, points, or lines and columns.

Figure 15.2: Summary of Setup options

But there are two other types of backup that can be made automatically—a timed backup and an original document backup. Let's look at these two first.

When you create or edit a document, WordPerfect stores it in the computer's memory. This memory is only temporary, so when you exit WordPerfect, or turn off your computer, anything in it is erased.

As long as you've saved the document on the disk, everything is fine. But say someone accidentally pulls the plug, or something causes your computer to go haywire. What's on the screen will be lost forever. To guard against this possibility, you can have WordPerfect automatically save a special copy of your document at regular intervals. So when disaster strikes, you'll only lose what you've typed since the last timed backup.

Of course, there are other ways to lose a document. Every semester I see students accidentally "save" one document with the same name as an existing one. They just press *Y* at the Replace prompt without even thinking that the original document will be overwritten, or erased. Or they make extensive changes to a document, save it, then change their mind. Too late—the original is gone.

An original document backup protects against these losses. When you save a document that's already on the disk, WordPerfect first makes a copy of the original version. So you can always go back to the unedited document.

Timed Backups

Here's how to set up WordPerfect for timed backups:

1. Press Shift-F1 to display the Setup menu.

2. Press *1* or *b* for the Backup option. The screen displays the Setup Backup menu (Figure 15.3).

3. Press *1* or *t* to select timed backups. The cursor moves to the Timed Document Backup option.

4. Press *Y* (or *N* to turn off the feature). The cursor moves to Minutes Between Backups option.

5. Type the number of minutes you'd like between backups.

```
Setup: Backup
        Timed backup files are deleted when you exit WP normally.  If you
        have a power or machine failure, you will find the backup file in the
        backup directory indicated in Setup: Location of Files.

           Backup Directory

        1 - Timed Document Backup                No
            Minutes Between Backups              30


        Original backup will save the original document with a .BK! extension
        whenever you replace it during a Save or Exit.

        2 - Original Document Backup             No




    Selection: 0
```

Figure 15.3: Setup Backup menu

6. Press ⏎ to accept the changes.

7. Press ⏎ twice if you are ready to return to the document.

At these intervals, a backup copy of your document will be saved on the WordPerfect disk (floppy or hard). The backups are stored as WP{WP}.BK1 (document 1) and WP{WP}.BK2 (document 2). You can change this setting to another drive, say drive B, or to the hard disk directory using the Location of Files option on the Setup menu. I'll show you how shortly.

These files will be erased when you properly exit WordPerfect but not if some machine failure or power problem occurs. In that case, you would start your computer again and use the DOS Rename command to change the name of the backup file to a document name. The *command syntax* (that is, the general form of the command) is

REN WP{WP}.BK1 *new-document-name*

So you might type

REN WP{WP}.BK1 OLDMEMO

then start WordPerfect. Before it starts you might see the prompt

Are other copies of WordPerfect currently running? (Y/N)

Press *N*.

If you don't rename the backup file, then when WordPerfect is ready to make the first timed backup after the failure, you'll hear a beep and see

Old backup file exists. 1 Rename; 2 Delete:

Press *1* and enter a name for the backup file or press 2 and the old backup file will be deleted.

Original Document Backups

1. Press Shift-F1 to display the Setup menu.

2. Press *1* or *b* for the Backup option and display the Setup Backup menu.

3. Press *2* for the Original Document Backup option.

4. Press *Y* (or *N* later if you want to turn off this feature).

5. Press ⏎ to accept the changes, and press it again if you are ready to return to the document.

When you save a document that's already on the disk, WordPerfect first adds the extension *BK!* to the original version. So suppose you save a document called LETTER. The original version will be stored as LETTER.BK!, and the new version as LETTER.

You now have a copy of the document that existed before you made any changes.

Changing Backup File Location

Follow these steps to change the default directory in which backup files are stored:

1. Press Shift-F1 to display the Setup menu.

2. Press *7* or *L* for the Location of Auxiliary Files menu (Figure 15.4).

3. Press *1* or *b* for the Backup Directory option.

4. Type the letter of the drive in which you want to store backup files. Remember to end the drive in a colon, such as *B:*.

```
Setup: Location of Auxiliary Files

     1 - Backup Directory

     2 - Hyphenation Module(s)

     3 - Keyboard/Macro Files

     4 - Main Dictionary(s)

     5 - Printer Files                    C:\WP5

     6 - Style Library Filename

     7 - Supplementary Dictionary(s)

     8 - Thesaurus




Selection: 0
```

Figure 15.4: *Location of Auxiliary Files menu*

5. Press ←⟋ twice to return to the Setup menu, then press it again if you're ready to return to the document.

Making DOS Backups

Even these automatic backups, however, won't help if the disk holding the document is destroyed. So the only real insurance is to save duplicates of important documents on another disk. If you have a hard disk, back up critical documents into a floppy. If you have floppy drives, back up copies onto another disk and store it in a separate location.

You can make copies of documents either from the DOS prompt or from the F5 directory listing.

From the DOS prompt, use the following syntax:

COPY *name-of-document destination-disk*

Suppose you want to make a copy of the document MEMO from the hard disk onto drive A. Your command at the DOS prompt should look like this:

C>COPY MEMO A:

With floppy drives, place the disk containing your document in drive A and the disk you which to copy it to (it must be a formatted disk) in drive B. Your command at the DOS prompt would look like

A>COPY MEMO B:

If you enter a name immediately after the destination drive letter, the copy will be given a new name.

If you are already in WordPerfect and want to copy a document, press F5 ← to display the directory listing. Use the arrow keys to highlight the document you which to copy, then press *8* or *c* for the Copy command. The prompt changes to

Copy this file to:

Type the drive designation (such as *B:* or *C:\BACKUPS*), press ←, then press F1 to return to the document.

*F*ast Save

When you save a document, WordPerfect doesn't format it on the disk as it appears on the screen. Saving it unformatted this way speeds up the process. But as you'll learn in the next lesson, saving it formatted may have some advantages.

If you record the document formatted, for example, you can print it directly from the disk drive without first displaying it on the screen. You can print specific pages of the document, or *batch print* a number of documents—tell WordPerfect to print a series of documents while you're working on another.

To save your documents formatted you must turn off the Fast Save feature on the Setup menu. To do this, press Shift-F1 to display the Setup menu, then *4* to select the Fast Save option. Press *N* for No (or *Y* later if you want to turn it back on) then ← to return to the document.

Fast Save does not affect the appearance of a document on the screen or in View mode.

*L*esson 61 – How to Set Print Options

So far you've printed all documents by pressing Shift-F7 1 for the full document or Shift-F7 2 for the current page. Well now it's time to look at some sophisticated printing options available on the Print menu.

With these options you can control the way documents are printed, print documents directly from the disk (as long as they've been saved formatted), print specific pages, and more. Refer to the Print menu displayed when you press Shift-F7. You're already familiar with options 1 (Full Document), 2 (Page), 6 (View), and S (Select Printer). Let's take a look at the other options (option 4, Control Printer, will be discussed separately in detail in Lesson 62).

*D*ocument on Disk

Using this command, you can print a document that's stored on the disk without first displaying it on the screen. The document must have been saved formatted (that is, with the Fast Save option on the Setup menu turned off).

Here's how to print a document:

1. Press Shift-F7 3 to select Document on Disk. The status line changes to

    Document name:

2. Type the name of the document you'd like to print, then press ←┘. If the document was saved formatted, you'll see the prompt

    Page(s): (All)

3. Press ←┘ to print the entire document, or type a page number or range of pages (as you'll learn next) then press ←┘.

    If your document is numbered consecutively, without a new page number set, print a range of pages according to these rules:

    - For a single page, type the number and press ←┘.

    - For a range of pages, type the starting page, a hyphen, the ending page, and ←┘. For example, to print pages 2 through 6 type *2–6* ←┘.

    - From a given page to the end of the document, type the starting page number, a hyphen, and ←┘. Type *8–* then ←┘ to print from page 8 to the end of the document.

    - From the first page of a document through a specific page, type a hyphen, the last page you want printed, and ←┘. Type *–6* then ←┘ to print pages 1 through 6.

No spaces are allowed in any of these entries.

If you restarted page numbering in your document, thus dividing it into sections, you must specify what sections contain the pages to be printed. Type the section number and a colon before entering the page number.

Here are some examples:

RANGE	WILL PRINT
2:1–2:8	The second set of pages numbered 1 through 8.
1:1–3:1	The first page numbered 1 through the third page numbered 1.
2:8–	From the second page numbered 8 to the end of the document.
–3:1	From the start of the document through the third page numbered 1.

If you try to print a document that was saved under the default Fast Save option, you'll see the prompt

Error: This document was Fast Saved—Must be retrieved to print.

Recall the document first then print it from the screen.

By the way, you can also print a document from the directory listing that's displayed by pressing F5. Highlight the name of a document not saved with Fast Save, then press *4* or *p* for the Print option. The Pages prompt line will appear. Enter the range of pages you want to print then press ◄──┘.

*T*ype Through

Another way to print documents is as you type them, just like a typewriter. You'll lose the editing powers of WordPerfect, but it is a convenient method of filling out complicated preprinted forms. If your printer is capable, each character or line you type will be printed immediately.

Press Shift-F7 5 or Y to select Type-Through printing. If you see the prompt *Feature not available on this printer* then your printer is not set up for this mode. Otherwise, you'll see

Type Through by: 1 Line; 2 Character:0

If you press *2,* you'll see a Character Type-Thru Printing screen (Figure 15.5) and each character you type will be sent immediately to the printer.

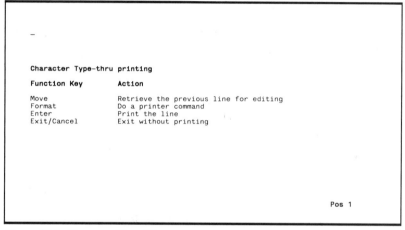

```
    —



    Character Type-thru printing

    Function Key          Action

    Move                  Retrieve the previous line for editing
    Format                Do a printer command
    Enter                 Print the line
    Exit/Cancel           Exit without printing





                                                              Pos  1
```

Figure 15.5: Character Type-Thru Printing screen

If you press *1,* you'll see a Line Type-Through Printing screen, identical to that shown in Figure 15.5 except for its title. When you press ⏎ to finish a line, the entire line will be sent to the printer. This allows you to backspace and correct errors before the line is printed.

What occurs when text is sent to the printer depends on your printer. Some printers, like daisy wheels, will immediately print each character or line. Most dot matrix printers will wait until the ⏎ key is pressed, even if you select Character mode. Laser printers wait until the entire page is completed. These are "page printers" that do not eject the paper until the page is filled or a Page Break code is sent to the printer from the word processor. This code, by the way, is not sent by WordPerfect when you have finished using Type-Through, so if you do not fill a page you'll have to eject the paper manually.

While you might want to check your printer's manual, most laser printers have buttons called *On Line* and *Form Feed.* Pressing *Form Feed,* which ejects the page, has no effect if the printer is on line, indicated by a light on or near the On Line button. So first press On Line until the light goes off, then press Form Feed to eject the paper. When the paper is ejected, press On Line until the light goes back on.

*B*inding

Documents normally start printing at the left margin. If you plan to bind the pages into a book, you'll need some extra margin space or *binding width*. For instance, with a three-ring binder, you should insert extra space or else the holes might be punched too close to the text, if not directly on it! With the binding option, you can add extra space to the left margin of odd-numbered pages and to the right margin of even-numbered ones.

From the Print menu, press *B* to select Binding. Type the amount of extra space you want to add to the left margin, then press ↵.

The value you enter stays in effect until you exit WordPerfect.

*N*umber of Copies

Change this option to print more then one copy of the text. With the Print menu displayed, press *N,* type the number of copies desired, then press ↵. Like binding, this option stays in effect until you exit WordPerfect. So change it back to 1 if you want to print a single copy later on.

*G*raphics Quality

As you'll learn in Chapter 18, you can add graphics to your documents for maximum impact. The Graphics Quality option determines whether you want to print the graphics, and, if so, the quality of the final printout.

Press *G* from the Print menu to display the prompt

Graphics Quality: 1 Do Not Print; 2 Draft; 3 Medium; 4 High: 3

- Press *1* to suppress printing the graphics and print only the text. Why would you want this option? Well, graphics take a long time to print, particularly on dot matrix printers. So for a quick rough copy, turn graphics off and print the document.

If you're using a laser printer, it might not have enough memory to print an entire page of text and graphics. So you can turn off graphics to print just the text. Then insert the same sheet of paper, turn off text printing (you'll see how soon), turn graphics printing back on by selecting option 2, 3, or 4, and print the document a second time. Now the graphics will be printed.

- Press *2* to print the graphics in low resolution. This is the fastest way to print graphic images.

- Press *3* to print the graphics in medium resolution.

- Press *4* to print the graphics in high resolution, the slowest method.

*T*ext Quality

Press *T* from the Print menu to display the prompt

Text Quality: 1 Do Not Print; 2 Draft; 3 Medium; 4 High: 3

These options work just the same as described above for graphics but only affect the text. So to print only the graphic images, select *1* from this prompt. Selecting option 2, 3, or 4 turns text printing back on and sets the quality.

All of the options discussed in this lesson are selected before your document is sent to the printer. In Lesson 62 you'll learn how to control the printing process after that has taken place.

*L*esson 62 – How to Control Printing

WordPerfect uses a *print queue* to control your printing. A queue is a "waiting line" where WordPerfect stores the names of documents that you've sent to the printer. Because of this, you can give the command to print a document even while one document is still being printed. Each document will be stored in the queue until the previous one is completed. You can also create or edit a document while printing another.

The fact that you've added documents to the queue, however, doesn't mean that you've lost control over the printing process. On the contrary, you can control the queue and the order of documents in it from the Control Printer menu (Figure 15.6). You can also use this menu to check on the progress of a document and see which page is currently being printed.

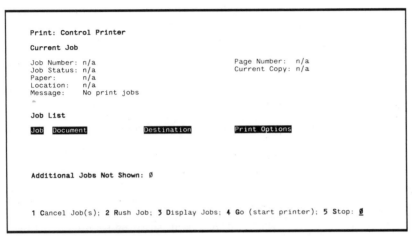

```
    Print: Control Printer

    Current Job

    Job Number:  n/a                    Page Number:  n/a
    Job Status:  n/a                    Current Copy: n/a
    Paper:       n/a
    Location:    n/a
    Message:     No print jobs


    Job List

    Job  Document                 Destination         Print Options




    Additional Jobs Not Shown: Ø



    1 Cancel Job(s); 2 Rush Job; 3 Display Jobs; 4 Go (start printer); 5 Stop: Ø
```

Figure 15.6: Control Printer menu

To display this menu, press Shift-F7 to reveal the Print menu, then press *4* or *C.*

The top of the menu reports on the status of the queue and the current print job. The page being printed, and the copy number if you're printing more than one, is shown on the right. On the left is the job number and a report of any problems encountered.

A numbered list of documents in the queue will be displayed in the Job List section. If you're printing a document from the disk, its name will appear. Documents being printed from the display are shown as *(screen).*

If you have more documents that can be displayed on the job list, you'll see the number in the Additional Jobs message.

Your queue control panel is the prompt line at the bottom of the screen. Here are the options:

1 Cancel job(s)	Press *1* or *c* to cancel a job, type the number of the document shown in the job list, then press ←. Cancel everything in the queue by entering an asterisk *(*)* in place of a number. Some

	printers have a built-in queue called a *print buffer*. Any text in the buffer waiting to be printed will still be printed even if you cancel the job. Turn your printer off then on again to stop printing what's in the buffer.
2 Rush job	Press *2* or *r* to move a document to the first spot in the queue. You'll be prompted to enter the number of the job you want to print next. This does not cancel the current job being printed.
3 Display jobs	This option lists the names of the documents in the print queue, if they cannot all be listed in the bottom of the menu.
4 Go (start printer)	Select this option to resume printing after a Stop Print command or when using individual sheets of paper.
5 Stop	This option halts the printing process. Restart the current job with the Go *(G)* command. Any text in your printer's buffer will continue to be printed.

If you try to exit WordPerfect while jobs are in the print queue, you'll see the warning

Cancel all print jobs? (Y/N) No

Press *N* to remain in WordPerfect and let the documents be printed. Press *Y* to leave WordPerfect, cancelling any jobs in the queue including the one currently being printed.

The next chapter takes you one step further into fast and efficient word processing. You'll learn how to reduce long series of keystrokes to simple commands.

16

Automating Keystrokes with Macros

*F*eaturing

Named, temporary,
and Alt-key macros
A macro library

*L*esson 63 – How to Create and Use Macros

Do you ever find yourself writing the same word or phrase over and over? For instance, you're writing a history paper and have to write *World War II* at least twice on every page. Or do you end every letter with the same closing, or start every letter with your name and address centered at the top of the page?

Are there special formats that you use time and again? Each time you want that format you have to repeat the same keystrokes, go through the same menus.

These are occasions to use macros. A *macro* is a special command that you create to "remember" a number of keystrokes. You can then repeat the keystrokes automatically by just repeating that one command. Macros can be used to repeat text, such as *World War II* in the example just given, or complex formatting commands, such as changing to an odd size of paper or inserting a header or footer. While all macros work basically the same way, there are three distinct types of macro commands.

Alt-key macros	These are convenient to use because they can be recalled quickly. The remembered keystrokes are linked with an Alt-key combination, such as Alt-A. The macro is defined, then saved on the disk. Just press the same Alt-key combination to repeat the keystrokes.
Named macros	These macros are also stored on the disk but under a name from one to eight characters long. To repeat the keystrokes, press Alt-F10, type the name, then press ◄─┘. While this requires more keystrokes than Alt-key macros, it's easier to remember a macro with a descriptive name.

| Temporary macros | Unlike the others, these macros are not stored on the disk, so they remain in effect only during the current session. |

Use Alt-key and named macros for keystrokes that you use often or in a number of documents. Reserve the temporary macros for text or formats needed in a specific document. Since temporary macros are not remembered after you exit WordPerfect, they do not take up disk space.

Before using a macro, you must first define it using the Ctrl-F10 key. This links the keystrokes to be repeated with either an Alt-key combination or a name. Since Alt-key and named macros are stored on disk, you must have the correct disk in the drive when you recall or use the macro.

*D*efining Macros

Let's create macros of each type to speed everyday correspondence. Normally, you would define the macro when you first want to use the keystrokes in a document. In this case, however, you will define a series of macros, clear the screen, then use them in the next section. Follow these steps:

1. Start WordPerfect. The first macro will be a named macro to quickly insert your name, your address, and the date, centered on the page. Thus, this macro will include both text and formatting (Center Text) keystrokes. You can use it to place your address on letters.

2. Press Ctrl-F10 to begin the macro definition process and display the prompt

   Define Macro:

   This is the prompt where you must enter either the macro's name or the Alt-key combination to be linked with the keystrokes.

3. Type *HEAD* (the name of the macro) and press ←. Word-Perfect doesn't distinguish between uppercase and lowercase in macro names.

    The prompt changes to

    Description:

4. If you want, type a brief description of the macro, up to 60 characters. This description is used for editing macro definitions, a function beyond the level of this book.

5. Press ←.

    Now enter the keystrokes of the macro, following steps 6 through 10 below. While you enter the keystrokes, the words *Macro Def* will blink on the status line.

6. Center the cursor with Shift-F6, type your name, then press ←.

7. Press Shift-F6, type your street address, then press ←.

8. Press Shift-F6, type your city, state, and zip code, then press ←.

9. Press ← twice to insert a blank line between the address and the date.

10. Press Shift-F6 Shift-F5 2 to center and insert the Date function, then ← twice. The extra ← will leave a blank line following the date.

11. Press Ctrl-F10. This ends the macro and *Macro Def* disappears from the status line. This particular macro is stored on the disk under the name HEAD.WPM. WordPerfect adds the .WPM extension to all stored macros.

    Now let's create an Alt-key macro to store a single word.

12. Press Ctrl-F10 to begin the macro definition.

13. Press Alt-D as the macro's "name." You can name up to 26 Alt-key macros, one for each letter of the alphabet.

14. Press ← at the Description prompt.

15. Type *Dear* (the text of the macro), press the Space bar, then press Ctrl-F10 to end the macro definition and save it on the

disk as ALTD.WPM. Now whenever you want the word *Dear* in a letter just press Alt-D.

Since the word *Dear* will always be followed by a space, you included the space in the macro itself.

Let's create another Alt-key macro. This one will contain the formatting commands to indent a paragraph 1 inch from both margins.

16. Press Ctrl-F10 Alt-Z ◄┘ to define a macro called *ALT-Z*.

17. Press Shift-F4 Shift-F4, the keystrokes needed to indent 1 inch on both the left and right sides.

18. Press Ctrl-F10 to end the definition. The macro will be stored on the disk as ALTZ.WPM.

    Finally, let's create a temporary macro for use with the next section only.

19. Press Ctrl-F10 for the Define Macro prompt.

20. Press ◄┘. When you name a macro with only the ◄┘ key it is not stored on the disk, but WordPerfect will remember it for the current session.

21. Press ◄┘ at the Description prompt.

22. Type *December 15, 1988* and press Ctrl-F10 to end the definition.

23. Press F7 N N to clear the screen.

You now have four macros defined and ready to use. The ALT-D, ALT-Z, and HEAD macros are saved on the disk.

It is not always necessary to insert extra lines or spaces after the text of a macro as you did in several cases above. For example, the word *Dear* in the salutation will always be followed by a space. So inserting the space within the macro will save entering that keystroke in the letter. However, no extra space was inserted after the date in the temporary macro, just in case it ends a sentence and needs a period.

*U*sing Macros

Now that the macros are defined, they can be used in any document. Remember, to use Alt-key or named macros, you must be using the disk that contains them.

You will now type a letter using the macros defined in the last section. When you want to repeat the keystrokes, just recall the macro. Here's how:

1. Press Alt-F10 to display the prompt

   Macro:

2. Type *HEAD* (uppercase or lowercase) and press ←. The text and formats in the HEAD macro will be loaded from disk and displayed.

3. Type the inside address of the letter:

   Mr. Terry Dershaw
   153 Sampson Lane
   Willow Grove, PA 19011

4. Press ← twice to leave a blank line between the inside address and the salutation.

5. Press Alt-D. The macro will be recalled and the word *Dear* displayed on the screen. Because you included a space in the macro, the cursor is positioned for the remainder of the salutation.

   Now complete the salutation.

6. Type *Mr. Dershaw:* and press ← twice.

7. Now start typing the body of the letter:

   Thank you for your interest in renting offices in our
   building for your legal practice. However, if you wish
   to occupy the space by

   This is the point where you want to insert the text in the temporary macro.

8. Press Alt-F10, then ←. The text of the temporary macro appears in the document.

9. Complete the sentence:

   please keep in mind the following:

10. Press ← twice. You want the next sentence to be indented on both sides. Rather than press the Indent command twice, use the ALT-Z macro just created.

11. Press Alt-Z, then type:

> **A two-month security deposit is required no later than one month prior to occupancy. The first three months of rent are due no later than seven days prior to occupancy.**

12. Press ⏎ twice. Pressing ⏎ cancels the Indent commands.

13. Now finish the letter by typing

> **Sincerely,**
>
> **Your Friendly Management**

Using macros can streamline typing and formatting. As a summary, here is how the three types of macros are recalled:

Alt-key macros	Press the Alt-key combination.
Named macros	Press Alt-F10, type the name, and press ⏎.
Temporary macros	Press Alt-F10 ⏎.

14. Press F7 N Y to exit WordPerfect without saving the document. The Alt-key and named macros are on your disk and can be used, or deleted, at any time.

As you type, consider whether certain keystrokes should be saved as a macro. Most users create a macro for their name and address, their company name, and other frequently used words and phrases. You might also create macros for special paragraph and page formats.

If you enter the name of an existing macro at the Define Macro prompt, the status line will show

(macro name) is Already Defined. 1 Replace; 2 Edit: 0

Press *1* if you want to replace the macro with other keystrokes or ⏎ to cancel the definition. Option 2, Edit, lets you change the macro definition or add special programming commands to it. This is a complex function that won't be of use to you until you've gained more experience with WordPerfect.

*L*esson 64 – A Macro Library

Macros are so useful that you should build libraries of them and store them on disk until needed. Floppy disk users should be prudent in the number of macros on their disks since they take room that may be needed for documents. If you have a floppy-disk system, you could create several libraries and store each on a different working copy of your system disk; use the disk containing the macros needed for that particular job. Hard disk users, however, can store an almost unlimited number of useful macros.

Let's look at some macros that many WordPerfect users find practical.

*G*o Command for Hand-Fed Paper—Alt-G

When using hand-fed paper, you must issue the Go command before printing each sheet. Rather than repeat all of the necessary keystrokes each time, create and use a macro.
Press

Ctrl-F10 Alt-G ↵ Shift-F7 4 4 ↵ ↵ Ctrl-F10

*M*acro for Resetting to the Default Format—Alt-F

This macro sets margins, tabs, pitch, and line spacing back to their default settings. After changing settings for a special format and typing the text, use this macro to resume typing with the default settings.
Press

**Ctrl-F10 Alt-F ↵ Shift-F8 1 6 1 ↵ 7 1 ↵ 1 ↵ 8 Home
Home ← Ctrl-End 0,.5 ↵ F7 F7 Ctrl-F8 3 Ctrl-F10**

*M*acro to Center Text on the Page—Alt-P

This macro centers text between the top and bottom margins.
Press

Ctrl-F10 Alt-P ↵ Shift-F8 2 1 F7 Ctrl-F10

*D*ouble Space Macro—*Alt-D*

This macro changes to double spacing.

Since an Alt-D macro has already been created in this chapter, you will be prompted whether to replace it. The *1* following Alt-D ↵ in the keystrokes below confirms the replacement.

Press

Ctrl-F10 Alt-D ↵ 1 Shift-F8 1 6 2 ↵ ↵ ↵ Ctrl-F10

*P*age Number Macro—*Alt-N*

This macro turns on page numbering at the bottom center of each page.

Press

Ctrl-F10 Alt-N ↵ Shift-F8 2 7 6 ↵ ↵ Ctrl-F10

*L*egal Paper Macro—*Alt-L*

Attorneys could use this macro to switch to legal size paper. The legal form must be defined as a form as explained in Chapter 8.

Press

Ctrl-F10 Alt-L ↵ Shift-F8 2 8 3 1 ↵ ↵ Ctrl-F10

*S*ave Named Text Macro—*Alt-X*

This saves the current document under an already given name and returns to the document. It can only be used for documents that have previously been saved, so make sure you are in a document that has already been saved before entering these keystrokes:

Ctrl-F10 Alt-X ↵ F10 ↵ Y Ctrl-F10

*F*ont Change Macros

Use these macros for a quick change to a new printing font. The letters used are on the top row of the keyboard running in order from the fine font to extra large. For example, Alt-Q changes to the fine font, the smallest, while Alt-Y is used for extra large. Each macro first resets the font to normal to avoid conflicting formats. Alt-E selects the normal font alone.

Fine Font—Alt-Q

> **Ctrl-F10 Alt-Q ↵ Ctrl-F8 3 Ctrl-F8 1 3 Ctrl-F10**

Small Font—Alt-W

> **Ctrl-F10 Alt-W ↵ Ctrl-F8 3 Ctrl-F8 1 4 Ctrl-F10**

Normal Font—Alt-E

> **Ctrl-F10 Alt-E ↵ Ctrl-F8 3 Ctrl-F10**

Large Font—Alt-R

> **Ctrl-F10 Alt-R ↵ Ctrl-F8 3 Ctrl-F8 1 5 Ctrl-F10**

Very Large Font—Alt-T

> **Ctrl-F10 Alt-T ↵ Ctrl-F8 3 Ctrl-F8 1 6 Ctrl-F10**

Extra Large Font—Alt-Y

> **Ctrl-F10 Alt-Y ↵ Ctrl-F8 3 Ctrl-F8 1 7 Ctrl-F10**

By planning your macros carefully, you can streamline the typing, editing, and formatting of your documents. In the next chapter, you'll learn about two other powerful tools, the Speller and the Thesaurus.

17
Word Tools:
The Speller
and
Thesaurus

*F*eaturing

Dictionary
Thesaurus

*L*esson 65 – How to Check Your Spelling

If you are as bad a speller as I am, you probably keep a dictionary near the computer at all times. But even if you win spelling bees, typing errors can still occur.

The WordPerfect spelling program will report if a word in your document is not found in its list of over 100,000 correctly spelled words. If the word is not found, it is reported as a possible misspelling. You can then tell WordPerfect that the word is properly spelled, correct it yourself, or select from a list of suggested spellings taken from the dictionary. The new word will automatically be inserted into the text.

Just like any dictionary, the list may omit some correctly spelled words. Many technical words and names, for instance, will be reported as possible misspellings. But if the word really is spelled correctly, you can add it to a supplemental dictionary of your own words so it will not be reported as incorrect again.

With a hard disk drive, the spelling dictionary and thesaurus will be installed on the same drive and directory as other WordPerfect programs. These programs don't require any special instructions.

*F*loppy Disk Systems

With floppy disk systems, however, there is no room for the spelling or thesaurus programs on the Program disk in drive A or the document disk in drive B. So you'll have to insert separate Dictionary or Thesaurus disks in drive B when they are needed. To do so, you must first set up WordPerfect so it expects to find the dictionary and thesaurus in that drive. Follow these steps:

1. Start WordPerfect.

2. Press Shift-F1 to display the Setup menu.

3. Press *7* to select Location of Files.

4. Press *4* for the Main Dictionary(s) option.

5. Type *B:* then press ←.

6. Press *7* for the Supplemental Dictionary(s) option.

7. Type *B:* then press ⏎.

8. Press *8* for the Thesaurus option.

9. Type *B:* then press ⏎.

10. Press ⏎ twice to return to the typing screen.

You can now insert the Dictionary or Thesaurus disk in drive B when you want to use either program.

Checking Spelling

You can check the spelling of individual words, blocks of text, specified pages, or the entire document. All spelling tasks begin by pressing Ctrl-F2. Here are the steps for checking your spelling:

1. Start WordPerfect and either retrieve a document or type a new one.

2. To check an individual word, place the cursor on or immediately following the word.

   To check a block of text, press Alt-F4 and use the cursor keys to highlight the block.

   To check a page, place the cursor anywhere on the page.

   To check an entire document, place the cursor anywhere in the document.

3. If you have a floppy disk system, place the Spelling disk in drive B.

4. Press Ctrl-F2. The message *∗Please Wait∗* will appear on the screen. If you are checking a highlighted block, skip to step 7. WordPerfect is now checking each word in the block.

5. If you do not have a block highlighted, the following prompt will appear:

   **Check: 1 Word; 2 Page; 3 Document; 4 New Sup.
   Dictionary; 5 Look Up; 6 Count:0**

   Press *1* to check an individual word.
   Press *2* to check all of the words on the current page.
   Press *3* to check the entire document.

6. If you are checking a page or a document, the message *∗Please Wait∗* will appear in the status line while each word is compared with those in the dictionary.

   If you are checking an individual word and the cursor moves to the next word in the document, the word is spelled correctly. The prompt will remain on the screen so you can select another option to continue the checking process or press F1 to stop.

7. When a match is not found in the dictionary, a word will become highlighted and the screen will change as illustrated in Figure 17.1. The line across the screen and the prompt line will appear first. Then some suggested spellings will appear as they are found in the dictionary.

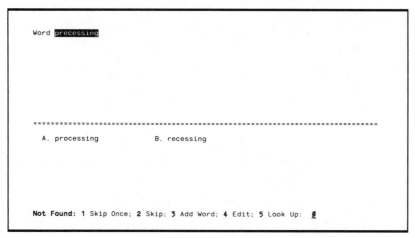

```
Word precessing




------------------------------------------------------------------------------
   A. processing          B. recessing




Not Found: 1 Skip Once; 2 Skip; 3 Add Word; 4 Edit; 5 Look Up:  0
```

Figure 17.1: Correction screen

Notice that each of the suggested spellings is labeled with a letter. If the correct spelling appears among the suggestions, press the appropriate letter. That spelling will replace the one in the document.

If none of the suggested words is correct, or nothing was found in the dictionary, then select another option from the prompt line. Here are the options:

- 1 Skip Once—Tells WordPerfect that the word is spelled as you want it in this one instance. The program will look for the next misspelled word.

- 2 Skip—Tells WordPerfect you want it to accept the word as spelled for the remainder of the current checking session. The checking will continue but will not stop if this word is encountered again.

- 3 Add Word—Lets you add a word to the supplemental dictionary. If a word is spelled correctly and you use it regularly, you will want to use this option.

- 4 Edit—Lets you edit the word. If you press *4,* the cursor will appear on the word. You can now press the right and left arrow keys, use Backspace and Del, or type new characters to change the word. (The up and down arrow keys, and other cursor-movement key combinations, will not work.) Press F7 to return to the spell checking after you have edited the word. If the edited word is still misspelled according to the WordPerfect dictionary, it will again be highlighted so you have to select an option on the prompt line.

- 5 Look Up—Displays the prompt *Word or word pattern:* on the status line. Enter a word that you want to search for. You can use the wild-card characters * and *?.* A *wild-card* character is one that stands for an undetermined character or several characters. Each *?* will be replaced in the search by a single character, each * by any number of characters. For instance, looking up *f?r* will display *for* and *fur* while *f*r* will result in words such as *fair, falter,* and *fascicular.* To stop the Look Up process, press F1 (Cancel) at any prompt to return to the Spelling selection line. Press F1 once more to exit the spelling checker and return to the document.

    You can really use the wild cards to take advantage of WordPerfect's dictionary. Say, for example, that you vaguely remember that the word you want to use starts with an *a* and ends with *gram.* Rather than taking a guess at the spelling, enter *a*gram* as the lookup phrase. The wild cards are also helpful to find related words based on the same root, such as entering *photo** or **meter.*

    I hate to admit it, but I even use this feature for solving crossword puzzles. If you know some of the letters in the word, enter them but use the question mark for the blank boxes, such as looking for a "unit of measure" to fit in *l???r.*

In two instances a different prompt will appear on the status line. If WordPerfect finds the same word twice in a row, the prompt changes to

Double Word! 1 2 Skip; 3 Delete 2nd; 4 Edit; 5 Disable Double Word Checking:0

Enter the appropriate selection:

- 1 2 Skip—keeps both words in the text.
- 3 Delete 2nd—deletes one of the pair.
- 4 Edit—moves the cursor to the text for editing.
- 5 Disable Double Word Checking—ignores paired words throughout the document.

When words contain numbers, such as *2nd* or *F10,* the following prompt appears:

1 2 Skip; 3 Ignore Words Containing Numbers; 4 Edit:0

Make your selection:

- 1 2 Skip—accepts the word as written.
- 3 Ignore Words Containing Numbers—tells the program not to bother checking any words with numbers.
- 4 Edit—places the cursor in the text so you can correct it manually. Press ⏎ when you're ready to continue the checking process.

When the spelling check is completed, the number of words checked will be displayed in the status line with the prompt

Press any key to continue

You can now press any key to return to the document. To exit the spelling checker quickly at any prompt, press F1 twice.

Other Spelling Options

In addition to checking a word, a block, a page, or a document, there are three other options on the main Spelling prompt line.

- 4 New Sup. Dictionary—Allows you to use a special supplemental dictionary. A supplemental dictionary is a list of your own words that are not found in WordPerfect's main dictionary. For example, say you often write articles containing technical words. To avoid having these words reported as misspellings, you add them to the supplemental dictionary using the Add Word option when you check spelling. The default supplemental dictionary is called WP{WP}EN.SUP and it is normally used whenever you check spelling. But since searching this dictionary takes time, why use it when you're writing non-technical documents that will not contain these words? In this case, create your own supplemental dictionary that you can use whenever you need it as a reference.

  To create or use your own supplemental dictionary, select option 4 to display the prompt

  Supplemental dictionary name:

  Type the name of the supplemental dictionary you'd like to use, or the name of a new dictionary you'd like to create, then press ◄─┘.

- 5 Look Up—Works in the same way as the Look Up option discussed earlier. Use it when you want to check the spelling of a word before typing it.

- 6 Count—Reports the number of words in the current document.

The spelling dictionary is a powerful aid in the writing process. While it is more convenient with a hard disk system, it can still be used to advantage with floppy disks.

*L*esson 66 – How to Use the Thesaurus

Sometimes the hardest part of writing is selecting just the right word. You know what you want to say but you're not sure of the best word. Other times, you find yourself repeating a word frequently in a paragraph and you'd like to find another way to say the same thing without sounding repetitious. These times call for the WordPerfect thesaurus.

The thesaurus displays synonyms—words with similar meanings—
and antonyms—words with opposite meanings. The WordPerfect
thesaurus has some 10,000 words, called *headwords,* that can be
looked up.

Like the spelling dictionary, the thesaurus requires its own floppy
disk. So if you do not have a fixed disk system, you must insert the
Thesaurus disk in drive B before using it.

To use the thesaurus, place the cursor on or immediately following
the word you would like to replace with a synonym (or antonym) and
press Alt-F1. Four lines of text will remain on the screen above a box
of three columns containing the synonyms. Figure 17.2 shows the
Thesaurus screen displaying synonyms for the word *help.*

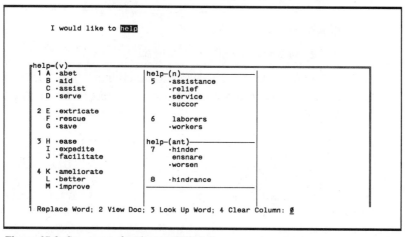

Figure 17.2: Synonyms for the word "help"

Note that, in this case, synonyms are given for the word *help* in both
the noun *(n)* and verb *(v)* form, along with several antonyms. The
words are listed in subgroups having similar connotations. Words preceded by dots are themselves headwords that can be looked up to find
additional possible substitutions. Press the letter next to a headword
to see more selections. For example, pressing *H* (before *ease*) changes
the screen as shown in Figure 17.3. Synonyms for the word *ease* now
appear in the second and third columns, and the letters have moved
from the first column to the second.

You can continue to search for the proper word by pressing the letter next to another headword. If you want to select a word in another

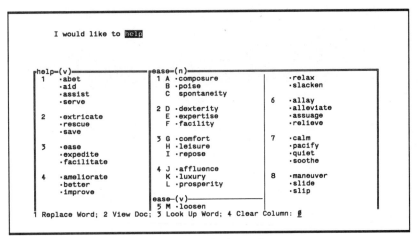

```
        I would like to help


  ┌help=(v)───────────────┬ease=(n)────────────────────────────────────┐
  │  1   ·abet            │ 1 A ·composure        │    ·relax           │
  │      ·aid             │   B ·poise            │    ·slacken         │
  │      ·assist          │   C  spontaneity      │ 6  ·allay           │
  │      ·serve           │ 2 D ·dexterity        │    ·alleviate       │
  │                       │   E ·expertise        │    ·assuage         │
  │  2   ·extricate       │   F ·facility         │    ·relieve         │
  │      ·rescue          │                       │                     │
  │      ·save            │ 3 G ·comfort          │ 7  ·calm            │
  │                       │   H ·leisure          │    ·pacify          │
  │  3   ·ease            │   I ·repose           │    ·quiet           │
  │      ·expedite        │                       │    ·soothe          │
  │      ·facilitate      │ 4 J ·affluence        │                     │
  │                       │   K ·luxury           │ 8  ·maneuver        │
  │  4   ·ameliorate      │   L ·prosperity       │    ·slide           │
  │      ·better          │ease=(v)───────────────│    ·slip            │
  │      ·improve         │ 5 M ·loosen           │                     │
  │ 1 Replace Word; 2 View Doc; 3 Look Up Word; 4 Clear Column: 0        │
  └─────────────────────────────────────────────────────────────────────┘
```

Figure 17.3: Synonyms for "ease" from the first column

column, you must first move the reference letters there by pressing the right or left arrow key.

The prompt line at the bottom of the screen can be used anytime. The four options are:

- 1 Replace Word—When you find the word you want to use, make sure it is preceded by a letter. If not, press the → or ← key until letters appear in that column. Press *1* to display the prompt

  Press letter for word

  Press the letter preceding your selection.

- 2 View Doc—This option returns the cursor to the document at the top of the screen and displays the prompt line

  Press EXIT to return to thesaurus

  Use the arrow keys to scroll through the text, then press F7 when you want to return to the thesaurus.

- 3 Look Up Word—Use this option to look up synonyms for words not listed on the screen.

- 4 Clear Column—The Thesaurus screen holds a maximum of three columns. To erase synonyms that you know are irrelevant, use the arrow keys to place the letters in the column you no longer need, then press *4*.

Press ↵ to select the default *0* option and leave the thesaurus.
If the word you are looking up is not a headword, the message

Word Not Found

will appear on the status line for a few seconds and then change to

Word:

Type another word with similar meaning that may be a headword or press F1 to display the prompt line.

You'll notice that the thesaurus also shows some words with opposite meanings—antonyms. Here's how you can use them.

There may be times when you're trying to find the correct word but can't even think of where to start. Or every word you try to find in the Thesaurus results in the Word Not Found message. In these instances, try to think of a word with the opposite meaning. If that is a headword, the suggested antonyms would be just what you're looking for.

This is particularly useful when you want to find synonyms for phrases. For example, perhaps you want to find a synonym for the phrase *put all your eggs in one basket*. Looking up synonyms for *put, eggs,* or *basket* certainly wouldn't help.

So try looking up a word with the opposite meaning, *diversify.* The antonym *consolidate* will be listed, and you can extend the search from that point on. Figure 17.4 shows how your screen would look.

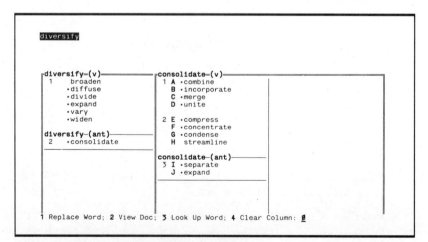

Figure 17.4: Searching for synonyms by antonyms

Of course, you'll have to use caution and judgement when selecting synonyms from the thesaurus. Not all synonyms are interchangeable in every context. Many words have connotations that make them unsuitable replacements for one in the text.

The next chapter will take you the last step into desktop publishing, as you learn how to add graphics to your WordPerfect documents.

18
Enhancing Your Documents with Graphics

*F*eatring

Adding horizontal and vertical lines
Enclosing text in boxes
Merging graphics and text

Warning! If you're like me, you may find the topics covered in this chapter to be habit-forming. But they are also interesting and powerful, enabling you to create finished-looking documents complete with drawings. If you produce newsletters, flyers, mail-order literature, or any document that can be improved with graphics, then this chapter is for you—especially if you have a high quality dot matrix or laser printer.

In this chapter, you'll learn the fundamentals of WordPerfect's potent graphics commands. I'll show you how to add vertical and horizontal lines to your documents, enclose text in a box, and add drawings and graphic images to your documents.

Because these commands are so powerful, you'll just get the basics here. But you'll learn enough to take advantage of these commands in a variety of documents. Go through this chapter, following each instruction carefully. Then, when you have time, return to the graphics menus that are shown here and experiment a little.

But first the small print. Your ability to print graphics, just like type sizes and fonts, is based entirely on your printer. If you have a daisy wheel printer, or a dot matrix printer without graphics capabilities, then many of the features in this chapter will not be very useful to you.

How can you tell what your printer can do? Just follow the lessons here and print out each of the examples. You'll see which features your printer supports.

*L*esson 67 – How to Add Vertical and Horizontal Lines

You can use horizontal and vertical lines to separate text on the page or simply to add some visual perspective. Using the Graphic Lines command, you insert lines before and after text, between columns, or along the margins. You won't see lines on the editing screen, but they will appear when the document is printed or displayed in View mode.

Let's use the command to create two different documents. First, we'll use a simple 2-inch horizontal line to separate two parts of the document MEMO, which you created in Chapter 4. This was a short memorandum followed by a brief list of items. Of course, you can add horizontal lines to any document.

*H*orizontal Lines

1. Recall MEMO.
2. Place the cursor where you want to insert a line, in this case between the memorandum and the list of items.
3. Press Alt-F9 to display the prompt

   1 Figure; 2 Table; 3 Text Box; 4 User-defined Box; 5 Line: 0

4. Press 5 or *L* for the Line option to display

   Create Line: 1 Horizontal; 2 Vertical; Edit Line: 3 Horizontal; 4 Vertical:0

   Options 3 and 4 are available with the 1/3/89 release.

5. Press *1* or *h* to select a horizontal line. The screen will show the Horizontal Line menu (Figure 18.1).

```
Graphics: Horizontal Line
    1 - Horizontal Position          Left & Right
    2 - Length of Line
    3 - Width of Line                0.01"
    4 - Gray Shading (% of black)    100%




    Selection: 0
```

Figure 18.1: Horizontal Line menu

These options are used to set the position and size of the line. The default settings call for a single solid horizontal line extending from the left margin to the right margin. But let's change this to a 2-inch line in the center of the page.

6. Press *1* or *h* to set the horizontal position. The prompt line changes to

   Horizontal Pos: 1 Left 2 Right 3 Center 4 Both Left & Right 5 Set Position:0

7. Press *3* or *c* to center the line.

8. Press *2* or *L* to set the length of the line. Selecting this option has no effect if the horizontal position is set at Both Left and Right, in which case the line extends between both margins.

9. Type *2* for a 2-inch line, then press ←.

 Let's accept the default width (thickness) and gray shading. But if you wanted, you could print a thicker line (option 3) or a line other than solid black (option 4) if your printer allows.

10. Press ← to return to the document. The code [HLine:Center, 2", 0.01", 100%] will be inserted in the text, showing the line type and specifications. Remember, you won't see the line on the screen.

11. Press Shift-F7 1 to print the memo (Figure 18.2).

12. Press F7 N N to clear the screen.

```
MEMORANDUM

TO:        All Department Chairpersons
FROM:      Rose Savage
SUBJECT:   Reserved Equipment List

Attached is a list of Class 2 equipment that must be reserved at
least two weeks before needed.


                    _____

                         Class 2 Equipment

Electron Microscopes
Fluorescent Microscopes
Cryostat
Serum Glutamic Pyruvic Transaminase Analyzer
Flow Cytometer
Nuclear Magnetic Resonance Scanner
```

Figure 18.2: Memo with horizontal line

To remove a line from the document, press Alt-F3 to reveal the codes and then delete the Line code. If you want to edit the line (starting with the 1/3/89 release of WordPerfect), press Alt-F9 5, and then either *3* or *o* to edit a horizontal line, or *4* or *e* for a vertical line. WordPerfect will search back through the text to locate the closest line code, and then display the Graphic Line menu. Make your changes and press ←.

Vertical Lines

Vertical lines are used to separate columns on the page or to highlight the left or right margin. They can provide a pleasing visual effect that breaks up large sections of text, particularly in bound books.

Let's see how easy it is to add vertical lines. In this case, you'll insert a line along the left margin.

1. Press Alt-F9 5 2 to select Vertical Lines. You'll see the Vertical Line menu (Figure 18.3).

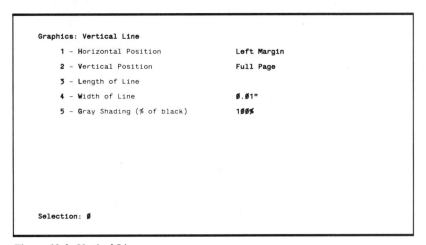

```
Graphics: Vertical Line
        1 - Horizontal Position           Left Margin
        2 - Vertical Position             Full Page
        3 - Length of Line
        4 - Width of Line                 0.01"
        5 - Gray Shading (% of black)     100%




    Selection: 0
```

Figure 18.3: Vertical Line menu

The options on this menu are similar to those for horizontal lines but with some important differences. The Length of Line setting determines the height of the line. Use the Horizontal Position option to place the lines either at the right or left margin, between columns, or at some specific position. The Vertical Position option controls where at that position the line appears: along the full length of the page, near the top, center, or bottom, or at a specific position that you can set.

You can only enter a line length if the vertical position is something other than full page.

2. Press ⏎ to accept the default settings and return to the document.

3. Press Shift-F7 V to view the document. (Figure 18.4).

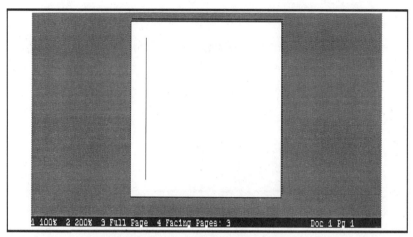

Figure 18.4: Vertical line in View mode with default settings

Any text you enter on the page will appear to the right of the vertical line.

4. Press F7 N N to clear the screen.

Vertical Lines in Columns

To print a line separating columns, start by defining the columns as you did in Chapter 12. Then create the line by selecting the Horizontal Position option to see the prompt

Horizontal Position: 1 Left; 2 Right; 3 Between Columns; 4 Set Position: 0

Press *3,* Between Columns, for the prompt

Place line to the right of column: 1

Press ⏎ if you want the line down the center of the page between two columns, then ⏎ again to return to the document. Turn Columns on and enter your columns.

By adjusting the vertical position and length, you can insert lines anywhere on the page, even between uneven parallel columns surrounded by regular paragraphs as shown in Figure 18.5.

You can even add lines to existing text by placing the cursor at the start of the document, pressing Shift-F9 for Line, then selecting the appropriate options. For complex lines, such as lines between

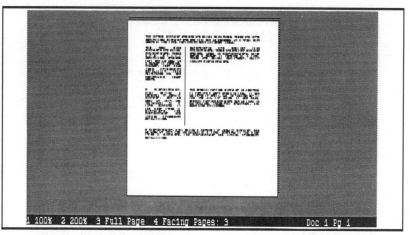

Figure 18.5: Vertical lines in columns

columns as shown in Figure 18.5, first print a copy of the document and draw in the lines by hand. Then measure the vertical and horizontal positions, and the length of the lines you want to add. Place the cursor at the start of the document and enter the appropriate measurements on the Line menu.

*L*esson 68 – How to Enclose Text in a Box

Let's now take lines one step further into complete boxes. Surrounding text in a box calls attention to it and draws the reader's eye to important points. Figure 18.6 shows the document CLASSES enhanced with a text box. The text in the box has been formatted as extra large to grab the reader's attention.

You can enclose any amount of text in a box, and even retrieve a document from disk into a box. Like all graphics, however, boxes are seen only when viewed or printed. But you can edit and format the text in the box easily.

In this lesson, I'll show you how to create the eye-catching announcement shown in Figure 18.7. (Of course, your own printout will depend on your printer.) The text will be enclosed in a box centered on the page.

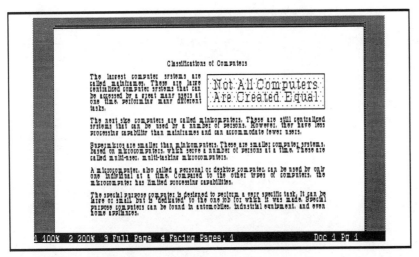

Figure 18.6: Combining font sizes and boxes

1. Press Alt-F9 for the Graphics prompt line. Notice the options other than Line. Each of these represents a type of graphic box that can be included in your document.

   The option names really have nothing to do with the type of text or graphics you place in the box. For example, you can have a table in a text box and text in a figure box. The names are just there to help you plan and control your document.

   For consistency, however, let's use the text box to hold text.

2. Press *3* or *b* to select Text Box and show the prompt line

   Text Box: 1 Create; 2 Edit; 3 New Number; 4 Options: 0

   Before creating a box, you should set any specific options you want.

3. Press *4* or *o* for Options to display the Text Box Options menu (Figure 18.8).

   The menu shows the default values used for text boxes—thick border lines on the top and bottom, nothing on the sides, and a ten percent shade. To make it a complete box, you have to add lines on the sides.

4. Press *1* for the Border Style option. The cursor moves to highlight the word *None* next to the left border style and the

Figure 18.7: Announcement using text box

```
Options:    Text Box

    1 - Border Style
            Left                            None
            Right                           None
            Top                             Thick
            Bottom                          Thick
    2 - Outside Border Space
            Left                            Ø.16"
            Right                           Ø.16"
            Top                             Ø.16"
            Bottom                          Ø.16"
    3 - Inside Border Space
            Left                            Ø.16"
            Right                           Ø.16"
            Top                             Ø.16"
            Bottom                          Ø.16"
    4 - First Level Numbering Method        Numbers
    5 - Second Level Numbering Method       Off
    6 - Caption Number Style                [BOLD]1[bold]
    7 - Position of Caption                 Below box, Outside borders
    8 - Minimum Offset from Paragraph       Ø"
    9 - Gray Shading (% of black)           1Ø%

    Selection: Ø
```

Figure 18.8: Text Box Options menu

prompt line changes to

> **1 None; 2 Single; 3 Double; 4 Dashed; 5 Dotted;
> 6 Thick; 7 Extra Thick:0**

5. Press *7* to select Extra Thick for the left border.

6. Press *7* three more times to select the extra thick border for the remaining sides.

   Take a moment to review the other options. They determine the space between the text and the border, and the numbering used to reference the boxes. The last option is used to shade the inside of the box, such as the light shading in the sample figure. On dot matrix printers, shading takes a long time to print. So if you didn't want any shading you would press *9* to select the option, type *0,* then press ←.

7. Press ← to return to the document.

You have just set certain characteristics that all text boxes now defined will have—an extra thick border and the default ten percent shading. All text boxes from this position on will have that format until you select new options or delete the [Txt Opt] code in the text.

Now that you've selected the optional format characteristics, you must describe the contents and position of the box itself.

1. Press Alt-F9 3 to select Text Box again.

2. Press *1* or *c* to create the box and display the Text Box Definition menu (Figure 18.9).

```
Definition: Text Box
        1 - Filename
        2 - Caption
        3 - Type                    Paragraph
        4 - Vertical Position       Ø"
        5 - Horizontal Position     Right
        6 - Size                    3.25" wide x 3.37" (high)
        7 - Wrap Text Around Box    Yes
        8 - Edit



    Selection: Ø
```

Figure 18.9: Text Box Definition menu

Graphics can be a complicated process, as you've seen by the many options in the menus. So I'll just briefly explain the purpose of these options.

- Filename—allows you to recall a document or graphic image to be inserted into the box.

- Caption—allows you to enter a caption to print under the box.

- Type—gives you a choice of Paragraph, Page, or Character. Paragraph boxes align with the paragraph where the box is defined; Page boxes can be placed anywhere on the page; Character boxes can be placed within lines.

- Vertical Position—allows you to change the position of the box in relation to the text or the top margin.

- Horizontal Position—allows you to position the box where desired between the right and left margins.

- Size—allows you to change the size of the box.

- Wrap Text Around Box—with text wrapped around the box, the default mode, prevents text outside of the box from printing over the box and its contents.

- Edit—allows you to add, edit, or format text in the box. With graphic boxes, this allows you to scale, move, or invert the image.

3. Press *3* or *t* to change the type of the box. The prompt line changes to

   Type: 1 Paragraph; 2 Page; 3 Character:0

4. Press *2* or *a* to select a Page box. The vertical position automatically changes to Top, the horizontal position to Margin, Right.

5. Press *4* or *v* to change the Vertical Position and display

   Vertical Position: 1 Full Page; 2 Top; 3 Center;
   4 Bottom; 5 Set Position:0

6. Press *3* or *c* to select Center.

7. Press *5* or *h* to set the horizontal position. The prompt line changes to

   Horizontal Position: 1 Margins; 2 Columns;
   3 Set Position:0

8. Press *1* or *m* to align the box between the margins and display

   Horizontal Position: 1 Left 2 Right 3 Center
   4 Both Left & Right:0

9. Press *3* or *c* to center the box between the margins.
   Finally, let's enter text into the box. You could insert the text of an existing document by entering its name at the Filename option. The box size will adjust automatically to accommodate the text. In this case, we're going to enter the text directly through the Edit menu.

10. Press *8* or *e* for Edit. The screen clears except for the status line and the prompt

    Press Exit when done, Graphics to rotate text

The length of the line you'll be able to type is controlled by the box width. The height will automatically adjust to fit the text that you enter. You can make the box larger than the text by using the Size option on the Text Box Definition menu.

11. Press Ctrl-F8 1 7 to select Extra Large font.

12. Press Shift-F6 to center the cursor, then type

    ATTENTION

13. Press Ctrl-F8 3 for Normal, then press ◄┘ twice.

14. Now type

    All members of Faculty Council are requested to submit their nominations for Student of the Year by Tuesday, May 24.
    Deliver nominations to room 205.

15. Press F7 to accept the text and display the Box menu. Figure 18.10 shows the completed menu.

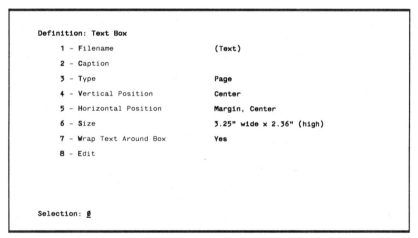

```
Definition: Text Box

        1 - Filename                (Text)

        2 - Caption

        3 - Type                    Page

        4 - Vertical Position       Center

        5 - Horizontal Position     Margin, Center

        6 - Size                    3.25" wide x 2.36" (high)

        7 - Wrap Text Around Box     Yes

        8 - Edit




    Selection: 0
```

Figure 18.10: Completed Text Box menu

16. Press F7 again to return to the document. The appropriate codes are in the text, but nothing appears on the screen. That's because the box is centered on the page.

17. Press ◄┘ until you reach line position 6.69". Notice that a box, with no text inside, appears on the screen indicating the presence of a text box (Figure 18.11).

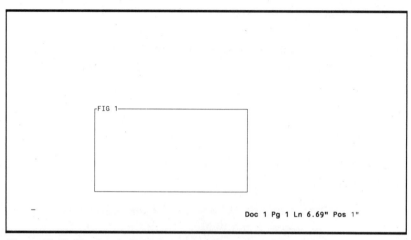

Figure 18.11: Text box indicated on the screen

18. Press Shift F7 1 to print the document, or Shift-F7 V to view it.

19. Press F7 N N to clear the screen.

Text boxes can be any size, so you can create a full-page border by selecting Full Page for the vertical position of a page type box. To divide the page into a number of smaller boxes, define each box with coordinated positions—one each on the top, center, and bottom.

Text boxes can add impact to any document if not overused. Plan your documents and reserve boxes for those elements that you want to emphasize.

*L*esson 69 – How to Add Graphics to Your Documents

This final lesson also creates a box. But in this case you'll insert a graphic image. WordPerfect supplies a number of sample drawings, which are stored as files ending with the extension WPG. You can merge any of these into your document as well as graphics files from many other programs, such as Lotus 1-2-3 or PC Paintbrush, a drawing program.

The techniques are almost identical to creating a text box, so most of the steps will be familiar to you.

In this lesson, you'll add a graphic image to the document CLASSES. In Figure 7.5 you saw the document in View mode, while Figure 18.12 shows a sample printout. Follow these steps to create that document:

Classifications of Computers

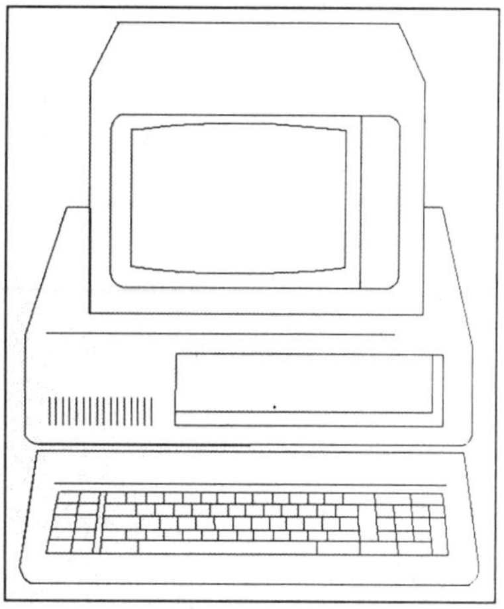

The largest computer systems are called mainframes. These are large centralized computer systems that can be accessed by a great many users at one time, performing many different tasks.

The next size computers are called minicomputers. These are still centralized systems that can be used by a number of persons. However, they have less processing capability than mainframes and can accommodate fewer users.

Supermicros are smaller than minicomputers. These are smaller computer systems, based on microcomputers, which serve a number of persons at a time. These are called multi-user, multi-tasking microcomputers.

A microcomputer, also called a personal or desktop computer, can be used by only one individual at a time. Compared to the other types of computers, the microcomputer has limited processing capabilities.

The special purpose computer is designed to perform a very specific task. It can be large or small, but is "dedicated" to the one job for which it was made. Special purpose computers can be found in automobiles, industrial equipment, and even home appliances.

***Figure 18.12:** Sample document with graphics*

1. Recall CLASSES. The document contains a number of paragraphs, each indented farther to the right.
2. Remove the indentations using the Replace command.
   a. Press Alt-F2.
   b. Press ↵ for unconfirmed replacement.
   c. Press F4, the Indent key.
   d. Press F2 twice to perform the replacement.

   All of the [->Indent] codes will be deleted, aligning each of the paragraphs at the left margin.

3. Format the title to extra large printing.

   a. Place the cursor at the start of the title.

   b. Press Alt-F4 to turn on Block mode.

   c. Press End to highlight the entire line.

   d. Press Ctrl-F8 1 7 for extra large printing.

4. Place the cursor at the start of the first paragraph.

5. Press Alt-F9 1 to select a Figure box. Remember, any box type could actually be used.

6. Press *4* or *o* to display the Figure Options menu. It is just like the menu shown in Figure 18.8 except for some different default values: figure boxes are already formatted for a single line border but with no shading. So let's add a ten percent shading to really make it stand out on the page.

7. Press *9* or *g* for the Gray Shading option.

8. Type *10,* then press ◄─┘ twice to return to the document. Now let's define the box itself.

9. Press Alt-F9 1 1 to create a Figure box. The Figure Box Definition menu appears. It is identical to the Text Box Definition menu shown in Figure 18.9 except for the title.

10. Now insert the graphics file PC.WPG, supplied on the Word-Perfect Graphics disk if you're using 5¼-inch disks. If you have a floppy drive system, insert this disk in drive B.

   a. Press *1* to select Filename. The prompt changes to

    Enter filename

   b. Type *PC.WPG* (or *B:PC.WPG* if you have floppy disks and did not change the default drive), then press ◄─┘. You'll see the message

    Please wait – Loading WP Graphics File

    as the file is retrieved.

11. Press F7 to accept the box and return to the document, accepting the default paragraph type and other options.

12. Press Ctrl-F3 ↵ to rewrite the screen. It will appear as in Figure 18.13.

13. Press Shift-F7 1 to print the document or Shift-F7 V to view it on the screen, then F7 to return to the document.

14. Press F7 N Y to exit WordPerfect.

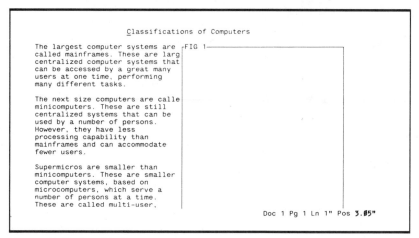

Figure 18.13: Graphic document

As you become more familiar with WordPerfect's graphics commands, you'll see that you can do some rather sophisticated formatting.

For example, you could use the Vertical Position option on the Definition menu to lower the position of the box. Figure 18.14 shows the box with a vertical position of 0.25". This lowers the box just enough so the top line of text runs across the page. You can also rotate, mirror-image, and scale the size of graphics.

Here's a closing idea. If you have a painting or drawing program, use it to sign your name. Save the file, then merge it into your document using the graphics commands, placing the drawing at the end of a letter. When you print the document, your name will be signed for you (as in Figure 18.15). Think of how much time this will save if you produce form letters!

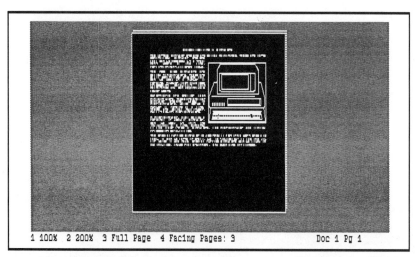

Figure 18.14: Position of box changed vertically

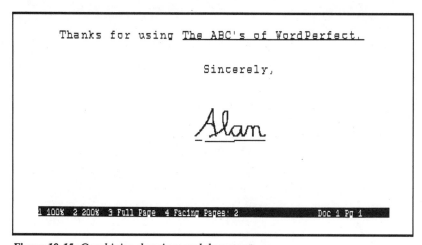

Figure 18.15: Combining drawings and documents

Appendices

A

How to Make Backups

It is unethical and illegal to distribute copies of your WordPerfect disks or manual to anyone. You should, however, make a copy of all your WordPerfect disks before attempting to use the program. Because disks can wear out from use, an extra set of disks is simply a precaution against losing this valuable program.

You'll need a DOS or OS/2 disk, all of your WordPerfect disks, and a number of blank disks, either 5¼-inch or 3½-inch depending on your computer. Make sure you have a blank disk for each disk supplied with WordPerfect. If you have two floppy disk drives, and no hard disk, you'll need an extra blank disk. This will be used to hold your own documents.

First, *write-protect* your WordPerfect disks as a precaution against accidentally erasing your WordPerfect program. With 5¼-inch disks, place a write-protect tab over the small notch on the edge of each disk. The write-protect tabs are the small rectangular stickers that are packaged with blank diskettes. If you have 3½-inch disks, protect the disk by pushing the small tab toward the end of the disk. If the small square is blocked, then the disk is unlocked and the files can be erased. Lock the disk by pushing the tab so the hole is uncovered.

DO NOT lock or write-protect the blank disks that you will be copying onto. You want these disks free so that you can transfer WordPerfect to them.

Systems with Two Floppy Disks

You will first *format* the blank disks according to the instructions below, allowing them to accept the WordPerfect programs. Then you will copy WordPerfect onto these new disks. Check with your DOS manual if you have any problems with the following procedure.

In this procedure, NEVER place one of your original WordPerfect disks in drive B. If you tried to copy with a WordPerfect disk in drive B and without a write-protect tab on, the WordPerfect program would be destroyed.

1. Insert a DOS disk in drive A, turn on your computer, and respond to the date and time questions, if they appear.

    Type the date in MM-DD-YY format—such as *10-19-88*—and press ←⏎.

    Type the time in HH:MM format—such as *10:16*—and press ←⏎. Past noon, use military time by just adding 12 to the hours. For example, if it is 2:30, enter *14:30*.

    The disk drive prompt *A >* will appear.

2. Type *FORMAT B:/S* and press ←⏎. DOS and OS/2 commands can be entered in either uppercase or lowercase.

    The screen will display

    Insert new diskette for drive B:
    and strike ENTER when ready

3. Place a blank disk in drive B and press ←⏎. It will take a few minutes, but the blank disk will be formatted.

    On some MS-DOS systems, the message

    Volume Label (11 characters, ENTER for none)?

    will be displayed. Press ←⏎.

    A *volume label* is a disk name that is displayed when you list the directory. By pressing ←⏎ you didn't name this disk. We're only skipping the names here to save time. Since each disk will be labeled on the outside, and each will have different programs on it, a name is not needed. However, later you might want to give your disks volume labels that identify their contents so when you display the directory listing its name will appear. The volume label could be "School Papers," "Annual Report," or any name that will quickly identify the nature of the documents on that disk.

    The screen will now display

    Format another (Y/N)?

4. Press *N*.

   With most versions of DOS, the disk in drive B will now contain enough of the operating system to start your computer. However, with a few versions of DOS, the FORMAT/S command does not place one very important, and necessary, file on drive B—COMMAND.COM. You should check to see if this file is on the disk and, if not, copy it from the DOS disk. Just continue following these steps.

5. Type

   DIR B:

   See if a program called COMMAND is displayed. It will be listed like this:

   COMMAND COM

   If it is on your disk, then skip ahead to step 7.

6. Type the following:

   COPY COMMAND.COM B:

   then press ←. This instruction copies the program onto the disk in drive B.

7. Remove the disk from drive B. If you have 5¼-inch disks, label it *WordPerfect 1*. With 3¼-inch disks, label it *WordPerfect 1/WordPerfect 2*.

   This first disk has been formatted to include enough of DOS or OS/2 so you'll be able to use it to start your computer and run WordPerfect.

8. Type *FORMAT B:* and press ←.

9. Place another *blank* disk in drive B, then press ←. When the formatting is complete, the *Format another (Y/N)?* message will appear again.

10. Replace the disk in drive B with another blank disk.

11. Press *Y* to format another disk, then ← to start the process.

12. Complete steps 10 and 11 until all of the blank disks have been formatted.

13. Press *N* to stop formatting.

Copying WordPerfect

Now that the disks are formatted, you must copy the WordPerfect programs. Remember, *never place one of your original WordPerfect disks in drive B.*

1. Remove the DOS disk from drive A.

2. Insert the original WordPerfect disk, labeled *WordPerfect 1* for 5¼-inch systems or *WordPerfect 1 / WordPerfect 2* if you have 3½-inch disks, in drive A.

3. Insert the newly formatted disk labeled *WordPerfect 1* or *WordPerfect 1 / WordPerfect 2* in drive B.

4. Type *COPY A:*.*B:* and press ←┘. All of the programs from the original disk will be copied onto the working disk in drive B.

5. When the *A >* prompt reappears, remove both disks.

6. Place another original WordPerfect disk in drive A.

7. Place one of your formatted disks in drive B.

8. Type *COPY A:*.*B:* and press ←┘.

9. When the *A >* prompt appears, remove both disks and immediately label the disk in drive B to match the one in drive A.

10. Now repeat steps 6 to 9 until you have copied all of the WordPerfect disks and labeled all of the copies.

    You should have one blank formatted disk left. Label this "Document Disk."

    Place the original WordPerfect disks in a safe location and use the copies for everyday work.

*H*ard *Disk Systems with One Floppy*

During this procedure, you must be very careful to follow the instructions displayed on the screen. Remember to install write-protect tabs on your WordPerfect disks as a precaution against accidentally erasing them.

1. Turn on the computer and respond to the date and time prompts if they appear. (See Step 1 of "Systems with Two Floppy Disks" if you need instructions.) Wait until the drive prompt appears. It will usually be *C>*.

2. Make sure the DOS program DISKCOPY.COM is on the current directory. If not, move to the appropriate subdirectory with the CD\ command.

   a. Type *DIR* then press ⏎ to display the programs on the main, or root, directory. If DISKCOPY.COM is not there, make a note of the subdirectory names (marked with <DIR>).

   b. Move to each subdirectory by entering *CD* followed by the subdirectory's name, then use the DIR command again to check for the copying program, DISKCOPY.COM.

   c. If you can't find it, insert a DOS or OS/2 disk into your floppy drive and continue below.

3. Type *DISKCOPY A: A:* and press ⏎. DOS and OS/2 commands can be entered in either uppercase or lowercase.
   The screen will display

   > **Insert source diskette in drive A:**
   > **Strike any key when ready**

   You will be making a copy using only one disk drive. During the process, you will be instructed to insert either the *source* diskette or the *destination* diskette into drive A. The *source* diskette is the original WordPerfect disk that you will be copying from. The *destination* disk is the blank diskette that you are copying onto. *Never* insert the original WordPerfect disk when you are asked to insert the *destination* disk. If the write-protect notch was not covered, the WordPerfect program would be erased.

4. Place one of your WordPerfect disks in drive A. This will be one of the original disks supplied with WordPerfect. You should have a write-protect notch on it, or with 3½-inch disks the tab should be moved to the locked position.

5. Press any key. Soon the message

   > **Insert destination diskette in drive A:**
   > **Strike any key when ready**

   will appear.

6. Remove the WordPerfect disk and insert a blank disk in drive A.

7. Press any key to begin the copy.

    You will be told several times to switch disks until all of the information on the WordPerfect disk has been copied onto the blank disk. Be certain that the original WordPerfect disk is in the drive only when the screen requests the source diskette.

    When the copy is completed, the message

    Copy Another (Y/N)?

    will appear.

8. Remove the disk and immediately label the copy accordingly. Write the name of the disk on the label before sticking it on the disk. If you write on the disk itself, the impression of a pen or pencil could damage the recording surface. If you must write on a disk, use a felt-tipped pen and write very lightly.

9. Press *Y* and repeat this process for all of your disks.

    Place the original WordPerfect disks in a safe location and use the copies for everyday work.

B

Installing WordPerfect

When you *install* a program, you get it ready for use with your own computer. With WordPerfect this is a really simple procedure that involves making a working copy of your program.

Configuration File

To use all of the features of WordPerfect you need a special file on your DOS (or OS/2) disk—the one that you use to start your computer—called CONFIG.SYS. The file must include a special command that allows the disk operating system to handle all of the special files that WordPerfect uses.

If you have a hard disk system, this file will be created when you run the Install program later. These instructions are for floppy disk users.

Follow these steps to add the proper commands to the file:

1. Start your computer, respond to the date and time prompts if they appear, then wait until the drive prompt appears. If you have a floppy disk system, start your computer with the WordPerfect 1 or WordPerfect Program disk that you created in Appendix A. This is the disk with the operating system—DOS or OS/2—on it.

   If your computer is already started, press Alt-Ctrl-Del. (Press down all three keys at the same time.) This ensures that the CONFIG.SYS file will be on the operating system disk.

2. Type the following then press ←:

   COPY CONFIG.SYS + CON CONFIG.SYS

   The drive prompt will not reappear.

3. Type the following then press ←:

   FILES = 20

4. Press Ctrl-Z. (Press and hold down the CTRL key, press the Z key, then release both of them.)

5. Press ⏎. The drive prompt appears on the screen.

*F*loppy Disk Systems

Except for selecting printers, which is discussed in Appendix C, WordPerfect is already installed. The disks labeled *WordPerfect 1* and *WordPerfect 2* (or just *WordPerfect Program* with 3½-inch systems) contain the WordPerfect program and some other necessary programs used during word processing.

Since these programs take up most of those disks, there is little room to store your own documents. The extra disk that you formatted in Appendix A will be used to store your documents. Because it has no operating system or other programs, you will be able to store the maximum number of documents on it.

Keep in mind that unless told otherwise, WordPerfect will store documents on the program disk or directory containing WordPerfect itself. To save them on the data disk you must enter the drive letter (B:) in front of all document names, for example, B:LETTER. When this document disk becomes full, you'll have to format another blank disk.

You can also start WordPerfect so your documents are stored in drive B without any special attention. This procedure is described in Chapter 1, Lesson 1.

*H*ard Disk Systems

You should follow the steps below to copy all of your WordPerfect disks into a special subdirectory of your hard disk. This way you'll have available every WordPerfect function, including the Speller, the Thesaurus, and the Printer files, without needing any floppy disks.

WordPerfect will also save your documents to that disk and subdirectory, unless you direct it otherwise. This is fine as long as you don't run out of space on the hard disk and as long as you regularly make backup copies of your important documents on a floppy disk. So you should also format a blank disk, as explained in Appendix A under "Systems with Two Floppy Disks." Then copy important documents from the hard disk onto the floppy disk for safekeeping. This floppy disk will serve as a backup in case of a hard disk problem or accident.

For now, however, follow these steps to install WordPerfect in a new subdirectory of your hard disk:

1. Turn on your computer, respond to the time and date questions, then wait until the drive prompt (*C>*) appears.

2. Place the Learning diskette in drive A.

3. Type *a:Install* and press ←⏎. You'll see the message

    Do you have a hard disk? (Y/N) Y

4. Press *Y.*

5. Follow the directions shown on the screen. Don't worry if you occasionally see a message telling you that a file was not copied. If this happens, just press *Y* to continue.

6. Place one of your WordPerfect Printer disks in drive A.

7. Type *COPY A:*.* C:* and press ←⏎. All of the programs on the WordPerfect Printer disk will be copied into the WP50 subdirectory.

8. When the copy is complete, remove the WordPerfect Printer disk from drive A. Repeat steps 6 and 7 for the remaining WordPerfect Printer disks.

Once you designate printers in Appendix C, you can free up valuable space on your hard disk by deleting the printer files you just copied. Do this at the drive prompt (*C>*) by typing

DEL WPRINT*.ALL

Make sure you keep the floppy disks handy, however, in case you later need to change printers.

C

How to Designate Printers

Appendix C: How to Designate Printers

You must tell WordPerfect what printer you have before using the program for the first time or if you change printers later. This is called *installing* your printer. It really isn't complicated, but it does take many steps. So be patient as I take you step-by-step through the process.

To get you up and running as quickly as possible, this appendix will give you only the steps needed to select printers. I won't take the time here to explain all of the choices on the several menus you'll be using. These will be explained in more detail, however, in Chapter 8.

Setting Up WordPerfect for Your Printer

To perform these steps you need the WordPerfect program and Printer disks, either as floppy disks or already installed on a hard disk. The Printer disks contain the codes and commands required by over a hundred different printers.

Follow these steps to tell WordPerfect what printer you have:

1. First, you must start WordPerfect. Go to Chapter 1, Lesson 1, follow the step-by-step instructions, and return here for step 2.

2. If you have a floppy disk system, place a Printer disk in drive B, removing the blank document disk. The WordPerfect program disk should be in drive A.

   You probably have several printer disks. Place any one of them in drive B.

3. Press Shift-F7. (Press and hold down the Shift key, press the F7 key, then release both.) This is the Print key, used to start printing or to change print options. You'll see the Print menu shown in Figure C.1.

```
Print
       1 - Full Document
       2 - Page
       3 - Document on Disk
       4 - Control Printer
       5 - Type Through
       6 - View Document
       7 - Initialize Printer

Options

       S - Select Printer
       B - Binding              Ø"
       N - Number of Copies     1
       G - Graphics Quality     Medium
       T - Text Quality         High




    Selection: Ø
```

Figure C.1: Print menu

4. Press *S,* for Select Printer. The screen changes to the Print: Printer Selection menu (Figure C.2).

   Notice that no printers are listed on either menu, so you won't be able to print a document until you designate a printer, as you'll do here. WordPerfect stores the information about all printers in the WPRINT.ALL files on your Printer disks. When

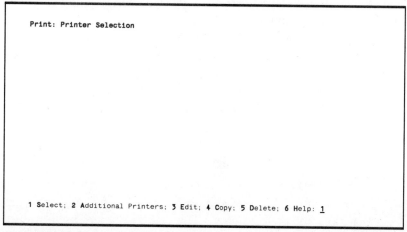

```
Print: Printer Selection




    1 Select; 2 Additional Printers; 3 Edit; 4 Copy; 5 Delete; 6 Help: 1
```

Figure C.2: Print: Printer Selection menu

you designate a printer, WordPerfect creates a separate file that contains just the data needed for that specific printer.

To use your own printer, you must go through a series of additional menus so your printer's PRS file can be placed on the disk.

You'll use the prompt line at the bottom of the screen to continue this process.

5. Press *2* or *a* to select Additional Printers. Floppy disk users will see the message shown in Figure C.3; press *2* or *o* to select Other Disk, type *B:* then press ←┘.

   The Additional Printers screen is displayed (Figure C.4). This screen lists the various printers WordPerfect has been designed to work with. You must select your own printer from the list.

6. Press the ↓ key. As you press the key, the highlight bar will move from printer to printer down the screen. When you reach the bottom of the screen, the list will "scroll" off the top to display more printers at the bottom. You can press the ↑ key to redisplay any names that have scrolled off the top of the screen.

```
Printer Selection: Additional Printers

Printer files not found

      Use the "Other Disk" option to specify a directory for the printer
      files.  Continue to use this option until you find the disk with the
      printer you want.










1 Select; 2 Other Disk; 3 Help; 4 List Printer Files: 1
```

Figure C.3: Message to floppy disk users that printer files cannot be found on the current disk

```
Printer Selection: Additional Printers

  AST TurboLaser
  Brother HR-20/Fortis DX21
  C. Itoh C310-EP
  Canon LBP-8 A1/A2
  Canon LBP-8II
  Citizen MSP-25
  Citizen Premiere 35
  Córdata LP300X
  Daisywriter 2000
  Dataproducts LZR-1230
  Diablo 620
  Diablo 630 ECS
  Diablo 635
  Diablo D80IF
  Epson EX-800
  Epson FX-80
  Epson FX-85/286
  Epson FX-86e/286e
  Epson GQ 3500
  Epson LQ-1500
  Epson LQ-800

1 Select; 2 Other Disk; 3 Help; 4 List Printer Files: 1
```

Figure C.4: *Additional Printers*

7. Press the ↓ or ↑ key to highlight your printer's name.

You might not see your printer's name even after scrolling the entire list. That's because the printer files are divided into more than one disk. In this case, remove the Printer disk from drive B and insert another Printer disk. Then press *2* or *o* to select Other Disk, type *B:*, then press ←. Now press the ↓ key to highlight your printer, or try the additional disk(s) if you still can't find your printer's name.

What happens if you don't see your printer listed? Look for a printer that may be compatible or one made by the same manufacturer. For instance, a great many dot matrix printers are compatible with the Epson MX, Epson FX, Epson FX-85, or IBM Graphics Printer. Many daisy wheel printers can emulate a Diablo 620 or another common printer. If you're not sure, look through your printer's manual to see if it emulates or uses the same commands as some other printer. If you're still unsure, ask the salesperson who sold you the printer.

Nothing drastic will happen if you select and attempt to use the wrong printer definition on the list. You might lose a few sheets of paper, or your printer might just do nothing. So if you don't see yours listed it's worth trying one that appears close.

8. Press ⏎ when your printer's name is highlighted. You'll see the prompt

   Printer Filename: *(your printer's name)***.PRS**

   at the bottom of the screen.

9. Press ⏎. You'll see the message

   Updating font:

   at the prompt line followed by a font number while WordPerfect loads the appropriate printer codes onto your disk. You'll see the Printer Helps and Hints screen, as shown in Figure C.5. Don't worry if your screen says *No help available.* Read the screen, wait until you see the message *Press Exit when done,* then press F7.

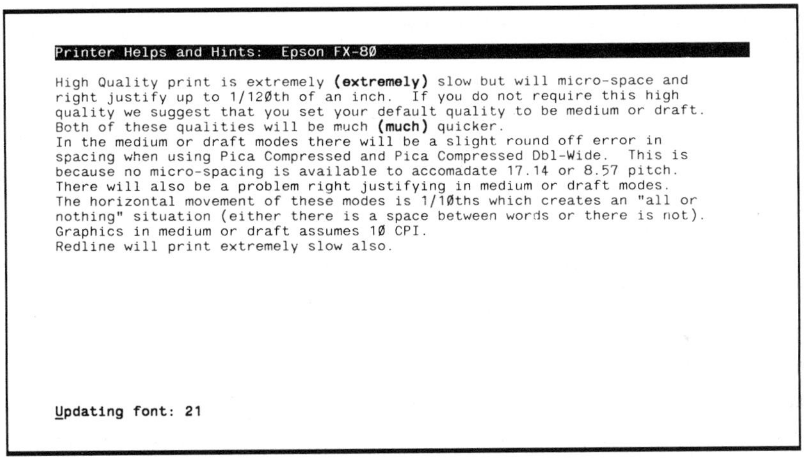

```
Printer Helps and Hints:  Epson FX-80

High Quality print is extremely (extremely) slow but will micro-space and
right justify up to 1/120th of an inch.  If you do not require this high
quality we suggest that you set your default quality to be medium or draft.
Both of these qualities will be much (much) quicker.
In the medium or draft modes there will be a slight round off error in
spacing when using Pica Compressed and Pica Compressed Dbl-Wide.  This is
because no micro-spacing is available to accomadate 17.14 or 8.57 pitch.
There will also be a problem right justifying in medium or draft modes.
The horizontal movement of these modes is 1/10ths which creates an "all or
nothing" situation (either there is a space between words or there is not).
Graphics in medium or draft assumes 10 CPI.
Redline will print extremely slow also.




Updating font: 21
```

Figure C.5: Printer Helps and Hints Screen

   After the file is loaded, you'll see the Printer Selection: Edit menu (Figure C.6).
   You have to check out two options on this menu: the type of paper feed you're using and the port your printer is attached to. Let's handle the paper feed first using the Forms option.

10. Press *4* or *f* to select the Forms option. The screen changes to the Printer Selection: Forms menu (Figure C.7). Look at the

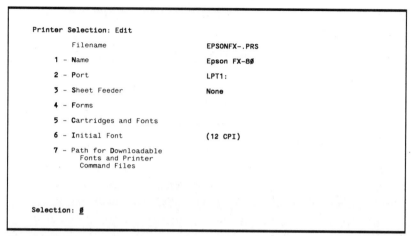

Figure C.6: *Printer Selection: Edit menu*

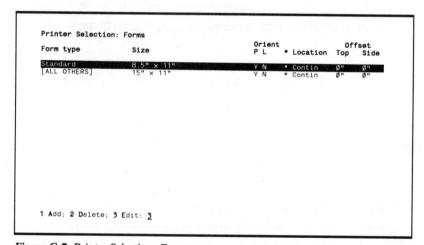

Figure C.7: *Printer Selection: Forms menu*

line starting with *Standard,* under the column marked *Location.* If it says *Contin* then WordPerfect assumes you're using continuous feed paper and it won't stop to let you insert individual sheets into the printer—*manual feed.*

If the location is correct, then skip to step 15. Otherwise continue here.

11. Press *3* or *e* for Edit to display the Printer Selection: Forms edit menu (Figure C.8).

```
Printer Selection: Forms

         Filename                 EPSONFX-.PRS
         Form Type                Standard
    1 -  Form Size                8.5" x 11"
    2 -  Orientation              Portrait
    3 -  Initially Present        Yes
    4 -  Location                 Continuous
    5 -  Page Offsets - Top       Ø"
                        Side      Ø"




Selection: Ø
```

Figure C.8: *Printer Selection: Forms edit menu*

12. Press *4* or *L* for the Location option to display the prompt line

    Location: 1 Continuous; 2 Bin Number; 3 Manual: 0

13. Press the number corresponding to the paper source. If you press *2* for *Bin Number,* you'll see the prompt

    Bin number:

    Enter the letter or number of the paper tray or bin containing the paper you'll be using.

14. Press F7 to display the Printer Select: Forms menu.

15. Press F7 to redisplay the Edit menu.

    Look at the Port option. This refers to the plug where your printer is attached to your computer. LPT 1 refers to a standard parallel printer port, the most common in use with PC's. Chances are you're using a printer attached to that port. If you have a parallel printer and the port listed on the menu says LPT 1, then just press ◄─┘ and skip to step 18. If you have a serial printer and the port says COM 1 then press ◄─┘ and skip to step 18.

    If you're not quite sure, read the explanation following the next step.

16. Press *2* or *p* to select the Port option and display the prompt line

   Port: 1 LPT 1: 2 LPT 2; 3 LPT 3; 4 COM 1; 5 COM 2; 6 COM 3; 7 COM 4; 8 Other: 0

   You can't tell a serial printer from a parallel one just by looking at it. But you might tell by seeing where it's connected to the back of your computer. You'll see a plug—called a *port*—where the printer's cable is attached. If the plug is labelled *Printer, LPT 1,* or *Parallel,* then your printer is a parallel printer. If it's the only port on the back of the computer then it's probably a parallel port as well.

   If the port is labelled *COM 1* or *Serial* you're using a Serial printer, so enter *4*. However, if you do have a serial printer, you'll have to read your manual for complete instructions.

   By the way, if you have more than one port of a type, they are called LPT 2, LPT 3, or COM 2. You would use these if you had more than one printer attached, say a dot matrix printer for quick rough copies and a letter quality printer for the final draft. If you do have this type of hardware, repeat this entire procedure for each printer you have.

17. Press the number corresponding to your printer's port.

18. Press F7 to display the Print: Select Printer menu. The printer you just defined is now added to the list and highlighted, although it is not yet selected.

19. Press ◄──┘.

20. Press F7 to return to the document window.

*C*hanging Printer Definitions

   If you purchase a new printer, you must add its definition to the list and select it. Just follow the steps shown above. If you have more than one printer, follow the steps above so they are all listed. Then, to use a specific one, press Shift-F7 S, highlight the printer you want to use, then press ◄──┘ twice.

*Q*uitting WordPerfect

You are now prepared to use WordPerfect, and since you have already started WordPerfect you are ready to continue with Lesson 2. But if you want to stop now, press the F7 (Exit) key, then answer *N* to the *Save Document?* prompt and *Y* to the *Exit WP?* prompt. (Since we'll be using this sequence of keystrokes at the end of most lessons, it will usually appear in an abbreviated form: F7 N Y.) Just turn to Lesson 1 when you want to start WordPerfect again.

Index

*, 231
+ key, 21
-, 110–111
− key, 21
->, 156
<-, 157
=, 58–59
?, 231

A

Align key, 89
aligning text, 88–90
Alt key, xxvii
Alt-F1 keystroke, 234
Alt-F2 keystroke, 159
Alt-F3 keystroke, 34
Alt-F4 keystroke, 70, 86–87, 229
Alt-F5 keystroke, 78
Alt-F6 keystroke, 89
Alt-F7 keystroke, 166
Alt-F9 keystroke, 241, 243, 246, 249, 254
Alt-F10 keystroke, 222–223
Alt-key macros, 218
Alternate key, xxvii
antonyms, use of, 234–237
appended blocks, 154
arrow keys, 8–11
asterisk (*), 231
automatic hyphenation, 112–113
auto-pagination, 5

B

Backspace key, xxvii, 6, 23, 26
backup disks, creating, 207–208, 259–264
Backup option, 202–208
backward-pointing arrow (<-), 157
backward search, 156
base fonts, 80
batch printing, 208
Binding option, 212

Block commands, 146–154
Block key, 70, 87–88, 146–154
block-protected parallel columns, 169–170
boldfacing text, 69–72
bottom margin, 118–119
boxes, 244–252

C

Cancel key, 12, 26–28
Caps Lock key, 4
centering text, 86–88
Character Type-Through Printing screen, 211
characters
    boldfacing, 69–72
    changing appearance of, 74–79
    lowercase, 74
    non-continuous underlining, 72–73
    underlining, 69–73
    uppercase, 74
    wild-card, 231
checking spelling, 228–233
codes
    listing of, 35–36
    revealing, 34–35, 37
    searching for, 158–159
color monitors, xxxii
Column mode, 165–166, 170–172
columns
    aligning, 90–91, 95–98
    defining, 164–166
    parallel, 168–173
    typing, 166–168
COMMAND.COM, 261
Comment prompt line, 65
comments
    adding to documents, 63–65
    converting text into, 150
    editing, 64–65
composite monitors, xxxii
CONFIG.SYS, 265

Control Printer menu, 12, 214
Copy command, 148–149, 202
COPY command (DOS), 262
copying disks, 262–264
Ctrl key, xxvii, 21–23
Ctrl- keystroke, 111
Ctrl-Backspace keystroke, 24, 26
Ctrl-End keystroke, 25–26
Ctrl-F2 keystroke, 229
Ctrl-F3 keystroke, 43
Ctrl-F4 keystroke, 150
Ctrl-F5 keystroke, 65
Ctrl-F6 keystroke, 97
Ctrl-F7 keystroke, 194
Ctrl-F8 keystroke, 75, 80
Ctrl-F9 keystroke, 185
Ctrl-F10 keystroke, 219–221
Ctrl-Home keystroke, 21–23
Ctrl-PgDn keystroke, 25–26
cursor
    finding location of, 4
    moving, 7–8, 20–23
cursor movement keys, 8–11
Cursor Speed option, 203
customizing WordPerfect, 202–208

D

dashes, double row of, 58–59
Date code, 45–46
dates, changing format of, 47–48
default settings, xxx, 50, 224
Del key, xxvii, 23–24, 26
Del Y keystroke, 150
Delete command, 147–148
deleting text, 23–26
destination disk, 263
dictionary, use of, 229–233
directories, displaying, 18–20
Directory Listing key, 19
disk drives, xxxiii
disks
    copying, 262–264
    floppy, xxxiii, 3, 228–229, 259–264, 266
    formatting, 259–261
    hard, xxxiii, 2–3, 262–264, 266–267

write protection of, 259
display cards, xxxii–xxxiii
Display option, 203
displaying two documents, 42–45
document number, 4
Document on Disk option, 209–210
DOS backup disks, 207–208
dot leaders, 90
Double Space macro, 225
double spacing, 57–58
down arrow key, 8
downloaded fonts, 80

E

Endnote Options menu, 199
Endnotes, creating, 196–199
Enter key, xxvii
envelopes, printing, 128–132
Esc key, xxvii, 21–22
Exit key, 3, 13, 19
exiting
    documents, 13–14, 29, 277
    WordPerfect, 3, 13–14, 29, 277

F

F1 function key, 12, 26–28
F2 function key, 157–158
F3 function key, 14–15
F4 function key, 102–105
F5 function key, 19
F6 function key, 69–71
F7 function key, 3, 13, 19
F8 function key, 69–71
F9 function key, 180
F10 function key, 29
Fast Save option, 203, 208
Field codes, 176–177
files
    handling missing information in, 183–184
    merging, 184–187
    variable information, 180–184
floating footnotes, 190
floppy disks
    copying, 262–264

formatting, 259–261
handling, xxxiii
loading, 3
and spelling program, 228–229
fonts, 80–84, 225–226
footers, 134–139, 141–142
Footnote Options menu, 194–195
footnotes, creating, 81–82, 190–196
form feeds, 124–125
form letters, creating, 176–180
Form Size Selection menu, 121
form types, setting, 119–125
Format Document menu, 62
Format key, 52
Format Line menu, 52–53
Format menu, xxxi
formatting
disks, 259–261
documents, 50–65
forward search, 156
forward-pointing arrow (->), 156
function keys, definition of, xxviii. *See also*
individual function keys

G

Go command, 224
GoTo key combination, 23
Graphic Line command, 240–245
graphics, adding to documents, 252–256
Graphics disks, 252, 254
Graphics Quality option, 212–213

H

hanging indentions, 106
hard carriage returns, 35, 37
hard disks, loading, 2–3
hard page breaks, 58–60
hardware, xxv–xxxiii
headers, 134–139, 141–142
headwords, 234
Help function, 14–15
Home - keystroke, 111
Home Backspace keystroke, 25–26
Home Del keystroke, 26

Home key, 20–23
Horizontal Line menu, 241
horizontal lines, creating, 240–242
hyphenation, 110–113

I

Initial Settings option, 203
Ins key, xxvii, 4–5, 32–34
Insert mode, xxvii, 4–5, 9–11
inserting text, 9–11
italic type, 76

J

justifying text, 109–110

K

Keyboard Layout option, 203
keyboards, introduction to, xxv–xxvi
keystrokes
combining, xxxiv
repeating, 39–40

L

landscape orientation, 122
Learning diskette, 14
left arrow key, 8
Legal Paper macro, 225
letters (form), creating, 176–180
line number, 4
line spacing, adjusting, 57–58
Line Type-Through Printing screen, 211
lines, creating, 240–245
loading WordPerfect, 2–3
Location of Files option, 203, 206–207
Look mode, 19–20
looking up words, 231
lowercase letters, 74

M

macros
defining, 219–221
definition of, 218

library of, 224–226
using, 221–223
Main Format menu, 52
manual hyphenation, 111–112
Margin Set codes, 55–57
margins
left and right, 51–57
setting for envelopes, 130–132
top and bottom, 118–119
temporary changes, 102
Mark Text command, 78
Math/Column prompt line, 165
menus, definition of, xxxi
Merge codes, 177–180
Merge E and Merge R, 180
Merge/Sort key, 185
merging files, 184–187
monitors, xxxii
Move command, 147–148

N

named macros, 218
naming documents, 13
newsletters, creating, 164–168
Newspaper Column feature, 164–173
Non-continuous underlining, 72–73
Num Lock key, xxix, 4, 8
Number of Copies option, 212
numbered paragraphs, 107–109
numbering footnotes, 195–196
numbering pages, 139–143
numeric keypad, xxix

O

orientation of printing, 122
original document backup, 204, 206
orphan lines, 126
Outline type, 76

P

page breaks, 5, 58–61
page feeds, 124–125
Page Format menu, 126–128
Page Number Position menu, 140

page numbers, 4, 139–143, 225
page offset, 122
pages
creating breaks, 5, 58–61
number of lines on, 5
numbering, 139–143, 225
setting size and shape, 119–125
paper
legal size, macro for, 225
selecting type of, 119–125
paper feeds, 124–125
paragraphs
combining, 38
hanging indentions, 106
indenting, 102–106
numbering, 106–109
orphan lines in, 126
splitting, 37–39
widow lines in, 126
parallel columns, 168–173
parallel printers, 276
personalizing form letters, 176–177
PgDn key, 20–21
PgUp key, 21
pitch, 74
points (fonts), 80
portrait orientation, 122
ports, 276
position number, 4
primary documents, 176–180
Print menu, 12
print queue, 213–215
Printer Control menu, 12, 214
Printer Selection Edit menu, 83, 274
Printer Selection Forms menu, 274
printers
installing, 269–276
introduction to, xxxii
merging form documents to, 186–187
printing
batches, 208
blocks, 152
comments, 64–65
control over, 213–215
documents on disk, 209–210
envelopes, 128–132

from keyboard, 210–212
from screen, 11–12
program disks, 3
prompt, definition of, xxx

Q

question mark (?), 231
queue control panel, 213–215
quitting WordPerfect, 3, 13–14, 29, 277

R

records, 180
Redline printing, 75–77
repeating keystrokes, 39–40
Replace command, 159
resolution of screen, xxxiii
restoring text, 26–28
Retrieve key, 18
Return key, xxvii
reverse video, 35
Rewrite command, 40–41
right arrow key, 8

S

Save key, 29
Save Named Text macro, 225
saving documents, 13–14, 28–29
scale line, 34–37, 44–45
screens
    adjusting after editing, 40–41
    clearing, 12
    merging form documents to, 185–186
    number of lines on, 5
    printing from, 11–12
    resolution of, xxxiii
    scrolling text, 5
    status line on, 4
scrolling text, 5
Search command, 156–159
secondary merge file, 180
selection line, xxx
serial printers, 276
Setup menu, 202–203
shading boxes, 248

Shadow type, 76
Shift key, xxxvii
Shift-F1 keystroke, 202
Shift-F2 keystroke, 157
Shift-F3 keystroke, 41–43, 74
Shift-F4 keystroke, 105–106
Shift-F5 keystroke, 45
Shift-F6 keystroke, 86
Shift-F7 keystroke, 11, 71, 83, 208–209
Shift-F8 keystroke, 52, 72
Shift-F9 keystroke, 180
Shift-F10 keystroke, 18
soft hyphen, 111, 113
soft page breaks, 58
source disk, 263
speed block function, 148, 150
spelling checker, 228–233
starting WordPerfect, 2–3
status line, xxx, 4
storing text, 150–152
Strikeout option, 75–77
subdirectory, installing WordPerfect on, 267
subscripts, 81–82
summary, adding to document, 61–63
superscripts, 81–82
supplemental dictionary, 231, 233
Suppress (this page only) menu, 142
Switch command, 41–43
synonyms, use of, 234–237

T

Tab key, xxvi, 9, 90, 97
tab stops
    changing, 98–99
    setting, 90–95
templates for keyboards, xxviii–xxxiv
temporary macros, 219
text
    aligning, 88–90
    appending blocks of, 154
    boldfacing, 69–72
    centering, 86–88, 224
    converting to comments, 150
    copying, 148–149
    deleting, 23–26, 147–148

enclosing in box, 245–252
hyphenating, 110–113
inserting, 9–11
justifying, 109–110
marking, 78
moving within a document, 147–148
moving between documents, 150–152
printing blocks of, 152
replacing, 159–162
restoring, 26–28
saving blocks of, 153
saving named, macro for, 225
scrolling, 5
searching for, 156–159
setting justification of, 109–110
storing, 150–152
underlining, 69–73
Text Box Definition menu, 249
Text Column Definition menu, 165
Text Quality option, 213
Thesaurus program, 228, 233–237
timed backups, 204–206
title page, creating, 126–128
toggle keys, 5
top margin, 118–119
type styles, 79–84
Type Through option, 210–212
Typeover mode, xxvii, 5, 32–34

U

Undelete key, 27
underlining text, 69–73
Units of Measure option, 203
up arrow key, 8
uppercase letters, 74

V

variable information file, 180
Vertical Line menu, 243
vertical lines, creating, 240, 243–245
View mode, 113–116
volume label, 260

W

widow lines, 126
wild-card characters, 231
Window command, 42–44
windows, clearing, 44
WordPerfect program
    customizing, 202–208
    installing into subdirectory, 267
    version of, xxiii
word-wrap, 6–7
WPG extension, 252
WPHELP.FIL, 14
write-protecting disks, 259

Alphabetical Summary of WordPerfect Commands

Block	Alt-F4
Boldface print	F6
Box	Alt-F9
Cancel	F1
Cancel printing	Shift-F7 4 1 *
Center text	Shift-F6
Center page	Shift-F8 2 1 ↵ ↵
Clear screen	F7 N N
Column definition	Alt-F7 4
Column off/on	Alt-F7 3
Copy text	Ctrl-F4
Cursor movement	
bottom of document	Home Home ↓
bottom of screen	Home ↓
left margin	Home ←
next screen	Home ↓
previous screen	Home ↑
right margin	End
specific page	Ctrl-Home (page number) ↵
top of document	Home Home ↑
top of screen	Home ↑
Date code	Shift-F5 2
Date format	Shift-F5 3
Date text	Shift-F5 1

Decimal tab align	Ctrl-F6
Delete to end of line	Ctrl-End
Delete word	Ctrl-Backspace
Double space	Shift-F8 1 6 2 ↵ ↵ ↵
Double underline	Ctrl-F8 2 3
Exit without saving	F7 N Y
Extra large print	Ctrl-F8 1 7
Fine print	Ctrl-F8 1 3
Flush right	Alt-F6
Font size	Ctrl-F8 1
Footnote	Ctrl-F7 1
Go to page	Ctrl-Home (page number) ↵
Hanging indentation	F4 Shift-Tab
Help	F3
Hyphen, optional	Ctrl -
Hyphen, required	-
Indent, both sides	Shift-F4
Indent, left	F4
Insert mode	INS
Italics	Ctrl-F8 2 4
Justification off	Shift-F8 1 3 N ↵ ↵